THE MALE IMAGE

Also by Ian Gregson and from the same publishers

CONTEMPORARY POETRY AND POST-MODERNISM
Dialogue and Estrangement

The Male Image

Representations of Masculinity
in Postwar Poetry

Ian Gregson

First published in Great Britain 1999 by
MACMILLAN PRESS LTD
Houndmills, Basingstoke, Hampshire RG21 6XS and London
Companies and representatives throughout the world

A catalogue record for this book is available from the British Library.

ISBN 0–333–76020–4

 First published in the United States of America 1999 by
ST. MARTIN'S PRESS, INC.,
Scholarly and Reference Division,
175 Fifth Avenue, New York, N.Y. 10010

ISBN 0–312–22246–7

Library of Congress Cataloging-in-Publication Data
Gregson, Ian.
The male image : representations of masculinity in postwar poetry
/ Ian Gregson.
p. cm.
Includes bibliographical references and index.
ISBN 0–312–22246–7 (cloth)
1. English poetry—20th century—History and criticism.
2. Masculinity in literature. 3. English poetry—Male authors–
–History and criticism. 4. World War, 1939–1945—Great Britain–
–Influence. 5. English poetry—Psychological aspects. 6. Men in
literature. I. Title.
PR508.M35G74 1999
821'.91409353—dc21   99–12112
                                                         CIP

This book is printed on paper suitable for recycling and made from fully managed and
sustained forest sources.

10   9   8   7   6   5   4   3   2   1
08   07   06   05   04   03   02   01   00   99

Printed and bound in Great Britain by
Antony Rowe Ltd, Chippenham, Wiltshire

Contents

Acknowledgements

My special thanks go to Deryn Rees-Jones whose idea it was originally to write a book on this subject. Thanks, also, to David Kennedy with whom I discussed the project at some length. I'm also grateful to my colleagues Lucie Armitt and Tony Brown who read some of the chapters and made valuable suggestions.

Introduction

Masculinity is increasingly being addressed as an issue. Even in
popular culture (where it tends not to speak its name) masculinity is
being treated with increasing self-consciousness. *The Full Monty*, for
example, directly concerns itself with a sense of what is currently
happening to men. Its male characters have all lost their jobs in
the steel industry in Sheffield and are shown to be suffering the
psychological consequences of this loss of a traditional source of
male power. The central character is estranged from his wife and
will be denied access to his son unless he comes up with £300. His
overweight friend is suffering from sexual problems which are
said to have started when he became unemployed. The film
assumes that gender roles are changing. An early scene shows a
woman using a male urinal. The men respond to their situation by
becoming strippers, by adopting a role traditionally regarded as
feminine, and the film therefore focuses on the male body and
male self-regard and finds much of its comedy in this implied role
reversal. This stresses the men's disturbing new vulnerability. The
older man among them is using anti-wrinkle cream; the over-
weight man laments the absence of an 'anti-fat bastard cream';
there is an anxiety throughout, explicit and implicit, about penis
size.

The men in *The Full Monty* are depicted as wounded and be-
wildered; its comedy works to present them, sympathetically and
affectionately, as the victims of current social changes. Barbara
Ehrenreich in her essay 'The Decline of Patriarchy' is much less
sympathetic to the male cause; she characterises those changes as
involving a decline of patriarchy but insists that this does not
mean any lessening of sexism, misogyny or male domination, but
a decline in the intimate power of men over women, a power
which is historically exercised within the family by the male as
breadwinner, property-owner, or armed defender of women and
children.[1]

Male power, according to Ehrenreich, is exercised less and less
from person to person – which involved women being patriar-
chally protected as men's familial property – and more and more
impersonally, corporately, bureaucratically, systemically. Where

1

The Full Monty depicts the feminising of men, Ehrenreich focuses on the masculinising of women. Men, she says, no longer even pretend to protect women so that it is now too dangerous 'to go about the world being femme' (289). As a result there is increasing support for female violence against abusive men – support by working-class women, for example, for Lorena Bobbitt – and growing cinematic representations of 'tough women, killer women, bitchy women, from *Thelma and Louise* to *Basic Instinct* to *Serial Mom* and *Bad Girls*' (290).

What lies behind these changes is the movement from a rigid set of gender relations that became most dominant in high capitalism and therefore modernism to a much looser set associated with late capitalism and postmodernism. Some of the characteristics of the former were already present in early capitalism when it arose in the mid-fifteenth to the mid-seventeenth centuries in Western Europe: an increasing emphasis on what R.W. Connell calls 'the conjugal household',[2] on individualism, and on a view of both Western civilisation and masculinity as distinguished by their rationality which allowed the forging of 'a cultural link between the legitimation of patriarchy and the legitimation of empire' (Connell, 187). Culture became increasingly urban and entrepreneurial and its values – those associated with the 'Protestant ethic' – were overwhelmingly if implicitly gendered, so that masculinity became 'institutionalised' in the form of 'gendered work and power in the counting-house, the warehouse and the exchange' (Connell, 188).

These are the historical origins of an ideology which has embedded itself so deeply in the modern West and moulded the identities of men and women to such an extent that those identities have seemed inevitable and obvious. This ideology has been so successful that it appears to have transcended history and established itself as common-sense and natural. However, it most strengthened its grip in the eighteenth century when social changes, most importantly industrialisation, resulted in 'an increasing separation of spheres, a sharpening of the differences between male and female social roles'[3] as middle-class women were increasingly excluded from public life and dedicated themselves to household responsibilities. Many historians have argued that, as a result of this, the family became more sequestered and family life was characterised as 'private and sentimental, and defined as feminine, in opposition to the masculine world of public affairs' (Shoemaker, 7). Concurrently with this and largely as a consequence of these economic and social changes, concepts of the body and sexuality underwent a crucial shift:

> Thomas Laqueur has argued that … while in the early modern period female bodies were seen as essentially similar to men's but less fully developed, in the eighteenth century there developed a 'two-sex' model. … The early modern view that lust was a fundamentally (though not exclusively) feminine vice was transferred to men, and women were increasingly seen as sexually passive. … Changes in actual sexual practice are difficult to study, but a recent argument posits a parallel change: Henry Abelove and Tim Hitchcock have argued that over the eighteenth century heterosexual intercourse came to focus exclusively on vaginal penetration, excluding previous practices of fondling and mutual masturbation. Concurrently, sexual practices such as homosexuality and masturbation were increasingly condemned. (Shoemaker, 9)

This is worth quoting at length because it emphasises that gender characteristics and behaviour which tend now to be regarded as natural and inevitable are actually the products of history. In fact it is increasing knowledge and understanding of this which characterise our own period: it is a constitutive aspect of the postmodern that what had been established as gender norms and hierarchies have been increasingly called into question, most importantly by feminists. What is fascinating about the poets I discuss in this book is the extent to which their work registers the changes in understanding of gender which have taken place over the past 50 years. Poetry is especially effective in this context because its techniques effect a radical defamiliarising of its material. Because gender norms had established themselves so rigidly during the nineteenth century their subversion requires especially subtle and complex aesthetic means, so that the grip of their familiarity can be broken.

Thomas Foster has examined how Emily Dickinson deconstructs gender expectations by focusing on her imagery of 'home' and thereby on how her experience is defined by reference to the woman's sphere.[4] He draws on Mary Ryan's book *Womanhood in America* and its description of the way that industrialisation created that sphere, that gendered geography, so that womanhood as a concept acquired 'a distinctive spatial character during the early stages of industrial capitalism'.[5] Foster then shows how Dickinson deploys poetic discourse to question assumptions about gendered space, so that the home is made to function 'as a position both inside and outside dominant social structures' (244) and is made to 'restructure radically the typical relations between time and space, inside and outside, public and private spaces, within modern industrial societies' (244–5).

Foster's essay is one of an increasing number written during the last decade in which men have addressed the sort of gender questions previously associated with women theorists and critics. This entry of men into what was previously – as it were – a female intellectual sphere is itself important because it draws attention to the *genderedness* of the male author, and therefore to masculinity as a gender. This has a representative significance in opposing the assumption that had arisen in the culture – for the historical reasons I have summarised – that masculine values are not masculine but universal, that masculinity is not a gender but a norm, not a perspective but the only coherent way to be and know.

This is a masculine self-consciousness which has arisen in response to feminism. It has led to an increasing amount and variety of work being done into what it means to be masculine, and into how masculinity has been historically and ideologically constructed. Throughout this book I have been concerned to show how each of the poets under consideration has responded to the demand to acquire a masculine identity as it has been traditionally understood, and how they have represented that demand and that identity. In other words I have been concerned to explore their response to their need, as boys and men, to acquire the 'ideal masculine qualities' as David T. Evans puts it, of 'dominance, activity, autonomy, impersonality and rationality' and to acquire the appropriate sexuality with its focus on 'release, needs, experience, fantasy and achievement'.[6] To expand this further, this traditional male role involves

(a) 'no sissy stuff' – the avoidance of all feminine behaviours and traits;
(b) 'the big wheel' – the acquisition of success, status, and bread-winning competence;
(c) 'the sturdy oak' – strength, confidence and independence;
(d) 'give 'em hell' – aggression, violence and daring[7]

I have been concerned above all with what Stephen Heath calls the 'sexual positioning'[8] of postwar male poetry, responding that is to modern theories of textuality by revealing how these authors and their sexualities are involved 'in the whole mesh of discursive orders of language, all the available forms and constructions with their particular positions, their particular terms of representation' (Heath, 25). When these poets are given this kind of attention they are revealed to be doing already what Alice Jardine calls for male authors to do 'after feminism' when she asks for a discourse that expresses

> men's relationship ... to death, scopophilia, fetishism ... the penis and balls, erection, ejaculation (not to mention the phallus), madness, paranoia, homosexuality, blood, tactile pleasure, pleasure in general, *desire* (but, please, not with an anonymously universal capital D) voyeurism, etc. Now this *would* be talking your body, not talking *about* it.[9]

These in fact are the recurrent themes of my book which treats the writing of poems as a form of gender performance. For gender, as Judith Butler has stressed,[10] can only be defined interactively and performatively: there are no underlying gender 'essences'. Gender can only be defined, that is, in terms of activity and social practices. Writing is best regarded as one such activity, as a 'bodily function' in which the male body becomes, as Calvin Thomas puts it, 'a material site of linguistic production' which expresses 'a corporeal tension between (gendered) identity and (self-) representation'.[11]

I have drawn on theorists like Calvin Thomas, whose focus is on 'discourse', when it has seemed most appropriate. This has been important to me because my subject is ideological and yet routinely regarded as not ideological, so the introduction of theory has significance, in itself, in insisting on elements of representation and power in thematic areas which may easily be regarded as innocent of them. Such innocence is most often assumed in the non-academic discussions that take place in the poetry world among contemporary poets themselves and the readers of poetry magazines such as *Poetry* in the USA and *Poetry Review* in Britain. This seems to me most conspicuously in evidence in the lack of discussion there has been in such circles of the gender ideology that shapes the work of Seamus Heaney and, until his death in 1998, Ted Hughes. More of this later, but it has led, for example, to Hughes' bizarrely bad and (in terms of gender) elaborately sinister book *Shakespeare and the Goddess of Complete Being*[12] receiving fulsome praise on its blurb from two of the most intelligent contemporary poets, Tom Paulin and Michael Hoffman.

The application of post-structuralist and gender theories to this area effectively calls into question aspects of postwar poetry which tend to be overlooked. The style of theorists like Thomas is often confrontationally difficult because the style is itself making the point that what can too easily be regarded as obvious is, in fact, deviously complex. Such a style would be counter-productive for my purposes because my aim is to throw light into some ignored male corners of postwar poetry. But I am also disturbed by what seem to me the blind spots of this kind of theory and agree with Peter Middleton that 'certain areas of masculinity remain unconscious within the linguistic projects of poststructuralism'.[13] This is clearest when, almost as an aside, Calvin Thomas says

> The problem is not simply that men like power more than sex, although that is obviously the form the problem takes and in which it is historically reproduced (20)

This is an unusually accessible moment for Thomas but it finds him making an enormous generalisation in an area which is far larger in significance than those where he characteristically makes relentlessly fastidious distinctions. The smaller areas he addresses, which are mostly to do with discourse and the body, do have their own importance, but that he brushes aside this larger question in order to get to them is very frustrating. His use of that word 'obviously' also suggests (although his kind of analysis represents an assault on 'common-sense' ways of thinking about gender) that it is itself actually the product of another, alternative kind of orthodoxy.

Thomas's positioning of himself here is characteristically masculine. He is writing in an area, gender theory, where women have been most powerful and his whole book reveals his consequent vulnerability which takes the form, most conspicuously, of his defensive need to write a book which is in every sense *hard* – vigorously analytical, rigorously theoretical, monolithic in its post-structuralist register. He perfectly exemplifies, that is, an aspect of the masculine which, by his own account, Luce Irigaray identifies when she indicates the link between Western rationality and the phallic precedence accorded to solids, and advocates in reaction to it a new metaphorical respect for liquids:

> A fluid argument, for Irigaray, is one that resists being subjected to the reified Western *ratio*, resists having its fluid qualities seg-

mented and parcelled out in a quantifiable and rigidified form. The formal rigidity of the phallic *ratio* dictates that whatever fluids escape this form be considered not only as nonphallic, and therefore feminine, but also as irrational, if not as madness itself. (52)

This idea seems to me extremely suggestive and helpful for discussing the gendered treatment of imagery in modern poetry. The demand for phallic hardness, for example, is central to Ezra Pound's prescriptions for Imagism (imposed by contrast with late Romantic impressionism) and is thereby one of the premises of male modernism. In my chapter on Robert Lowell I describe his development away from a creative outlook similarly based on a sinewy solidity towards an increasing acceptance of oceanic fluidity, and see this as symptomatic of a crucial shift in his gender attitudes.

Calvin Thomas focuses on abject male fluids but his style effectively immunises him against their associations through its solid consistency. It is only slightly unfair to describe him wanting to be *impenetrable*, so that, though he is occupying what is most often a feminine position (theorising gender) his own masculine authority is linguistically guaranteed. When his argument backs him into a corner and he has to adjudicate – almost crudely, it seems, comparatively – between the relative importance, for men, of sex and power he declares that men 'obviously' prefer power. However, in reassuring his feminist sisters of his own correctness, Thomas makes a generalisation that is actually useless to them because it ignores the variety of masculine behaviour and sensibility.

My own project has been to focus on this variety. The one generalisation I would make as a result of studying the poets I have written about directly concerns the masculine attitude to power. What most typifies the masculine, it seems to me, is precisely the defensiveness that Thomas displays in response to vulnerability. *Male Matters* is a humourless display of brain power: men tend to flex their muscles most when they are feeling weak. The poet in my book with the most masculine swagger is Derek Walcott and my chapter on him explores how this arises directly out of the gender insecurity he reveals in relation to the colonial experience. Men in *The Full Monty* position tend to react by being oppressive: men who are powerless outside the home are most likely to be tyrannical inside it. The male characters in *The Full Monty* are lovable precisely

because of their implausible willingness to discuss and even choreo-
graph their unmanly powerlessness.

The best illustration, at the cultural level, of this defensive re-
action is the 'mythopoetic' men's movement in the USA which was
initiated by Robert Bly's bestseller *Iron John*.[14] Its basic premise is
that feminism, and the social changes to which it is linked, have led
to a softening of men. Bly says that in the 1970s he started to see an
increasing number of young men who were commendably gentle –
pacifist and ecological in their political outlook and concerned in
their personal life above all to please their mothers and girlfriends –
but also lacking in energy: 'They are life-preserving but not exactly
life-giving. Ironically, you often see these men with strong women
who positively radiate energy' (3). What most appals Bly and his
followers is their sense that men and women are becoming too
alike, and their anxious and angry reaction to this is a noisy
insistence on gender polarities:

> One can feel the resonance between opposites in flamenco
> dancing. Defender and attacker watch each other, attractor and
> refuser, woman and man, red and red. Each is a pole with its sep-
> arate magnetic charge, each is a nation defending its borders,
> each is a warrior enjoying the heat of extravagant passion, a dis-
> tinguished passion which is fierce, eaglelike, mysterious. (175)

The gender assumptions of this movement are essentialist and it is
concerned above all to penetrate to the truths of the psychobiologi-
cal self that lie below the deceptive surface of social interactions. Its
outlook is primitivist in the sense that it mistrusts the version of
human identity which emerges in civilised societies, regards this as
'unreal' and wants to insist that real instincts underlie this civilised
self. Its use of so-called 'Wild Man' workshops and initiation rituals
are clearly the product of this belief and are meant to re-introduce
men to a lost strenuousness which is necessary for masculinity to be
fully acquired.

It is not an accident that Bly is a poet because versions of this
primitivism have been present in the poetic tradition ever since
Romanticism with its assertion of 'natural' values against the baleful
confinements of capitalist society. Robert Lowell is characteristically
brilliant, in 'Waking Early Sunday Morning',[15] in his invoking of
this impulse (the desire to 'break loose, like the chinook / Salmon')
while also being ruefully sceptical about it. For Ted Hughes it was a

crucial idea and crucially linked to his views of gender. He was a far more sophisticated thinker than Bly and a far better poet, and his primitivism led him, towards the end of his life, to a version of eco-feminism – in other words to a celebratory embracing of that new ascendancy of the feminine which he and Bly both identify. This was in some ways the opposite of Bly's backlash response, but it was nonetheless based on a similar essentialism, similar beliefs in psy-chobiological drives, and similar invoking of Jungian archetypes.

This was a much more cogent ideology in Hughes' hands than it is in Bly's, but that made it all the more intellectually dangerous. I have never seen it discussed in these terms in the poetry world even though it has a powerful presence there – versions of it are also present in the work of Seamus Heaney and Peter Redgrove, among others. Where Bly's emphasis is on the power of the authen-tically masculine, Hughes's emphasis is on that of the archetypally feminine, on the concept of a fertility goddess who has been eschewed in Western culture since the rise of the Protestant ethic. This is potentially a very damaging view of gender relationships at a time when they are being constructively reassessed. At the most trivial level it leads to some cringe-making moments in Hughes's poems, as when he describes the Grand Canyon as

> America's big red mamma!
> Now letting the sun, with changing colours,
> Caress her, as she lay open.[16]

At the most significant level it is responsible for the gender ideology that transforms *Birthday Letters*, the collection of poems written over a long period but collected and published when he knew he was dying. Here, implicitly and occasionally explicitly in this sequence of poems about the Plath/Hughes relationship, Hughes claims that the two poets were in a sort of mystical threesome with a goddess who shaped their lives and poems:

> It was a visit from the goddess, the beauty
> Who was poetry's sister – she had come
> To tell poetry she was spoiling us.
> Poetry listened, maybe, but we heard nothing
> And poetry did not tell us. And we
> Only did what poetry told us to do.
> (66)

In 'Isis' the goddess is said to have occupied Plath's body which she then uses like a 'soft mask' (112). Always the implication is that there are transcendent forces which are determining how the man and woman relate to each other and what they mutually create. Their lives are not in their control because they are driven by creative compulsions. In 'Trophies' these take the metaphorical form – metaphorical but so powerfully believed it seems far more than that – of a panther that carries Plath in its jaws which it later locks into Hughes's face.

All of this is linked to the invention of an idealised femininity which is then treated with exaggerated respect, and a fear which is regarded as a spur to creativity. It is premised upon a stark division of the genders which are then depicted in a melodramatic and primordial struggle. This is a great pity – even aside from its unhelpfulness in terms of gender attitudes – because it mars what is otherwise a compelling account, in *Birthday Letters*, of the relationship between Plath and Hughes, an account that conveys a subtle and complex sense of both their personalities. What is representative in this for me is how vividly poetry enacts gender attitudes and relationships even when the ideology that lies behind it is a sinister one.

This is what makes it so worthwhile to study poetry and masculinity together. Masculine values have been so dominant that masculinity has been, as it were, hidden in plain sight – so difficult to see, paradoxically, because it is so pre-eminently there. What poetry does, through its habit of wrenching language into defamiliarising shapes, is to make masculinity aesthetically open to discussion. Poets like C.K. Williams and Paul Muldoon, who are young enough to have been influenced by the cultural impact of feminism, react in explicit, if subtle ways to the newly self-conscious business of being masculine. The best poets of the generation before them, Robert Lowell and John Berryman, identify a form of gender sickness in themselves and explore it in their poems in great detail. They are both open to the charges of misogyny and macho posturing but their confessional poetic deconstructs gender assumptions so that misogyny and macho posturing are both interrogated. I found myself in the end immensely impressed by their sensitivity about gender, their insight even into their own masculine insensitivities. Occasionally, too, they display an insight into the damage inflicted on women by patriarchy which in their own time was likely to be ideologically ignored. In 'His Helplessness', for example,

Berryman describes a woman friend who has been psychologically damaged by the sexual abuse she suffered as a child from her father. What is clear to readers of his other *Dream Songs* is that he is understanding her experience by analogy with his own, with a parallel kind of abuse he suffered from his father's suicide. Berryman and the woman both consequently have low self-esteem, both are promiscuous, alcoholic and suicidal. This, then, is masculine fellow-feeling for a specifically feminine experience:

> & I look with my heart, in her darkness over there:
> dark shroud the clouds on her disordered soul
> whose last letter flew like a prayer.[17]

1

Men and Mermaids: Robert Lowell's Martial Masculinity and Beyond

The major concern of confessional poets with exploring their own identities inevitably involves an exploration, explicit or implicit, of their gender identities. When Robert Lowell turned to confessional writing the evidence, in particular, of the prose piece '91 Revere Street'[1] indicates that gender was among the most pressing of his concerns – in depicting his ancestors, his parents and his childhood self he is obsessed with what constitutes manliness. Within its first two pages Lowell is worrying about the complex mixture of masculine and feminine in his ancestral inheritance and doing so in terms of the imagery which he associates – throughout his poetic career – with each. His father's ancestor, Major Mordechai Myers was a military man who successfully wooed Miss Charlotte Bailey, 'thus proving himself a better man than his rivals, the united forces of Plattsburg' (19). Yet there was was 'something undecided, Mediterranean, versatile, almost double-faced about his bearing' and his 'suffering, almond eye rested on his luxurious dawn-coloured fingers ruffling an off-white glove' (20). Most importantly, 'these relatives of my Grandmother Lowell seemed to have given my father his character' and this by contrast with the ancestors of his maternal grandfather, the 'iconoclastic, mulish Dunbarton New Hampshire Starks' with their *granite back-countriness*'. The imagery on his mother's side is all hard masculinity, while on 'the joint Mason-Myers bookplate, there are two merry and naked mermaids – lovely marshmallowy, boneless, Rubensesque butterballs, all burlesque-show bosoms and Flemish smiles. Their *motto, malo frangere quam flectere*, reads "I prefer to bend than to break"' (20).

The mermaid figures crucially again, near the end of Lowell's career, in *The Dolphin*[2] as he tries to understand his relationship with two women and his daughter. It is linked to a larger pattern of

12

imagery which associates sea creatures and the sea generally with the otherness of the feminine and which provides the most important clue to Lowell's gender attitudes – I'll be exploring this in detail. What is most important here, though, is the intensity of focus bestowed on the mermaids which are bombarded with adjectives that evoke feminine softness and exotic sensuality, and how this focus is deployed as part of Lowell's insinuation that his father was less masculine than he should have been.

The hybrid nature of the mermaids refers partly to the combining of the Mason and Myers families and what is involved here, too, is the combining of racial strains. Mordecai Myers, Lowell says, was 'a dark man, a German Jew' (20). This has its own importance but it is also linked to Lowell's gender preoccupation – his description of Myers introduces language that refers to his race but at the same time questions his gender, to the extent of implying a kind of duplicity – 'undecided, Mediterranean, versatile, almost double-faced'. The preoccupation with colour ('almond eye', 'dawn-coloured fingers', 'off-white glove') is partly justified by this being a portrait, but it again combines suggestions of the exotic (in which the poetic and the dubious mingle) with the fussily feminine ('ruffling'). What may well lie behind this is the centuries-old dominance of cultural assumptions which are both caucasian and masculine – anything outside those assumptions can easily be conflated, the feminine and the foreign can easily acquire associations of each other. But Jewish men seem particularly to have been open to questioning of their gender. As Victor J. Seidler has said, 'the idea of a "Jewish man" was experienced by me as a kind of contradiction in terms. Jewishness was related to the emotional, and so with the feminine'.[3]

What should be stressed above all about Lowell is how conscious an artist he is, how intelligent and aware of different facets of what he is doing. The comic element in his work tends to be overlooked but it is important, especially because it is linked to his knowingness. The mischievous and comic tone of the passage I've analysed suggests an authorial double-take on its material, which is connected to his own part in all of this. Confessional writing helps him to distance himself and control his subject-matter but it is intimately linked to who he is. The descriptions of Mordecai Myers and the mermaids are overblown as part of an almost satirical attitude to his father, but his wry tone also hints at his knowledge that he is himself implicated – this is his genetic inheritance too.

This has a representative significance in a literary idiom that is focused on how identity is constituted. The simultaneous complicity and distance which I have described are also the crucial components in the child's relationship with its parents, especially that of boys who learn their masculinity by separating themselves emotionally from their mothers and identifying with their fathers. This process is characterised at every point by its own double-facedness, as Judith Butler has described:

> Although Freud introduces the Oedipal complex to explain why the boy must repudiate the mother and adopt an ambivalent attitude towards the father, he remarks shortly afterward that, 'It may even be that the ambivalence displayed in the relations to the parents should be attributed entirely to bisexuality and that it is not, as I have represented above, developed out of identification in consequence of rivalry'. But what would condition the ambivalence in such a case? Clearly, Freud means to suggest that the boy must choose not only between the two object choices, but the two sexual dispositions, masculine and feminine. That the boy usually chooses the heterosexual would, then, be the result, not of the fear of castration by the father, but of the fear of castration – that is, the fear of 'feminization' associated within heterosexual cultures with male homosexuality.[4]

Lowell was deeply versed in Freud and described himself in a letter to his second wife Elizabeth Hardwick as 'a slavish convert': 'every fault is a goldmine of discoveries. I am a walking goldmine. … It's all too much (especially while staying with mother)'.[5] Confessional poetry itself partly evolved by analogy with the Freudian 'talking cure', and the authorial double-take I have referred to is connected with the confessional habit of presenting psychic material and simultaneously hinting at interpretation of it (though in Lowell's case this was also linked to his early exposure, as a student of John Crowe Ransom, to New Criticism). The form this knowingness takes in '91 Revere Street' is that the proper Freudian roles of mother and father are assumptions, they are taken for granted as norms, implied in similar nudges to the reader as the parenthetical one Lowell gives to Hardwick '(especially while staying with mother)'. It is against the background of this implied norm that Lowell's comic near-satirical treatment of his parents works.

Lowell implies that he inherited a kind of femininity (or, at least, mermaid ambiguity) from his father, and masculinity from his mother. It is Mrs Lowell who sets the standards for masculine behaviour: her hero 'dove through the grottoes of the Rhine and slaughtered the homicidal and vulgar dragon coiled about the golden hoard' (27). By contrast, she found her husband 'savourless, unmasterful, merely considerate', imagined him when he was away 'sublimed' like Siegfried (27) but when he was home emasculated him in the process of trying to make him more masculine – tells him 'A *man* must make up his *own* mind' and then, in her next sentence, tells him what to do: 'Oh Bob, if you are going to resign, do it *now* ...' (29).

There is comedy in this but Lowell is aware that, because he is implicated in it genetically and through the constitutive experiences of childhood, the joke is also on him. His work as a whole is characterised by what might be called refusal of denial, refusal that is to dissociate himself from the most disturbing aspects of his own psyche. '91 Revere Street' is charged with Lowell's sense of the problematic nature of gender in general and his own gender identity in particular. When his mother turns to him for solace when his father is away, saying 'Oh, Bobby, it's such a comfort to have a man in the house', he replies 'I am not a man ... I am a boy'.

His own interpretation of this rejection of the Oedipal role is to relate it to a rejection of the responsibilities of conventionally domestic adult masculinity. Italicising the word, he says that being a *boy* 'had private associations for me, it meant weakness, outlawry, and yet was a status to be held on to' (34). This helps to explain the curious reference in 'Waking Early Sunday Morning' to 'the criminal leisure of a boy':[6] he is celebrating there the freedoms he associates in '91 Revere Street' with his maternal grandfather 'whose unchecked commands and demands were always upsetting people for their own good – he was all I could ever want to be: the bad boy, the problem child, the commodore of his household' (38). So 'criminal leisure' refers to the rebellion against being tramelled like Mr Lowell: 'to judge from my father, men between the ages of six and sixty did nothing but meet new challenges, take on heavier responsibilities, and lose all freedom to explode' (38). It is by contrast with this vision of maleness severely in control of itself that Lowell evokes the need to hang on to an uncivilised Huckleberry Finn-like boyhood – the implication is that it is impossible for males *not* to yearn for 'natural' unconstraint. Yet they will also inevitably

feel guilty about such 'weakness, outlawry' to the extent that Lowell
links this 'criminal leisure' with 'squatting like a dragon on / time's
hoard before the day's begun', so associating himself with the
symbol of evil whose conquest by a more righteous masculine hero
is fantasised by his mother.

Guilt is one of Lowell's most recurrent and characteristic emo-
tions so it is not surprising that he feels it in relation to his masculin-
ity. Ambivalence, though, is equally characteristic and in this
context lays him open to the charge that his guilt is confessed in a
merely token or even self-glamourising fashion. Certainly this evo-
cation of boyishness has about it a self-consciously roguish element,
especially because it is linked in the poem to the natural energy of
the salmon 'jumping and falling back'. This is related to the refer-
ences to the private life in Marvell's 'Horatian Ode Upon
Cromwell's Return From Ireland', Lowell's prototype for 'Waking
Early Sunday Morning', where the pressures of public life are con-
trasted with the contentments of the Horatian 'happy man' in his
garden retreat. Marvell suggests that, for Cromwell, these content-
ments had to be put aside because of the pressing political circum-
stances. Nonetheless, they do represent an important cultural value
with an ancient tradition behind them, and it is clear that Lowell's
American and mid-twentieth century equivalent receives a parallel
sanction, albeit ambivalently.

The garden retreat will become an option again for Marvell's hero
– by contrast Lowell's boyish leisure is regarded with a tinge of nos-
talgia in a poem whose central concern is with what citizenship has
become in the modern period, how it imposes a narrowing of
human potential. Lowell is concerned throughout his career to take
up the themes adumbrated in modernism and he refers repeatedly
to the imagery of fertility, which is deployed as a controlling
metaphor in *The Waste Land*. The breaking loose Lowell yearns for
in 'Waking Early' is associated at the same time with boyhood and
with the heroic fertility of the chinook salmon which is 'alive
enough to spawn and die' and 'breaks / water' (13). These in turn
are connected with the breaking loose of the president 'swimming
nude, unbuttoned, sick / of his own ghost-written rhetoric' (16).
These are atavistic freedoms only sabbatically allowed to modern
men and their maleness is stressed in the presidential context by his
matey relationship with his aides ('this Sunday morning, free to
chaff / his own thoughts with his bear-cuffed staff') and their link

with the sudden insistence that 'All life's grandeur / is something with a girl in summer' (16).

The poem ends with an apocalyptic vision of planetary sterility, of 'the pruner and his knife / busy about the tree of life', the earth a 'sweet volcanic cone' and 'a ghost / orbiting forever lost' (16). This must be read by contrast with the imagery of the salmon, the boy, 'time's hoard' and the swimming president. The implication is that the nuclear waste land Lowell fears will result, at least partly, from the directing of male energies away from natural freedoms into a militarism which he describes in obsessively phallic terms ('Hammering ... top-heavy Goliath ... elephant and phalanx ... a million foreskins stacked like trash'). This destructive translation of sexual energies will not regenerate us as sexual release would: 'little redemption in the mass / liquidations of their brass' (15).

To some extent, then, 'Waking Early Sunday Morning' can be regarded as continuing the modernist tendency identified by Gilbert and Gubar:

Because texts like *Women in Love* and *The Waste Land*, *Ulysses* and 'The Second Coming' have been universalised and privileged as documents in a history of cultural crisis, the sexual anxieties they articulate have been seen mainly as metaphors of metaphysical angst. But though they do, of course express such angst – God did, after all, disappear in the nineteenth century and the smoke of dark Satanic mills did shadow Europe – it is significant that modernist formulations of societal breakdown consistently employed imagery that was specifically sexual and, even more specifically, imagery of male impotence and female potency.[7]

However, Lowell's differences from this tradition are more important than his similarities. He rarely expresses fears about female potency – 'Near the Ocean' (*Ocean*, 25–7) is a significant exception to this which I'll be exploring. What is crucially characteristic of him is his ambivalent attitude to male potency; it could be said that 'Waking Early' is a critique of patriarchy, but Lowell is too impressed by the president's maleness and too excited by his own appalled depiction of militarism for that to sit comfortably as a description of the poem. What makes his gender attitudes so fascinating is precisely this ambivalence. Like Eliot and Lawrence, Lowell does depict cultural breakdown in 'Waking Early' in terms of sexual imagery – but he is much more focused than them on males and what might be called lost boyishness, whose values are roughly those of his maternal grandfather and his 'granite back-countriness', and also of Theodore Roosevelt:

> 'As it is with the individual', Theodore Roosevelt observes in his 1899 men's club speech, 'The Strenuous Life', 'so it is with the nation'. And confronting the wilderness, Roosevelt continues, re-generates 'that vigorous manliness for the lack of which in a nation, as in an individual, the possession of no other qualities can possibly atone.' Linking together anxieties about the male natural body and the body of the nation – linking together, that is, body-building and nation-building – Seton's or Roosevelt's program for the making of men posits not merely that the indi-vidual is something that can be made but that the male natural body and national geography are surrogate terms. The closing of the frontier, announced by Frederick Jackson Turner in 1893, ap-parently foreclosed the regeneration of men through 'the trans-forming influence of the American wilderness' – a transformation that, Turner argues, makes 'a new product that is American'.[8]

It is precisely these values that Lowell alludes to in *Life Studies* when he wants to contrast his savourless unmasterful father with his back-country maternal grandfather. The first stanza of 'My Last afternoon with Uncle Devereux Winslow' (73–8) – the first confes-sional poem in the book – is already preoccupied with that contrast as the boy Lowell refuses to leave his 'Grandpa' to travel with his parents. They are soft and sophisticated. Their 'watery martini pipe dreams' are the cultural opposite of his grandfather's farm which seems precariously poised between civilisation and the wilderness: 'its alley of poplars / paraded from Grandmother's rose garden / to a scary stand of virgin pine, / scrub, and paths forever pioneering' (73). These images appear to place the farm right on the frontier itself, except that the last phrase transfers an epithet that can only be transferred in the boy's mind (pioneering is unnecessary where there are paths) and so hints at the boyish nostalgia that has created this impression. So too 'forever pioneering' is effectively an oxy-moron and as such reveals that it is an atavistic desire that perceives the paths in this glamorous light. These paradoxes again indicate Lowell's ambivalence which both mourns and mocks lost boyish-ness. His grandfather is still admired but his grandfather's possessions comically juxtapose the wild and the tame – his 'Edwardian cuckoo-clock' is 'slung with strangled, wooden game' (73), he has 'a Rocky mountain chaise longue, its legs, shellacked saplings' and a 'pastel-pale Huckleberry Finn' who 'fished with a broom-straw in a basin' (74).

Lowell is clearly aware of the gender aspects of all this:

> Like my grandfather, the décor
> was manly, comfortable,
> overbearing, disproportioned.
> (74)

The cooked is feminine (the rose garden is labelled as his Grandmother's) while the raw is what must be confronted, pioneeringly, by males. He is also aware of how much these boyhood experiences are structured – by both his childhood and adult selves – around his need for gender identification, his need to construct himself as masculine. Having introduced his grandfather in 'My Last Afternoon' he goes on in the second confessional poem in the book, 'Dunbarton', to recount how his grandfather's employees and even his grandmother referred to his grandfather as his father: 'He was my Father. I was his son.' (79) So it is important that Lowell shows himself learning masculinity – and choosing to learn it – from the frontier values he attributes to his mother's father. For the ambivalence in his retrospective account of this process insists on how much gender insecurity lies behind it and how comically, mock-heroically inappropriate this version of masculinity appears for contemporary males.

The nostalgia implied in 'paths forever pioneering' also implies that to be a modern man is to feel that a part of yourself is ill-attuned to your circumstances. In rejecting his father as a role model Lowell also rejects the burden of full twentieth-century male citizenship, which means endlessly to 'take on heavier responsibilities, and lose all freedom to explode' (LS, 38). It is exactly this freedom Lowell yearns for in 'Waking Early Sunday Morning', where the phrase 'criminal leisure of a boy' suggests guilt at feeling an immature yearning – but also confrontational sarcasm towards a culture so unnatural that a yearning so harmless can be denigrated. There is also contrast between the natural energy of the salmon (which represents the freedom to explode) and the deathliness of the culture which suppresses such freedoms and promotes phallic

militarism in their place. The vision of the president swimming nude
briefly hints at the possibility of the male natural body and the body
politic in harmony with each other, but a heavy stress is laid on its
brevity, on this being something only possible 'this Sunday
morning', as an alternative to going to church. Briefly, the president
can swim free 'of his ghost-written rhetoric', but mostly the dead
hand of the repressive social otherness of politics and language will
weigh on him. To feel this as repressive is to feel that your desires as
a man may be regarded as 'criminal' in contemporary society. To
want to be a chinook salmon on weekdays is to be a fish out of water.

* * *

Ambivalence is crucial, however, even here in a moment that seems
most purely masculine. As Alan Williamson has pointed out, with
typical acuteness:

> There is the same link between the will-to-power and the elation
> of sexual fulfilment ('something with a girl in summer'), borne
> out in the homoerotic, or at least exhibitionistic, implications of
> the President floating naked in a pool while lecturing to a sur-
> rounding circle of aides. The overtones of the word *girdled* add to
> the sense of a hidden femininity in the ostentatious stag-party
> masculinity of the occasion.[9]

That last point is perhaps confirmed by the fact that Jack Kennedy
(the predecessor of Lyndon Johnson, who is the president referred
to in the poem) did actually wear a kind of girdle to help his chronic
back problems. Williamson's insight into these lines provides a clue
to Lowell's gender attitudes in general: he is consistently concerned
to hint at elements of gender ambiguity in those moments where
men appear to be most conventionally masculine. Williamson links
this to Lowell's obsession with tyranny, and especially with
Caligula: 'masculinity and power are things Caligula deviously
seeks to incorporate from without, because he feels them to be
absent from his proper being' (101). Then he speculates in a
footnote:

> The frequent link between tyranny and homosexuality undoubt-
> edly has complex underpinnings. Psychological views of homo-
> sexuality as extended narcissism, or as an attempt to acquire

selfhood and strength from another person through incorporation, are obviously relevant. (But perhaps it is only our civilisation that would find the link strange to begin with, tending as we do to associate homosexuality with external weakness, effeminacy, passivity. To the Greeks, it was perfectly logical that a man preoccupied with military things, strength, and violence, would love people for related qualities, and despise – even fear – antithetical ones. Cf. Lowell's 'Epigram' on Thermopylae.)

The lines Williamson refers to in this aside were later incorporated in 'The Spartan Dead at Thermopylae', one of the sonnets in *History*.[10] In that context they become part of its linked motifs of war and tyranny and help to make explicit the extent to which Lowell's concern with those motifs is a gendered concern. Leonidas' hoplites, before battle, 'combed one another's / golden Botticellian hair', they are 'friends and lovers'. This is all the more significant because it represents for Lowell an attitude to life which he finds especially admirable. His wish to celebrate it is evident from its repetition, and its first incarnation is in *For the Union Dead*[11] where the hoplites share much in common with the eponymous soldiers of the title poem – both, in particular, rejoice in 'man's lovely peculiar power to choose life and die'. This is a central tenet in the existential outlook that Lowell increasingly holds from the 1950s onwards and which takes the place of his earlier Catholicism – an insistence on the human ability simultaneously to mould a destiny through life choices and, in that process, forge an identity. This may lead, as it does for both the Spartan and the Union dead, to the choice, *in extremis*, of an heroic death. But the terms of Lowell's praise clearly indicate that he regards this kind of heroism as specifically masculine, as representing the masculine at its most sublime. His use of the normally generalised 'man's' does not seem inadvertent because the statues of Colonel Shaw and his infantrymen are characterised by that hardness and sharpness which are always markers of maleness in Lowell's work (as in his grandfather's cane, and his recurrent references to harpoons):

> Their monument sticks like a fishbone
> in the city's throat.
> Its Colonel is as lean
> as a compass-needle.
>
> (71)

Shaw and his regiment are contrasted with contemporary Boston. They are surrounded by mid-twentieth century urban sprawl and mess but stubbornly retain their hard definitiveness, and their selfless courage contrasts with the 'savage servility' and venality of contemporary capitalism that uses a photograph of Hiroshima in an advertisement for a Mosler safe. When Lowell spreads the vision of the poem more broadly, to 'a thousand small town New England greens' he does so mostly to tie in a reference to their 'stone statues of the abstract Union Soldier' with the Boston monument which is the poem's central image. Like Colonel Shaw these figures are characterised by their youthful maleness, but their abstractness is important because it makes explicit what a weight of representativeness Lowell wants these statues to carry. This indicates that, among other things, 'For the Union Dead', is an elegy for a lost, and (in Lowell's view) deeply valuable, form of masculinity. The values they represent are of a piece with those advocated by Theodore Roosevelt: their male natural bodies, so lovingly described by Lowell, are made to represent an heroic virility that characterised American men before the closing of the frontier, and which is conspicuously lacking in the scene of civic sterility, with its 'Sahara of snow', which characterises modern Boston.

It is as if to balance this that two references to statuary elsewhere in *For the Union Dead* grieve over a lost feminine principle. The 'hundred marble goddesses' that 'wept like willows' in 'Buenos Aires' (60–1) are contrasted with the statues of 'leaden, internecine generals'. The bleak militaristic culture these male statues represent leaves Lowell so desperate for feminine succour that he 'found rest' from the female statues by 'cupping a soft palm to each hard breast'. In 'The Neo-Classical Urn' the 'stone statue of a nymph, / her soaring armpits and her one bare breast' looks on as the boy Lowell performs his acts of feverish cruelty against turtles. In both these poems the references to stone breasts serve to rebuke further a masculine obsession with violence. What they share with the statues in 'For the Union Dead' is the paradoxical sense that they are the most human things in the landscape, that the fully human has been lost and replaced with simulacra.

Both genders are represented in these elegies, but the masculine is mourned in and for itself whereas the feminine is depicted mostly in terms of the value it has for the masculine as a source of idealised kindness and comfort. The Spartan dead are celebrated by Lowell because they incorporate feminine strengths alongside their

obvious masculine ones and they may even implicitly share this
with Colonel Shaw and his infantrymen – self-sacrifice for a collec-
tive good is a quality with traditionally a more feminine reputation.
Lowell does suggest that the most admirable moments combine the
strengths of both genders. But there is another powerful motive
behind this combining of masculine and feminine: a kind of wish
fulfilment of a masculinity which, by absorbing the feminine,
immunises itself against it. The freedom the Spartan dead feel –
they are 'glittering with liberation' – is partly an existential
fulfilment that comes from shaping a destiny through choice, but it
is also a freedom that arises from a purely masculine transcendence
of the demands of the feminine.

This interpretation is confirmed by Lowell's explicit wish for this
masculine autonomy in an unpublished poem, 'Death and the
Maiden', included in the drafts of 'Memories of West Street and
Lepke' and printed by Terri Witek in her book on Lowell.[12] Here
the poet imagines himself split into halves, one a woman, the other
a black boy:

> He thinks his masculinity
> Only created to be free
> Of entangling alliances –
> To turn all women's hands from his,
> He swings a cane on which he's seared
> Norwegian mountains he has cleared ...
>
> (108)

Typically, though, because the wish here is at its most explicit, it is
also at its most repudiated – it is attributed to a caricatural figure, a
cool dude who is everything Lowell is not (his bearing is 'single-
angled to appear / Simple, sensuous and sincere'). By a heavy irony,
too, he is not a real man, not even a real person, and even more
entanglingly allied to a woman than most males, being literally
spliced with one:

> Thank God my better self is woman:
> All night she screams "*Nihil humanum* –
> I'm alien to no alien thing,
> The thousand thousand languishing,
> Poisoned devils of conscience drowse
> Outside my open floodgate house

And throbbing, glowing, reddened whole,
We burn together, one live coal."

(108)

This unpublished poem shows that the desire for an auto-
nomous masculinity is undoubtedly a part of Lowell's psychology,
and helps to explain some of the impulse behind his praise of the
Union and the Spartan dead, and his half-ironised nostalgia for
the spirit of the frontier. What it also indicates, however, is that he
recognises both the impossibility of such autonomy and the
destructiveness caused when it comes close to being achieved.
When he insists that his better self is woman he is not being merely
chivalrous: he is associating his attributes as a writer with this 'fem-
inine' part of his nature. This shows that he does not regard the
feminine as simply a matter of passive, anti-violent nurturing
which can be thoroughly evoked by references to stone breasts –
the qualities of conscience and imaginative sympathy which he
depicts as feminine here rank for Lowell as amongst the most
heroic human qualities.

To some extent Lowell is involved, in this poem, in what Terri
Witek calls a 'takeover', 'an alternative possibility of identity that
must be dismantled, or, rather, reconstructed as a version of
himself':

> the poet wants to see whether there is something beyond his own
> identity and, in a curious way, beyond his power. Feminist Luce
> Irigaray would argue that such a desire is both generically male
> and inevitably doomed, for male identity depends on creating a
> relentless series of others who are not truly 'other', but are mirror
> images of the central ego. (4)

However, this notion of the 'takeover' seems to me reductive. It is
undoubtedly part of Lowell's impulse in his depiction of historical
and contemporary figures, but there is an equally powerful impulse
towards reflecting on the otherness of the other, on exploring ways
Lowell will never be. From *Life Studies* onwards there is a painstak-
ingly realist concern to evoke – whatever ragged-edged asymmetry
it involves formally and linguistically – a sense of the lived particu-
larity of other people. And a large part of the motive of *History* is to
evoke modes of being that are impossible not just to Lowell but to

everyone in the twentieth century. Again and again in his characterisations Lowell could be saying, as he does explicitly in 'The Spell', 'He was not my double, and haunts me.'[13] Sometimes in fact the main point of his poems is to enact Lowell's struggle to differentiate himself from others. In 'Waking in the Blue' (LS 95–6), for example, Lowell is defined in opposition to the 'thoroughbred mental cases / twice my age and half my weight'. 'Stanley' and 'Bobbie' are passive and compared to sea creatures (respectively a seal and a sperm whale) and so prey to the metaphorical 'harpoon' which Lowell imagines is 'sparring for the kill': the poet himself, by contrast, is all masculine vigour, 'Cock of the walk' he struts in his 'turtle-necked French sailor's jersey'. It is only in this context that the poem's ending can acquire its irony – after all this insistence that Lowell is different, he concedes that he has become identified with the others through their shared fate: 'We are all old-timers, / each of us holds a locked razor.'

The crucial point here is the characteristic way Lowell balances the poem between identification and differentiation. It is in the dialogue between the two that he explores the issue of identity – and not simply, as Witek suggests, through a specular process of repeatedly taking over the identities of others. Witek's account of the process is accurate up to a point:

> Lowell leaves behind old styles and the mentors associated with them, but writers are not the only influential figures he attempts to discard. What these figures have in common is that they are similarly imposing and convincing males (the exception, Lowell's mother, is a telling addition to the list) who offer highly organised and indeed rigid models of identity. Lowell demonstrates an attraction to the 'highly metrical' in his choice of such figures similar to his attraction to highly structured poetic forms, in other words. (14)

Witek is very convincing in her emphasis on the power associated with these figures but what she does not draw attention to is the extent to which Lowell, in depicting them, also depicts himself in a power relationship with them which already differentiates him from them at the moment of his apparent identification. This is most explicit in his treatment of his grandfather in 'Dunbarton' (LS, 79–81). The boy Lowell turns to his grandfather as a model because his father seems insufficiently masculine – paradoxically, though, in identifying with his grandfather's imposing maleness, he responds to it in a 'feminine' and submissive way:

> In the mornings I cuddled like a paramour
> in my Grandfather's bed
> while he scouted about the chattering greenwood stove.

   Lowell is clearly fascinated by the notion of potent maleness but the figures he erects as such themselves ward off the possibility of true identification because their very maleness takes the form of emphasising its own stubborn and rigid particularity. No-one else could resemble these men because their power and style is thoroughly *sui generis*. Lowell at the same time admires their orderly purity and is disturbed by it, and reminded of his own mingledness and consequent comparative vulnerability. This is again most explicit in the unpublished 'Death and the Maiden'. By declaring the woman his better self Lowell can be said, up to a point, to be taming the otherness of the feminine and so immunising himself against it. This would help him more closely to resemble his masculine heroes, and it would confirm Witek's notion of the 'takeover' where, by implication, the poet is involved in controlling otherness. But Lowell is remarkable for his insistence on, even obsession at times with control – in combination with his ability to relinquish it at others. Witek herself refers to his 'double attraction toward the highly fixed and the highly free' (16). His development as a poet shows him acquiring growing flexibility not just in technique but in outlook and this importantly involves him in a continual exploration of gender roles and an increasing tendency to deconstruct gender stereotypes, so that he deliberately eschews a controlling insistence on presenting himself as purely masculine. When in 'Waking in the Blue' he calls himself 'Cock of the walk' he does so self-mockingly – he parodies his own manly insistence on his independence from the other inmates.
   It is exactly such independence which 'Death and the Maiden' is finally sceptical about. The male part of the self disentangles itself from women by displaying its frontier spirit, its ability to broach virgin territory ('Norwegian mountains he has cleared'). The female part, by contrast, embraces entanglements: instead of trying to tame otherness it allows itself to be penetrated by it, is 'alien to no alien

thing'. It is by dwelling on these stereotypes and by making them components of one personality that Lowell dismantles them, displays the pretentious impossibility of the masculine self-image, and insists on the necessity of messy entanglement, especially for creative artists. He is taking very seriously the idea that writers must be androgynous, as he also does in his prose piece 'Sylvia Plath's *Ariel*'[14] where he is excited by reading a poet whose concerns are so close to his own – 'personal, confessional, felt, but the manner of feeling is controlled hallucination, the autobiography of a fever' (122) – but who was a woman. His references to her gender are gauche at times but Mary Ellmann is unfair when she refers to his 'general pelting away at the single fact that Sylvia Plath belonged to a sex (that inescapable membership) and that her sex was not male'.[15] His gaucheness itself indicates the earnestness of his attempt to understand what is gendered about these poems and which is an essential part of their power. He is also aware that this is a very complicated issue: 'This character is feminine, rather than female, though almost everything we customarily think of as feminine is turned on its head'. That last point is important because it is the key to how Lowell in this piece is again both identifying and distancing himself. The subtext throughout is that Plath is like Lowell but then again unlike because she is a woman. He is tempted by her work but resists: 'In her lines, I often hear the serpent whisper, "Come, if only you, too, could have my rightness, audacity, and ease of inspiration." But most of us will turn back.' (123–4). Lowell is stirred by Plath's achievement to the extent of wanting to learn from it, especially from the last book whose 'title *Ariel* summons up Shakespeare's lovely though slightly chilling and androgynous spirit', and the whole piece is implicitly about imagining a poetic whose potency arises from its mingling of the 'masculine' and the 'feminine', imagining both turned on their heads.

***

These repudiations of the desire for an autonomous masculinity acquire special importance in the context of Lowell's repeated writings about tyranny, which he himself diagnoses as a symptom of a masculinity allowed to express itself with disastrous fullness. In order to understand this, however, it is worth reflecting briefly on what drives men to disentangle themselves from women. Tom

Ryan links it to the manner in which masculinity is constructed by
the early insistence on difference from the mother. As a result,

> To ensure a separateness many men deny feelings of need or de-
> pendency, finding them a threat to an already fragile identity. To
> indicate a need of or dependence on a woman for some men
> would be tantamount to self-annihilation. Such is the dilemma
> for men with their maleness and masculinity. To have a sense of
> separateness, a difference must be fortified and defended; hence
> the demonstration by many men of an exaggerated virility
> paraded as autonomy. Any expression of need or desire carries
> with it the threat of succumbing to a wish to be united with, or
> the same as, the woman.[16]

This leads, Ryan says, to 'machismo behaviour with its emphasis on
competitiveness, strength, aggressiveness, contempt for women
and emotional shallowness' (26).

One of Lowell's most remarkable achievements as a poet is that
he diagnosed this tendency in himself, allowed it to express itself to
a certain cathartic extent in his work but also learned how to dis-
tance himself from it and counter its effects. His early work is char-
acterised by what Gabriel Pearson has called 'the omnipotence of
manic verbal control' (quoted in Hamilton, 105). The poet seems to
want to tyrannise his material by obsessively man-handling it
through rhyme, heavy alliteration, compulsive punning, into hard
sinewy shapes. The poetic technique does seem exaggeratedly virile
and yet Lowell learned to write entirely differently – and what is
revealed in that process is what motivated the early style in the first
place. Confessional writing, like the psychotherapy of which it is
the creative kin, helps Lowell to know himself and so to change.
The hard shapes of the early poems seem to be about fortifying and
defending the poet, warding off any disturbing otherness: increas-
ingly with *Life Studies* and after the confessional Lowell allows in
an otherness which also interrogates the central ego.

As part of this process Lowell faces up to his fascination with
omnipotence and tyranny and explores it repeatedly, especially in
History. Ambivalence is again a crucial feature here. The knowing-
ness that lies behind this endeavour is linked to the interest in psy-
choanalysis and both are motivated, at least partly, by a desire to
control whose sources are similar to those of Lowell's obsession
with power. More disturbingly, the tyrants Lowell focuses on

arouse in him – alongside his liberal feelings of repulsion and horror – obvious feelings of identification and excitement. This is all the more important because it is so closely tied up with his mental illness, his manic depression. Repeatedly, during his manic phases, Lowell (as well as becoming fixated on a younger woman) became obsessed with figures like Napoleon, Hitler or Mussolini:

> troublingly for those who cared for him, his enemies could all too easily construct from accounts of his delusions a portrait of Lowell as a sort of near fascist – How was it, they could disingenuously wonder, that this renowned spokesman for correct liberal causes persistently 'revealed', in mania, a fascination with tyrants and monsters of the right? (Hamilton, 343)

The omnipotence which the early Lowell exercises, through manic verbal control, over his poetic materials is exercised by these tyrants over the world itself – they can create the world around them in their own image.

In 'Caligula' (UD 49–51) Lowell faces the problem of his own identification directly by asking why, at school, he took the name of the mad Roman emperor, and worrying that in Caligula's face he sees his own 'lowest depths of possibility'. Caligula is the opposite of the heroic selflessness Lowell celebrates in Colonel Shaw and Leonidas' hoplites, his megalomania is above all about imposing himself through destroying what is around him. The statues that surround him all have his head because he has smashed those of the gods and replaced them with his own. So Caligula is repeated everywhere, even by the poet himself looking in the poem for a mirror of himself. Except that Lowell himself rejects the idea of the 'takeover' when he insists, in the last line, that this tyrant was his 'namesake, and the last Caligula'.

That this last line is altered, in its sonnet version in *History* (48), to 'my namesake, not the last Caligula', shows again how Lowell wavers between identification and distancing. It also suggests that Lowell takes Caligula as the prototype for the tyrants who appear after him in that volume – for example for Attila and Hitler whose joint poem appears only three pages later (51) and who are also shown defining themselves through destruction ('old tins, dead vermin, ashes, eggshells, youth'). It is part of Lowell's own psycho-analysing tendency that he defines the tyrannical personality as consumed by compensatory activity designed to cover weakness: in describing Caligula he stresses his physical weakness and ugliness and diagnoses this as the source of his egomania. It is in these terms too that Lynne Segal characterises the authoritarian personality, seeing it as

> quintessentially masculine – the masquerade of power conceal-
> ing weak and dependent feelings through the assertion of
> strength and the rejection of everything gentle, spontaneous,
> soft, relaxed, chaotic (seen as intrinsically connected to the body,
> rather than the mind).[17]

In Lowell's case the fascination with tyrants is linked to his fascina-
tion with violence and war, as in his poems on Napoleon (*History*,
77–8) and both fascinations are expressed in terms that stress that
these are masculine preserves. In one of his poems about Vietnam,
for example, the emphasis is specifically on the destructiveness of
men: 'we was to burn and kill, then there'd be nothing / standing,
women, children, babies, cows, cats' (*History*, 199). The speaker of
this poem is ordered to shoot a woman and finds she is holding a
baby he 'thought was her gun. It kind of cracked me up.'

Much of the power of this writing comes from the complex feel-
ings that are seen to lie behind it when it is taken in the context of
Lowell's work as a whole. Taken in isolation these poems seem to
be simply about horror and protest but the obsessive repetition of
this material reveals Lowell's feelings of guilty complicity in it, his
disturbance that his mind excitedly dwells on and returns to it. Far
from treating these tyrants and soldiers as 'takeovers' Lowell is
involved in a psychological process that recognises elements of
himself in them and also feverishly repudiates those elements. In
doing so Lowell seems to be acutely aware of his own psychological
motives, related as they are to the family background he carefully
details in '91 Revere Street', a background whose circumstances
were startlingly close to those described by John Munder Ross as
the causes of 'martial masculinity'. Lynne Segal summarises his
argument tellingly when she refers to the 'sadistic narcissistic
fixations' of this outlook, and continues:

> This is a type of masculinity, Ross believes, related to the unavail-
> ability of the father early on as a libidinal object and figure for
> identification. Sons of fathers who are absent emotionally, who
> act like oppressors, or are entirely inhibited and ineffectual

compared with a powerful mother (especially in a relationship where the mother disparages or fears men), are led to create their own exaggerated, artificial, brittle and aggressive version of manhood as a protection against their identification with the powerful mother. (Segal, 75)

The boy Lowell seems almost too exactly defined by 'martial masculinity':

I was afraid Father's leaving the Navy would destroy my standing. I was a churlish, disloyal, romantic boy, and quite without hero worship for my father, whose actuality seemed so inferior to the photographs in uniform he once mailed us from the Golden Gate. My real *love*, as Mother used to insist to all new visitors, was toy soldiers. For a few months at the flood tide of this infatuation, people were ciphers to me – valueless except as chances for increasing my armies of soldiers. (LS, 22)

This was combined, slightly later, with his obsession with Napoleon, so that he spent 'whole vacations lugging home his hundred *Lives*' (*History*, 77). In 'Waterloo' Lowell perfectly captures the mingling of sadism and narcissism in these obsessions when he describes an 'aide-de-camp' toy soldier, 'Napoleon's perhaps' who 'wore a cascade of overstated braid, / there sabered, dying, his standard wrenched from weak hands' (*History*, 78).

***

Lowell's harping on tyranny and violence is best seen as part of his tendency to repeat material and best explained as such in the terms employed by Katherine Wallingford:

Lowell's uses of repetition were complex and various. Freud … saw repetition both as a terrible compulsion that drives many people to reenact painful experiences over and over again, and also as a therapeutic 'working-through' by means of which we can make sense of and come to terms with our experience.[18]

He is at the same time indulging his obsession and trying to shed a sickness. It is in 'Near the Ocean' (*Ocean*, 25–7) that the sources and

effects of Lowell's 'martial masculinity' are worked through most
fully, although the strain of this is evident in the poem's phantas-
magoric difficulty. The figure of the powerful mother is represented
first of all by Medusa, the sight of whose head is terrifying because,
as 'Freud argues ... it threatens by association with both castration
and female genitalia'.[19] However, in a scene of dreamlike wish-
fulfilment this powerful threat is shown being triumphantly over-
come by a 'hero' who has killed the monster and 'lifts her head to
please the mob'. This is a narcissistic fantasy of the son as Perseus –
of the son, in other words, who responds to the threat of the
mother's power by acquiring soldierly prowess and displaying it for
the admiration of others. In the third stanza Lowell refers to the
more general effects of martial masculinity when he suggests
that the source of wars lies in this masculine repudiation of the
feminine:

> Lost in the Near Eastern dreck,
> the tyrant and tyrannicide
> lie like the bridegroom and the bride;
> the battering ram, abandoned, prone,
> beside the apeman's phallic stone.

The reference to the bridegroom and the bride recalls a similar line
in Lowell's two poems about the Spartan dead but its effect is the
reverse of the celebratory one there – the shared maleness of the
tyrant and tyrannicide produces a destructive impoverishment. It
is paradoxical that they are like lovers because the dynamics of their
purely male relationship produce a sterile cycle of violence repre-
sented by the encounter of two phalluses, the battering ram and the
stone. In the terms of Gilbert and Gubar, Lowell is here relating
sexual anxiety and societal breakdown (Gilbert and Gubar, 202) but
that is not because he wants the one to be read simply as the other,
but because he wants to show, in his own way, that the personal is
political. He is diagnosing a male sickness and indicating its social
consequences.

Alongside the self-aggrandisingly mythic repudiation of the
mother Lowell places a more realist account of the son's desperate,
half-guilty attachment to her, and his doomed attempts to replace
her, ever afterwards, with his lovers. It is this element that then
becomes the main subject of the poem, so that the references to
tyranny and violence in 'Near the Ocean' are best seen as an

element that Lowell tries to 'work through' so that he can move beyond them into a healthier accommodation of the feminine and an acceptance of the demands, however entangling, of mature sexual relationships. Nonetheless, the course of these relationships is necessarily envisaged as largely predetermined by the male's previous, deeply ambiguous, experiences with the mother, and dogged with consequent confusions between need and suspicion, desire and squeamish repulsion:

> then high delirious squalor, food
> burned down with vodka ... menstrual blood
> caking the covers, when they woke
> to the dry, childless Sunday walk
>
> (26)

There are misogynistic images in 'Near the Ocean' but that is because it is a confessional poem *about* misogyny. That it is an attempt to work through these feelings is also evident from the fact that it is dedicated to Elizabeth Hardwick, Lowell's wife at the time.

What is perhaps most important about the poem is that it counters its own misogyny by explicitly associating feminine values with the ocean for the first time in Lowell's work. It is with the introduction, in its seventh stanza, of its oceanic references that 'Near the Ocean' grows lyrical (if still equivocally). And the growing presence of the ocean/woman association after this poem is the most important sign of the extent to which Lowell has worked through his martial masculinity. In 'Near the Ocean' it partly expresses masculine frustration at feminine unfixedness, but it also celebrates that same quality, and it is the celebratory note that is increasingly struck thereafter. It is precisely by contrast with phallic hardness that oceanic values are preferred. The battering ram and the phallic stone symbolise rigid responses to history: the ocean, on the other hand, collapses rigidities, 'grinding stones' it 'can only speak the present tense' (27).

Increasingly for Lowell the ocean is used to represent both the feminine and the overwhelming of pretentious masculine attempts at control. In 'Redskin' (*History*, 163) he uses it to measure the smallness of the penis when compared with the ambition of the phallus. Having contemptuously referred to the 'redemptive bat and balls' he asks in the last lines 'when earth and ocean merge, / who wants to hold his weapon to the whale?' This hints retrospectively that the references to whale-hunting (and therefore to all the forms of violence) in 'The Quaker Graveyard in Nantucket'[20] should be read as indictments, specifically, of masculine desires for slaughter – as well as making even more explicit the phallic dimension in Lowell's repeated references to harpoons. So, too, in 'Ocean', he says:

> Mostly its colour must adulterate,
> sway, swelter; earth stands firm and not the sea,
> one substance everywhere divisible,
> great bosom of salt. It floats us – less and less
> usable now we can fly like the angels.
>
> (*History*, 176)

The attributes Lowell evokes when he refers to this 'great bosom' are precisely those Luce Irigaray evokes in her sardonic account of masculine attempts to tame, control and limit the sea:

> So this sea where he is, or at least seems to be, lost, that overwhelms him on every side and so puts his life in danger, what is she? Considered coldly, she consists of an *extended corporeal thing*. Probably immense. Which explains why the gaze at least is drowned, saturated in her. But from this place where he is now assured of existing, he can cut the sea into any number of pieces. … The 'I' can subject the sea to a whole range of techniques that will transform her into an *object of use*: into a means of transport for example. … Nonetheless, he must harden his heart to the glorious assault of her colours, to the fascination of her sheer size, to the seduction of her smells and sounds. … Let him therefore call upon his will, *which also has no bounds*, and disdain such ultimately secondary modes of being in order to concentrate on the sea's essential attribute: extension. … The 'I' thinks, therefore this thing, this body that is also nature, that is still the *mother*, becomes an extension at the 'I' 's disposal for analytical investigations, scientific projections, the regulated exercise of the imaginary, the utilitarian practice of technique.[21]

The masculine discomfort and inhibition in the face of the sea which Irigaray depicts are also in evidence in Lowell's response. As early as 'The Quaker Graveyard in Nantucket' he described man's agonised attempts to impose his dominion over the sea which is an alien force whose 'high tide / Mutters to its hurt self, mutters and

ebbs' (Poems, 21). In 'Ocean', his description of the sea as 'one sub-
stance everywhere divisible' refers to the attempt to turn it into a
matter merely of 'extension' which can then be defined and
quantified. And the oceanic references in 'Near the Ocean' suggest
an attempt to use the ocean-as-mother for the 'regulated exercise of
the imaginary' – to accommodate the feminine guiltily and only up
to a point, subjecting it to a kind of repressive tolerance.

Surprisingly, though, Lowell does manage, in his later work, to
allow freer play to this oceanic imaginary – as though his obsessive
working through of his martial masculinity produces at least a
partial cure. Through the linked figures of the mermaid and the
dolphin, and an increased preoccupation with sexual love, Lowell
learns not to harden his heart to the sea, to 'the seduction of her
smells and sounds', and, as Jonathan Raban has suggested, substi-
tutes this healthy obsession for the previous sick one: 'he took to
going down the Kings Road and buying incredibly expensive stone
dolphins from places like the Antique Hypermarket, where he dis-
covered these things were going for hundreds of pounds' (quoted
in Hamilton, 413). This was in 1971, when Lowell had separated
from Elizabeth Hardwick and was living with Caroline Blackwood,
who was pregnant with his child. At her country house he had
dolphins placed

> at either side of the front door, dolphins in the garden, dolphins
> as hatstands. … Dolphins were his high obsession at that time.
> What was interesting about it was that it was a manic attack
> which this time he fought off. … It was a rather remarkable time,
> because I think it was almost the first manic attack Cal had which
> he actually fought off – sort of saw through to the end without
> actually going over the top. So the obsession was with dolphins –
> it never got into great men. Which was a triumph. (Raban quoted
> in Hamilton, 413)

This greater accommodation of the feminine in later Lowell may
even require from his readers a retrospective re-reading of his
earlier attitudes to it, if only in the direction of even greater ambiva-
lence. The link between the hoplites, with their homoerotic associa-
tions, and the soldiers in 'For the Union Dead' is important here
and is reinforced by the extent to which Lowell's loving apprecia-
tion of the latter's male physiques paradoxically feminises them –
the 'abstract Union soldier' is described as 'wasp-waisted'. What is

most significant in this thematically is the shared element of self-sacrifice: here by far the most influential prototype, given Lowell's Catholic, and then vestigially Catholic outlook, is Christ. In 'The Quaker Graveyard' Warren Winslow and Jonah are presented as retrospective and prospective types of the Christ figure and hence as scapegoats whose self-sacrifice can lead to salvation. As such they represent an ideal combination of 'masculine' and 'feminine', active and passive, and are pitted against the purely masculine destructiveness, vividly depicted in the poem, of whaling and war. The oceanic references prefigure this element in later Lowell when he becomes much more explicitly impressed by the hybrid expressiveness of dolphins and mermaids.

So where the earlier 'Water' ends, after its dream of a mermaid, with an abashed drawing away – 'In the end, / the water was too cold for us' (UD, 4) the poems in *The Dolphin* are much more prepared to take the plunge:

> 'I am a woman or I am a dolphin,
> the only animal man really loves,
> I spout the smarting waters of joy in your face –
> rough weather fish, who cuts your nets and chains.'
>
> (54)

At times the writing is sentimental, and awkward with the feeling that Lowell is writing against his own grain, and untypically sure of his touch – as in the dolphin referred to as a 'fish'. That seems to confirm the suspicion that this is only a specular dolphin, an obsessive fantasy of a man wanting to domesticate an other and who knows too little about the actual animal to know it is a mammal. If he thinks the dolphin is a fish, what about the woman? But the awkwardnesses are themselves indicators of the struggle Lowell is undertaking in these poems, a struggle of an explicitly gendered kind involving a masculinity that has grown conscious of itself and is concerned to negotiate with a changed sense of the feminine. When he refers to 'the smarting waters of joy' Lowell summons up the paradoxical idiom of courtly love and the idealised Petrarchan lady, who is the poet's 'sweet enemy'. But this register is very consciously mingled with the realist one that predominates elsewhere and insists on Caroline Blackwood as a particular woman, and this mingling draws attention to the shifts that have occurred in attitudes to love and gender. Moreover, the image of the dolphin cutting nets and chains suggests how much she insists on her freedom and the value that has both for her and for the poet if he genuinely responds to her otherness rather than trying to net or chain it.

By far the most awkward aspect of *The Dolphin*, though, is its inclusion, as poems, of letters written to Lowell by his ex-wife Elizabeth Hardwick. Adrienne Rich, reviewing *History, For Lizzie and Harriet* and *The Dolphin* expressed contempt for the first two books, but she was especially appalled by this aspect of the third:

> There's a kind of aggrandized and merciless masculinity at work in these books, particularly the third, symptomatic of the dead-end destructiveness that masculine privilege has built for itself into all institutions, including poetry … what does one say about a poet who, having left his wife and daughter for another marriage, then titles a book with their names, and goes on to appropriate his ex-wife's letters written under the stress and pain of desertion, into a book of poems nominally addressed to the new wife?[22]

Rich's argument would be valid if Lowell had incorporated Hardwick's words into poems that contain his own, and controlled their impact by creating a defining context for them, or responded to them directly. Instead they are allowed to stand on their own. As a result they are deeply unsettling because they are so thoroughly unreconcilable with Lowell's love poems to Blackwood: together these two conflicting kinds of poem subvert any sense of definitive control and produce an uncomfortably open text in which it is impossible to focus simultaneously on Lowell's guilt and his love. Hardwick was herself a writer and Lowell allows her to represent her position with great eloquence – the power of her pieces is at least as great as Lowell's, as when, in 'Records' she says she prefers his latest letter to the 'detached unreal ones' he wrote before and then refers to Blackwood as

> doomed to know what I have known with you,
> lying with someone fighting unreality –
> love vanquished by his mysterious carelessness.
>   (31)

Hardwick's letters are a part of this book but they are not digested by it: they stick like a fishbone in *The Dolphin*'s throat.

The metaphor of the mermaid that lies behind the book is crucial because it indicates how much it is a hybrid made up of conflicting languages, one of which belongs to Hardwick. The effect of this is to some extent like the deliberately mixed metaphors that Lowell deploys increasingly throughout his career – but mixed metaphor writ large so that it destabilises all metaphysical assumptions. By allowing feminine perspectives into the book alongside his own, Lowell places the genders in dialogue with each other so that the whole issue of gendered perspective is raised. As a result it is not, as Rich says, 'aggrandized' masculinity at work, but anxious and inter-rogated masculinity. Where the early Lowell tyrannised his mater-ial, the later Lowell questions his own control over it and lays his relationship with it open to doubt. Rich herself refers to this, if scathingly, when she says 'in poem after poem, at the moment when you thought Lowell was about to cut to the bone, he veered off, lost the thread, abandoned the poem he'd begun in a kind of verbal *coitus interruptus*'. That may not be *jouissance* but at least it's not a goal-oriented drive towards definitive closure.

2

John Berryman and the Buried Women

At the heart of John Berryman's work there is an image of violence against women:

> But never did Henry, as he thought he did,
> end anyone and hacks her body up
> and hide the pieces, where they may be found.
> He knows: he went over everyone, & nobody's missing.[1]

This is from *Dream Song 29*, his most memorable poem. In their particular context these lines form what seems a culminating metaphor for the 'thing' which has sat down on Henry's heart and whose heaviness is both unappeasable and indefinable. The word 'thing' is conspicuous because it offends poetic expectations of rigorous definitiveness, and it is because of its deliberate vagueness that the poem organises itself as an attempt to overcome that vagueness and pin the thing down. The first stanza ends with what might seem very specific images – 'the little cough somewhere, an odour, a chime' – these are insinuatingly unsettling but fall short of definitiveness because they are so thoroughly deprived of a context. They are introduced, instead, via that characteristically oblique Berryman syntax, 'Starts again always in Henry's ears'. This places 'Starts' at the start of both a sentence and a line so that the question of why is both mooted and unanswered; it juxtaposes 'again' and 'always' so that the question of when is frustrated by generalisation and hints of repetitiveness; and it suggests only a partial answer by evoking the subjectivity of Henry's ears.

Berryman seems almost explicitly to be flouting Eliot's demand for an 'objective correlative': whatever this 'thing' is, only self-consciously approximate correlatives can be found for it. Having failed to pin it down in the first stanza, Berryman starts the second incorrigibly – 'And there is another thing'. This time, however, he seems to get closer to the source of the psychic problem in the word 'reproach'. This hints for the first time that the heaviness Henry suffers has its origins in guilt feelings, so that 'a grave Sienese face' can seem to accuse him. If the word 'reproach' is treated as pivotal the poem can be read in a linear way, with a beginning, middle and end rather than merely as a list of approximate images of heaviness. For it is then possible to move consecutively to the nightmare of the last lines and to find there definitiveness of a paradoxical sort – the source of Henry's problem is an act Henry denies ever having performed but which he nonetheless feels guilty about.

The word 'never' is a key one here because it is the most important reference to time in a poem that is obsessed with such references: 'once', 'a hundred years / & more', 'in all them time', 'again', 'always', 'a thousand years', 'too late', 'never', 'Often', 'in the dawn', 'ever'. The poem desperately wants to discover when the thing occurred that caused the problem but ends up by denying that the most vivid thing ever did. Elsewhere Berryman repeatedly locates the origin of his pain in his father's suicide, that is in something out of his own hands but with a very specific date and setting. Here the location is diffuse because it is scattered across the landscapes of Berryman's psyche and, similarly, the date is both never and always. For the same reason, it is unsatisfactory to describe these murderous images as a metaphor for Henry's sadness because it is part of the premise of *Dream Song* technique that subjective tenor and objective vehicle intermingle or cross-dress.

The hacking up of women's bodies is neither the source of Henry's pain nor a metaphor for it – and, at the same time, it is both. This is an important part of its point, which is that at a level as subjective as this it is impossible psychoanalytically to locate a simple source, and impossible aesthetically to define one kind of material as 'expressing' another. This is linked to that aspect of Berryman's work which John Bayley characterises when he refers to 'a terrifying and comforting image of the poet as *there* – wrestling in his flesh and in his huddle of needs – while at the same time poetry is engraving itself permanently on the page' and a sense of 'extreme singularity, the Berrymanness of Berryman, which we and the poet stare at together'.[2] Though what this does not sufficiently refer to is that it is unconscious Berrymanness we are staring at much of the time. *Dream Song 29*, on first reading, seems to say that Henry feels so bad that *it is as though* he thinks he has hacked up women's bodies and seems to say that of course actually he doesn't think that. But that is to forget the dream part of the title. The point about dreams is that, as Freud insisted, they cannot depict a negative – whenever a dream says no it is also saying yes. There is an important sense in which Henry really does think he is a murderer. This is reinforced by the recurrence of this image in Berryman's work and by its link to his actual dream life: John Haffenden quotes the poet's account of a dream he had on 30 April 1948:

> Another terrible night, and my dreams of the cached murdered bodies returned – under houses, bound finally to be discovered. E. says I am naive not to recognise some *disguise*, but I can't shake off the feeling that it is my daysense of *not* having having [*sic*] murdered that is false, – not my nightmare of having murdered.[3]

Haffenden does not link this dream to *Dream Song 29*, which is especially strange given how much the first sentence sounds like a paraphrase of 'hide the pieces, where they may be found'. This is because he is preoccupied at this point with discussing the link between Berryman's psychology and the one Berryman imputes to Stephen Crane (this means that he identifies the dead bodies as those of Berryman's parents). Haffenden's discussion here is of crucial general importance, but the link with the Crane biography is a surprisingly esoteric one to make given the much more obvious link to one of Berryman's most famous poems. It is even stranger considering that in his earlier book *John Berryman: A Critical Commentary*[4] Haffenden mentions the same dream (19) in the context of another reference to murdered women in Berryman's poems, this time in 'Homage to Mistress Bradstreet'.[5] His emphasis here is on Berryman's personal involvement, his self-investment in the poem, evident in his injection of material from his own dream life. Explaining stanza 34 he had already paraphrased another Berryman dream, this time from 6 June 1952, that he 'had murdered a number of women and was burning their bodies on bars over a fire, an action which merited capital punishment' (18). And certainly the lines in question are closely related:

> I trundle the bodies, on the iron bars,
> over the fires backward & forth; they burn;
> bits fall. I wonder if
> *I* killed them. Women serve my turn.
>
> (22)

Haffenden has been by some distance the most important critic of Berryman's work but he seems to me shockingly wrong in his treatment of this issue. He is certainly right to stress the poet's personal involvement in this imagery, but that makes it all the more important not to explain away its thematic meaning as Haffenden does, saying merely that this stanza expresses 'Berryman's own feelings of having exploited women: "Women serve my turn", after a section detailing the association of murder and sexual opportunism' (19). He refers to 'the association' of the two as though it was natural and obvious, and compounds this by suggesting that the 'sense of guilt' is one shared by the 'poet' and Anne Bradstreet – this time equating murder and adultery.

The effect of this is complacently to soft-pedal the horror which these dream images of murder evoke. The poem may encourage Haffenden's response by the bizarreness of its premise as it imagines a version of Berryman embarking on an affair with the seventeenth-century poet, and Haffenden is characteristically astute in his general interpretation of the poem as to do less with 'the travails of either the historical or the fictive Anne Bradstreet than the emotional turmoil of the poet himself' (10). But he is again complacent when he continues by saying that 'Berryman is in fact treating his own guilt feelings by shedding them in the person of Anne Bradstreet' (10).

Berryman's own attitude to the images of murder is the opposite of complacent – his emphasis, constantly, is that his feelings of guilt about them refuse to be shed. Anne Bradstreet's response to his account of burning bodies parallels that of 'E' – Berryman's first wife Eileen – to his account of 'cached murdered bodies'. Eileen insists on the element of 'disguise', of dream metaphor: in the more recent biography of Berryman by Paul Mariani[6] she is said to have 'tried to persuade him to forget his nightmares and reassured him that he was indeed a good man' (210). Anne Bradstreet says 'Dreams! You are good' (22). But Berryman refuses to be soothed: he rebuts Eileen's point about disguise by insisting that he 'can't shake off the feeling' that it is his daysense of innocence that is wrong and not his nightsense of guilt; to Bradstreet he simply says 'No' (22).

To say, as Haffenden does, that the point of this exchange 'is that the "poet" is in effect saying to her that, while other women were prey to him, she could count herself safe' (19) is grotesquely wrong. ('I'm in the habit of burning women on iron bars but I'll make an exception in your case'). Both Haffenden and Mariani attest to Berryman's sexual predatoriness and his guilt about it, and his poems deal with this extensively, but the issue here is altogether different and more sombre. Haffenden's obtuseness about this is remarkable given his acuteness almost everywhere else and itself suggests how deeply disturbing and difficult this issue is – Haffenden's response is itself gendered in its disguised or unconscious concern to exonerate the poet he has spent so much time on. This, however, is misguided because what makes Berryman so compelling as a poet is his refusal to exonerate himself, his determination to explore and expose even the darkest corners of Berrymanness. It is important, moreover, to see his introduction of the murderous nightmare in 'Homage to Mistress Bradstreet' as a part of his explicitly gendered project in that poem which involves placing notions of the feminine and the masculine in dialogue with each other. The poem's most conspicuous strategy is to imagine Bradstreet's life and to speak (part of the time) in her voice, it involves 'writing the feminine', and, as Christopher Benfey has pointed out

> The distinction between the poet and the woman speaker seems, at critical points in the poems of Jarrell and Berryman, to break down, or to be put in question. The female speakers in these poems seem deeply uncanny, as though the primary aim of the poets was less to create believable women characters than to produce a truly bisexual poetry, a poetry in which male poets allow their femininity to speak.[7]

Given this context it is crucial that Berryman also introduces material which suggests what most troubles him about his masculinity, because it shows that he was not, as Benfey suggests, simply using Bradstreet as a mouthpiece for sentiments that would have been regarded as 'effeminate' if he himself had expressed them:

> Poems that appear, at first glance, to be sensitive and empathetic attempts to find an androgynous voice for poetry, and to allow a woman's voice to be heard at a time when the most influential and widely published American poetry was written by men, reveal, on closer analysis, new evasions, new repressions. For, what Jarrell and Berryman have done is to define a supposedly typical range of 'feminine' experience: looking into the mirror,

shopping, giving birth, and so on. The result is the opposite of a sensitive integration toward some ideal bisexuality. In speaking explicitly as a woman, the male poet may, in fact, be enforcing an even stronger distinction between the sexes. (134)

What this ignores is the thoroughly 'dialogic' nature of the poem, how it juxtaposes the voices of two poets, male and female, and so interrogates the gender issue through the open-ended interaction between the two perspectives. This works against the enforcing of distinctions because it hints constantly at the strategy of a male author writing the feminine, and at the same time insinuates self-consciously 'masculine' material into this context. The violent images from his dream life are especially important because they hint, in this explicitly gendered context, at how much the poet's masculinity is experienced by him as a problem and unsettles his ability to live with himself, let alone a woman. Benfey's point is similar to that made repeatedly in feminist literary criticism that, as Thais E. Morgan puts it in her introduction to the volume where Benfey's essay appears, 'men always reaffirm their masculinity – their superior placement in the "sex / gender system" or "patri-archy" – when they write the feminine' (3). But Berryman's intro-duction of deeply troubling images from his own dream life into the poem indicates how little his preoccupation is with asserting easy control, how much he is willing to rock the patriarchal boat by speaking with a raw genuineness. Masculinity has traditionally asserted its superiority by stressing its cool rationality and powerful self-control – but here are manifestations of it which insist on the opposite.

Morgan speaks of 'the precarious balance between men's appro-priation of the category of femininity in order to strengthen their own authority and men's attempts to critique masculinity through adopting a feminine (and, in some cases, feminist) position in the system of sexual difference' (3). Berryman's project falls more on the side of critique because 'authority' is repeatedly called into question by his insistence on the problematic ground on which the self is based. The central figure of Henry is the only feature of *The Dream Songs* that gives them any coherence and yet his own coherence is undermined by continuous interventions from his unconscious. Berryman's premises for this are largely Freudian and, as Helen Vendler has pointed out 'there is no integrated Ego in *The Dream Songs*: there is only Conscience at one end of the stage and the Id at the other, talking to each other across a void, never able to find common ground'.⁹ This makes poetry writing analogous to psychotherapy, so that each *Dream Song* is

> eighteen lines long, and is divided into three six-line irregularly rhyming stanzas – an isometric form one might associate, looking backward, with Berryman's debt to the meditative Petrarchan and Shakespearian sonnet sequences or, looking forward, to the therapeutic fifty minutes, with the inflexible and anecdotal psychiatric hour. (Vendler, 36)

Such a poetic may be open to the charge that is also levelled at psychoanalysis – that it represents a masculinist drive at all costs to order and control threateningly irrational psychic elements.¹⁰ But order and control are continually subverted in *The Dream Songs* where Henry's dream life is depicted as a flickering and jumbled phantasmagoria whose sources vary from mundane references from his quotidian consciousness through to wildly expressionist or surreal references that tap into his unconscious, and where there is a conspicuous refusal ever to arrange these materials hierarchically. So Berryman seems to accept Freud's psychic categories, his naming of the parts of the self, but not the Freudian architecture, the surface/depth model. Instead of Freudian structure, *The Dream Songs* present a self laid open and spread out on a flat surface where neither the conscious nor the unconscious can adopt a privileged position, where the status of the poetic materials is constantly in question – metaphorical or literal, fantasy or memory – and where 'dream' and 'reality' interfuse. This may largely explain why Berryman took so long to evolve his mature manner: in order to say what he had to say he had to find a style that would, through the use of multiple punning and open and radically ambiguous syntax, allow him in a sense to say everything at once and then enlarge upon that everything – allow it to ramify and double-back on itself – in the labyrinth of an unravelling long poem.

One of the major achievements of *The Dream Songs* is the invention of a long poem that is so much more than the sum of its parts and which is so because of, rather than despite, its deliberate eschewal of conventional patterns of order. This is largely because of the permission which its title bestows on it, or rather the use that is made of that permission. The presence of the word 'dream' in that title permits Berryman to omit it almost everywhere from the poem but still to leave open to question the status – 'dream' or 'real' – of all of its content. This, too, contributes to the flattening of hierarchies of meaning; nothing in the poem can be dismissed as merely fantasy and at the same time nothing can privilege itself as the last word in conscious and rational comment or interpretation.

So while the connection between the ending of *Dream Song 29* and Berryman's dream of 30th April 1948 is clear, it is also valid to question the status of this imagery even further by linking it, as Lewis Hyde does, to alcoholic *blackout*,

> a phenomenon of heavy drinking in which the drinker goes through periods of unremembered activity. In a blackout one is not *passed* out; he goes to parties, drives home, has conversations, and so forth, but afterwards he has no memory of what he has done.[11]

Hyde backs up his argument further with a reference to *Recovery*, Berryman's autobiographical novel about alcoholism, and then speculates, very helpfully for my purposes, about the link between alcoholism and gender:

> The main character is a teacher (so close to Berryman that we needn't maintain the fiction) who reports, 'My chairman told me one day I had telephoned a girl student at midnight threatening to kill her – no recollection, blacked out.' This incident may be the actual basis of the last stanza here. (The misogyny of the *Dream Songs* would take another essay to unravel. Suffice it to say here that sexual anger and alcoholism are connected through similar misconceptions of human power. As it has been men who 'get into power', men have traditionally outnumbered women alcoholics. This will change to the degree that women mistake feminism for a route to centralised power.) (217–18)

The gender problem diagnosed by Hyde is one shared potentially by all men, even if it only leads to alcoholism in a few. It arises from the expectations that are given to men by patriarchy that, as members of the powerful sex, they will naturally be powerful in their relationships with women. Yet as individuals all men inevitably find these expectations to be often frustrated and therefore to feel themselves less 'masculine' than they should. This may partly be because men have been encouraged to make themselves 'masculine' by belittling the emotional life and thereby making themselves ignorant about it; as a result it is possible for women, as Tony Eardley has pointed out, to exercise power in relationships because 'they possess arcane skills of emotional intensity and expression – all the feelings men have learnt to deny but which they now look at with some envy'.[12]

Men's bewilderment about their resultant and unexpected powerlessness may lead them to respond violently:

> if men's dependence and their emotional weakness within a relationship is exposed and challenged they may well perceive it as a deep threat to their identity and their security. All men's worst fears about themselves and all the ambivalent feelings they have towards women can emerge at these moments, and they may react with defensive hostility or outright violence. It is as though men attempt to exercise, in the only way they know how – by force – the fear of accepting what they are and what they may have lost in the process of becoming what they are. (105)

Throughout *Recovery* there are hints of sexual anger arising from a sense of powerlessness, and this despite the self-congratulating celebrity which is bestowed on the central character who manages to be, in a sense, both John Berryman *and* 'Alan Severance, M.D., Litt.D., formerly Professor of Immunology and Molecular Biology, now the University Professor, Pulitzer Prize winner etc. twice-invited guest on the Dick Cavett Show (stoned once, and a riot)'.[13] How galling that this genius, who is also charismatic, etc etc, should find his fate taken out of his hands! Especially when the agents of this seem to be mostly women. The novel starts with Severance's wife giving him a drink (registered as too small) and telling him it is going to be his last, and Severance realising glumly, despite his initial thought ('Screw that') that she might be right (3). Then he finds himself in hospital and resuming the Alcoholics Anonymous program he has previously abandoned, and assigned to a group whose Counsellor will be Louise: 'a goodlooking pale tall black-haired girl (thirty-eight?), rather stiff and pleasant, but would she confront?' This complaint about her inability to 'confront' (11) comes two pages after a paragraph where, by contrast, the attitude of her male patients is described. There Severance tells Charley Boyle (who had been a 'pro hockey player') about his classmate Johnson, holder at nineteen of two national records, and his

formula for running the 440: 'I run the first 220 as fast as possible to
get in front. Then I run the second 220 even faster, to stay in front.'
(9). His audience laugh, and Severance knocks over his coffee in
'self-appreciation' and then

> They pointed out to each other the broad relevance of this attack
> on life's problems but its peculiar application to the present task
> of Severance, who had been through treatment twice before and
> ought to be desperate but wasn't, but was. He quoted Lautrec's
> remark, 'I paint with my penis,' and explained in one fancy sen-
> tence (bypassing a Matisse anecdote) who Lautrec was. (9)

What is conspicuous in this passage is its depiction of a self-
defensive male camaraderie that is mutually supportive but alarm-
ingly unhelpful in its implication that traditionally 'masculine'
qualities of toughness and determination will suffice, however
complex the psychological task involved. Its deludedness is espe-
cially transparent when it says that the running example applies
peculiarly well to Severance – who appears to have dropped out
twice before completing one metaphorical circuit. This also draws
attention to the redundant but revealing competitiveness of the
analogy: Johnson runs to get in front and then to stay in front.
These alcoholics are competing only inwardly but the analogy com-
forts them by pretending that what they are contending with is not
subjective and irrational, but concrete, external and fully known.
Moreover, Berryman/Severance seems to want to convince himself
he can 'beat' alcoholism because of his specialness, and the macho
narcissism of this passage seems primarily designed to flatter him
into believing that what is actually weakness (powerlessness against
alcohol) is a form of paradoxical strength. This is confirmed by the
outlandish *non sequitur* from the running analogy to the Lautrec ref-
erence – this is very much an associative leap and its conspicuous-
ness as such is remarkable, especially when almost the only
association between this and the running analogy is their shared
overt masculinity. But more specifically they both evoke role
models of distinguished masculine achievement and suggest the
amount of achievement was attained in proportion to the amount
of testosterone.

Fiercely determined and competitive running, grand-masterly
painting with the penis: these are the analogies for winning against

alcoholism that please Severance. Louise's failure to 'confront', by contrast, is deeply frustrating to him, and this, too, is very revealing:

'A tea party,' he said violently in the Snack Room after the one-forty-five lecture, to Charley B. (Charley B. was a carroty fag from Houston. Apparently. Severance was not censorious. Like many or some others, he had endured his doubts. He heard himself seated in his red leather chair drunk, desperate, shouting across their livingroom at his first wife, after seven or eight years of mostly happy marriage and two years of depth-analysis high in a building on Fifth Avenue in the 80's facing the park, 'I'm a homosexual, damn you. I just don't do anything about it!' and saw her kind look.) 'Louise presides at a tea party. I'll never get anywhere except on my own. Okay.'

The sweet hockey pro looked sweetly at him, earnestly too. 'I hear different, Alan. Take it easy, my boy, as they say around here. You haven't been in but one day yet. Last time don't count, you know. Start all over. 'Even faster' but *gently*, son.'

'It's true what you say, pal.' Severance relaxed, dismissing images of female torsos dismembered and strewn. 'Besides, they've put me in Mini-group, which they didn't do before and I could never find out heads or tails of about. Maybe that's something.'

What is remarkable in this passage is its juxtaposition of materials which at the same time betray Berryman's inexperience (and inadequacy) as a novelist, and display the pattern of his mental associations. It follows a gap in the text to indicate that it is meant to be a scene of its own, and yet after only three words of direct speech and sixteen words of narrative it plunges into a lengthy parenthetical aside. As in the passage I quoted before the relationship between these elements is conspicuously problematic. The direct speech expresses Severance's violent dismissiveness of Louise, and the tea party reference seems meant to suggest she has insufficient aggressiveness to maintain her position of authority. However, instead of enlarging on this the prose gets distracted by homosexuality, an aspect of Charley which could easily have been mentioned earlier. This is referred to first of all in homophobic language ('carroty fag') but then we are told that Severance is 'not censorious' about this because of his own doubts on the subject, and this leads to a flashback, still inside brackets, to his own marriage and confession to his wife of his gayness. By the time we exit from the brackets Charley's homosexuality has been transformed into a positive feature, so that the words 'sweet' and 'sweetly' are applied to him. He refers to the running analogy but modifies it with the word 'gently' and it appears to be this which allows Severance to dismiss from his mind images of dismembered women which are reminiscent of *Dream Song* 29.

All in all this is structured less like a passage in a novel than a Dream Song. It seems to be driven, like *Dream Song 29*, by an enigma: what, exactly, is Severance's problem? His reaction seems out of all proportion to what has really happened, so that the narrative components of the passage seem actually to be not narrative so much as images which Berryman evokes to express some indefinable 'thing' which upsets and angers him. The passage seems to be about an obscure agitation which homes in on different possible causes for itself – the only definite thing is that all of these causes hover around the issue of gender. The narrative source appears to be Louise's 'tea party', the reference that frames the brackets. Berryman/Severance seems violently disturbed by this experience of a woman in authority, which makes him think, first, and at some length, about homosexuality and then, briefly, about dismembered women's bodies.

That last reference is, if anything, more disturbing in this passage than similar ones which I have discussed in Berryman's poems and which are treated much more seriously and head-on. The brevity, suddenness and casualness of the reference here, and the way it seems blithely unaware of its outrageous disproportionateness is very unnerving. What it does confirm, however, is the point about violence arising as a masculine response to bafflement in the face of powerlessness, and disoriented shock as a response to women's power.

That Severance's first reaction is to think of homosexuality is significant because it hints at how threatened, as a man, he feels by Louise's authority. Its actual importance to Berryman was very limited. It is possibly a minor component in his appreciation of his literary heroes and rivals, as in the first line of one of his elegies for Delmore Schwartz – 'Flagrant his young male beauty' (*His Toy*, 83). It is referred to by W.D. Snodgrass who was impressed by Berryman's teaching but shocked by his behaviour:

> My impression is that as soon as he liked you he began making your life difficult by tampering in your love life and sometimes by

trying to tamper with your wife (much of this seemed to have a heavy homosexual bent and some of it seemed deliberate mis-behaviour to get slapped down). (Life, 240)

Berryman confirmed this interpretation in a letter to a friend: 'writers are likely to have more masked-homosexual-component around than other people, and heading for friends' wives or girls is really a way of getting closer to friends' (Life, 240). But a homosex-ual component whose main manifestation involves chasing women hardly seems very significant, and the likelihood is that Berryman was no more bisexual than most people. What is important is that he thought about it. In this passage in *Recovery* Severance's exasper-ation with Louise gets quickly turned into homophobia directed at Charley, and then it is implied that his homosexuality has made him shout at his wife. All of this suggests that homosexuality is much less of an issue between Berryman (and his personae) and men, than it is an issue in his relationships with women – that it is not about homosexuality so much as about deeply troubled hetero-sexuality.

It is important that it is Charley who succeeds in placating Severance, but this is largely because he provides a brief alterna-tive to the threat represented by Louise by becoming his 'pal'. Severance's violent fantasy is not directed specifically at Louise but at all women ('images of female torsos'). Charley is able to help Severance forget these feelings by representing a version of masculinity (he has been a professional sportsman) which at the same time offers 'feminine' comfort (sweetness, gentleness). Crucially, too, Charley adopts a paternal attitude to Severance: in calming his petulant over-reaction he refers to him as 'my boy' and 'son'.

What emerges with almost shocking clarity from this passage, then, are the components of Berryman's gender disturbance. This was profound and the most important source of the relentless unhappiness whose causes he spent his life analysing, and which he always traced back to his father's suicide. Hearing of the death of Saul Bellow's father, Berryman told him he was lucky to have had his father so long and contrasted his own experience, saying the 'trouble with a father's dying very early (not to speak of his killing himself) is not so much just his loss as the disproportionate & crip-pling role the mother then assumes for one' (Life, 274). John Haffenden describes Berryman's preoccupation with this only two

years before the poet's own suicide, how he marked the passage in
Freud's *Civilisation and its Discontents* that said 'I could not point to
any head in childhood so strong as that for a *father's protection*'
(Berryman's emphasis); how he marked in Erik H. Erikson's
Childhood and Society the passage that said 'For we may be sure that
whatever deep "psychic stimulus" may be present in the life of a
very young child, it is identical with his mother's *most neurotic
conflict*'; and he then links these astutely with Berryman's own diag-
nosis of his psychological weakness:

> 'An individual feels isolated and barred from the sources of col-
> lective strength when he (even though only secretly) *takes on a
> role considered* especially evil, be it that of drunkard or a killer, a
> *sissy* or a sucker, or whatever colloquial designation of inferiority
> may be used *in his group*' (Life, 385)

The Dream Songs continually grieve over a loss which is related,
implicitly or explicitly, to the suicide of Berryman's father: this loss
always seems to lie behind any other Berryman mentions, forming
for him the paradigm of loss. So when the first Dream Song refers to
'a departure' after which 'nothing fell out as it might or ought',
experienced readers of his poems think automatically of that first
departure. But there are also repeated explicit references where the
repetition, with verbal differences and additions, of the same true
story enacts the obsessive psychological process of 'working
through'. *Dream Song 76* refers to the setting – 'a concrete
stoop/close by a smothering southern sea'; 143 refers to the story
that his father was going to swim out with the young Berryman and
drown them both 'in the phosphorescent Gulf' but opted instead
'for lead'; 145 refers to how close to Berryman's room it happened,
'outdoors by my window'; and in 384 he is said, dismissively, to
have 'shot his heart out in a Florida dawn'. The emotional
responses similarly vary – from grieving to sympathy to moral dis-
approval to the anger of 384, the penultimate Dream Song, where
Berryman imagines himself spitting on his father's grave.

Berryman harps so much on this that it is tempting to think, as
Haffenden does, that he harps too much, that he was too ready 'to
credit the theory that he himself had been psychologically crippled
by his father's default, and to give his mother proportionately more
of his own guilty adulation for her heroic endurance.' (Life, 248).

But in the sentence after this Haffenden provides evidence – as he does throughout his biography – of the truth of Berryman's interpretation, saying that one of the poet's analyses of his own dreams contains the sentence: 'So dream is my bloody father looking down at me, whom he's just fucked by killing himself, making me into shit: and taunting me before he flushes me away.' This confirms the evidence from Berryman's other writings: that the loss of his father has undermined his own sense of ontological security, and the imagery of the dream suggests that his father's suicide makes him 'abject' in the Kristevan sense[14] that it turns him into an expelled bodily product ('shit') and then scatters him into nothingness ('flushes me away'). For Kristeva, abjection relates to an anxiety about being engulfed by the mother and this is the implied fear in Berryman's dream – that the loss of his father hands him over entirely to her. By making him abject it makes him feminine, since it is women who are coded as 'abject' (64) and his father by killing himself has 'fucked' Berryman and so aggressively pushed him into his mother's role. The feeling of abjection aroused by bodily products that are regarded as polluted – according to Kristeva – is related to a shying away from the maternal body, and to a fear 'of being swamped by the dual relationship, thereby risking the loss not of a part (castration) but of the totality of his living being', to a fear of 'his very own identity sinking irretrievably into the mother' (64). Calvin Thomas very suggestively explores the relevance of these theories for masculinity[15] and later theorises the relationship between parturition and excretion in a way that helps interpret Berryman's dream, where his 'bloody' father reverses all the associations of childbirth by aggressively tying together fucking, death and shit:

> insofar as it follows the logic of the *corps propre*, phallogocentrism must exclude the excremental as such and identify that devalued element with the feminine. Centering (on) the fecal thus entails an unavoidable contradiction. Moreover, the centering by which the feces-penis-baby triad is finally stabilised is perhaps only the effect of reversing a logically and chronologically prior state of affairs in which, for the infant, the mother's body occupied center stage. I refer to this crucial reversal, this founding denial of constitutive alterity, as *primontological*: it is primary or primordial to the establishment of a certain masculine ontology that thereafter

depends on the rigorous maintenance of this reversal to remain ontological, to retain a masculine being, and to protect itself from the encroachment of a scatontological anxiety. (83–4)

So Berryman's dream suggests how his father's suicide has ruined the son's masculinity by associating him with the excremental and thereby with abject femininity – with everything that masculinity struggles hardest against in order to maintain its sense of integrity.

That Berryman's mother played a disproportionate role in his life is all too obvious. In the mid 1940s Berryman confided to his diary how he recoiled when re-reading the letters he had written to his mother from England ten years earlier: 'how desperately, then, almost obscenely, I was bound to Mother' (Life, 98). There is a disturbing tendency on the part of Berryman's mostly male critics to blame her, either implicitly or explicitly, for Berryman's psychological problems in later life: there does seem to be some misogyny in this response, which involves ignoring the difficulty of her own position as a woman with a deeply inadequate husband. Paul Mariani even insinuates that she may have killed him and made it look like suicide: 'while there were bloodstains on Smith's shirt, there were no powder burns, impossible in the case of a self-inflicted gunshot wound' (12). On the other hand, as Mariani says, the link between the intense mother / son relationship and the son's later problems is starkly clear:

> Women remained – always – more problematic and terrifying for Berryman in large part because of his attachment to and hatred of his mother, a woman every bit as complex, devious, and self-destructive as he himself was. He was engaged twice and married three times, yet he never seems to have learned to engage women as true partners. He either idolized them or savaged them, turning afterward to remorse and then to fear. (Mariani, xxiv)

Alongside the theme of his father's suicide, this theme is repeatedly treated in the *Dream Songs*. In 270 he seems convinced that the problems he has suffered have inflicted a kind of arrested development. He refers to Oskar, the central character in Gunther Grass's *The Tin Drum*, calling him a 'german' and so punning on the sense of 'having the same parents' and suggesting a kinship between Henry and the German dwarf who refused to grow into an adult.

This German context also suggests that the demand that his mother 'make room' is a reference to the Nazi search for 'lebensraum' but here applied surreally to her womb, a sense reinforced by the significant pattern of rhymes – 'room', 'bloom', 'tomb' and then 'womb'. This implies that the womb was invaded while Henry was inside it and is combined with the suggestion that he was tricked into leaving the womb and that this departure leads to death. This imagery implies there was something wrong from the start, and something located in his mother: as a result Henry is forced to adopt a sort of mask during his adult life (though one which indicates the damage he has suffered, being 'slightly wrecked') and is drawn towards death as a return to the security of the womb, a security he never had. Significantly, these feelings lead him towards those images of dismemberment I have been focusing on, this time applied directly to his mother:

> There was no time, in the end, to finish her off.
> Halfway he left her, with the right side of her head
> a' gone,

There is a characteristic shifting of pronouns in this poem – the first stanza has 'you' and 'we', indicating the mother/son intimacy; the second stanza has 'I', indicating adult independence; this last stanza has 'he' which, like the Henry persona, half-dissociates Berryman from these thoughts or actions. There is also something disorientingly inappropriate about the registers of the stanza, considering its violent content. The first line is matter-of-fact; the second attempts a kind of fastidious precision which is insidiously undercut by the awkward opposition between 'left' and 'right' and by the lightheadedness which is introduced by the very short third line with its dismissively colloquial over-simplicity. The fourth sounds quasi-medical; and then this inappropriateness widens to psychopathic proportions in the last two lines with the conviction that she has been 'cured'. The lack of fit between the event and the response is especially clear in 'her hair wind-blown' where the everyday association is still complacently affirmed but at the same time erased by the idea of hair blown completely away.

The dominant meaning of violent murder is slightly adjusted, then, by turning it almost, but not quite, in the direction of brain surgery and healing (the references to 'left' and 'right' sides of the head and their link with the ability to speak confirm this). This seems designed to ward off Henry's guilt feelings. These, however, are the focus of attention in other *Dream Songs*. In 320, Henry lies awake hearing footsteps approaching his door, worrying 'Was it his mother? Might it be a whore / out of his youth?' His guilt and fear are then summed up in the idea that he is being haunted by Pentheselia, the Amazon queen who represents a nightmare for Berryman with her associations of awesome female power and her mission to avenge the wrongs done to her sex. Her phallic power ('cold in steel & sworded') and her association with both his mother and his previous lovers, indicate that she sums up what it is, in femininity, that most threatens Henry. He feels his identity so menaced by her that he cries out 'I am – ' as he wakes in a significantly abject condition – 'sweated & sordid'. The rhyme 'sworded/sordid' and, even more, the use of the past tense of 'sweat' suggest these two words are both being used transitively to imply that Henry has been wholly reduced to sweat and dirt.

Berryman's violent fantasies against women are a direct response to the ontological threat which they pose, a threat which is repeatedly expressed in imagery of disintegration, as in *Dream Song 311*:

> Hunger was constitutional with him,
> women, cigarettes, liquor, need need need
> until he went to pieces.
> The pieces sat up & wrote.

Jerold M. Martin examines the cluster of images of disintegration in the *Dream Songs* and shows how the sexual obsessiveness of those poems can be read as an attempt to overcome the psychological problem from which those images arise, by counteracting 'experiences of inner deadness and self-fragmentation ... in an effort to find an eroticized replacement for the selfobjects who in [the subject's] formative years were traumatically absent'.[16]

Sex offers a compensatory fulfilment. Similarly, violence offers a compensatory revenge. The images of dismembered women reverse the nightmare where the woman is 'sworded' and the man 'sordid', where the woman is phallic and the man abject. Identifying this tormented desire to break the fearfully powerful integrity of women's identity (as it is perceived by this version of deeply anxious masculinity) also helps to interpret the 'grave

Sienese face' of *Dream Song 29*. That is, it confirms the suggestion made by George F. Wedge[17] that it refers both to the Sienese figure in Dante's 'Purgatorio' and to Eliot's reference to that figure in *The Waste Land*. The key words here are Dante's 'disfecemi' (Canto V, line 134) and Eliot's 'Undid me' (line 294): these are both used by women speakers who are referring to being un-made, to having had their being dismantled. This image clearly looks towards the hacking to pieces of the final lines, especially considering that Dante's Sienese woman was imprisoned by her husband and then murdered.

This image of undone women is driven both by wishing and guilty fearing. The pun on 'grave', and the insistence that the pieces are hidden but may still be found, point to a fear that what is buried may rise up and accuse him, may speak like Dante's murdered woman. And since the Sienese face also refers to painted images of the Virgin it enforces the sense that Henry is being reproached by a principle of transcendent and eternal femininity. The guilt that this arouses is specifically masculine and leads to a suggestion in Berryman's work that masculine drives can be experienced as so disturbing that they feel, in themselves, criminal. The sharp but routine lust described in the famous *Dream Song 4*, which hungers after a woman eating chicken paprika, leads to the idea that 'There ought to be a law against Henry' and the interlocutor's characteristically terse reply that 'there is'. So, too, Berryman identifies 'with Speck, who murdered several nurses in Chicago, with the insane Texas sniper Whitman (whose father taught him "respect for guns but not for people"), and with Loeb, who gave himself wholly to crime'.[18] The latter identification arises, in *Dream Song 95*, from Berryman's angry confrontation with a 'surly cop' and his resentment at the cop's power to intimidate another man – the implication is that this manner of imposing civic order ('A meathead, and of course he was armed') entails a form of suppression that is actually a daily humiliation so that Berryman becomes transformed, like the figure in Kafka's 'Metamorphosis', into an insect. His response to this is to fantasise about a life outside the law which would unloose everything that civilisation suppresses and allow him, like Loeb, to 'baffle, torment, roar laughter'.

Berryman's discussion of Fatty Arbuckle's crime ('if crime it were') takes him even closer to the source of his own anxiety and guilt. This takes place in *Dream Song 222* where the violence is almost as casual as it was in the throwaway reference in *Recovery*, and disturbing for that reason because it suggests that men's violence towards women is routine, part of the natural course of events, and wonders whether killing and sex are cognate drives ('Is it: to make or kill / is jungle-like what constitutes my I, / so let's thrust?') Arbuckle was accused of the murder of a young actress called Virginia Rappe after the two of them had gone to a bedroom during a party and she had died of peritonitis four days later. Berryman wonders whether she was merely unlucky, or 'was there shoved ice?' What takes this close to the heart of Berryman's gender concerns is how the poem generalises from this incident and when it does so reveals what is clearly crude and simplistic in his attitudes. For here, more clearly than anywhere else, he adopts a model based on biological roles:

> around the planet men are erect
> and girls lie ready:
> a bounce, toward pain. Melons, they say, though
> are best – I don't know if that's correct –
> as well as infertile, it's said.

This is the worst moment in Berryman's work, as he moves from discussing, in partly graphic and partly oblique terms, what may have been a sex crime, to blithely defining sex roles in unthinkingly conventional images, to facetiously referring to what is said to afford men the greatest sexual pleasure (and also, pal, no worries about pregnancy).

This poem seems untypically obtuse because it is emptied of the anxiety which characterises Berryman's treatment of this issue almost everywhere else. Somehow, though, this makes the issue more clearly defined, especially when he wonders whether Arbuckle was 'so made / as to be dangerous?' For it suggests that many men experience – indistinguishably from their sexual desire (this 'burning to sheathe it') – violent urges which make them feel themselves to be dangerous, to feel that their psychology does not sit comfortably in civilised society. The evidence of Berryman's work indicates that he felt that about himself, and this is surely the main point of his exchange with Anne Bradstreet when he describes his nightmare of burning women.

It is for this reason that Berryman identifies with serial killers and feels haunted and hunted: as J.M. Linebarger says, 'One of Henry's recurring delusions is that he is under attack, as when he imagines himself being lynched (10, 236), or substitutes himself for the hounded criminal in *High Sierra*, the 1941 Humphrey Bogart–Ida Lupino movie'.[19] What is crucial here, though – however unexpected it might seem given the sombre and sinister issues I have been exploring – is the black and satirical comedy that Berryman discovers in this theme. This is unlike the mere facetiousness in the Arbuckle poem, which seems shockingly absent-minded, because it is comedy that enforces a double-take on the central theme of hounded guilt and paranoia and so mocks the masculine self-regard which drives the Bogart persona in this film. This is achieved almost as soon as the Bogart character Roy Earle (who holes up in the mountains after a robbery and is hunted there and killed) is transformed into 'horrible Henry, foaming'. But it deepens as Berryman wryly melodramatises the story in a fashion that invents a macho version of camp. The poem's use of parody, for instance when it mimics Bogart's vocal mannerisms as 'his girl' is brought in to test 'if he's still human, see: she love him, see' is important because it opens a dialogue between the cultural values offered as a premise by the Hollywood film and the wider and much more sceptical values implied in Berryman's poetic. For in parody, as Bakhtin says,

> two languages are crossed with each other, as well as two styles, two linguistic points of view, and in the final analysis two speaking subjects … every parody is an intentional dialogized hybrid. Within it, languages and styles actively and mutually illuminate one another.[20]

This is important because it hints at how Berryman, throughout the *Dream Songs*, simultaneously expresses and parodies 'masculine' values. On the one hand, the plight of 'Roy Earle' provides an accurate analogue for Henry's feelings of persecution, and his courage and toughness are half-admired: on the other Bogart's impersonation of these qualities is parodied so that the extent to which such qualities are a self-conscious mask is wittily exposed. Once the character is dead, 'Bogart's duds / truck back to Wardrobe', the pun on 'duds' (reinforced by the reference, in the same line, to the rifle shot that killed him) revealing how much all this glorification of hunted masculinity is actually just an enjoyment of empty style.

In describing this as macho camp I am drawing attention to the extent to which Berryman is using parody to deconstruct gender roles, styles and assumptions, but still from a straight (and even exaggeratedly straight) masculine perspective. Berryman draws, repeatedly throughout the *Dream Songs*, on his characteristic black comedy in order to explore what it is that is masculine in Henry's behaviour and at the same time to bemoan and mock it. The references to, and parodies of caricature and cartoon (as in 22: 'I am Henry Pussy-cat! My whiskers fly.') are similarly deployed, satirically reducing Henry's personality to a ragbag of inflated drives but at the same time pumping it up to mock-heroic, larger than life proportions. Drawing upon the resources of this idiom allows Berryman to question identity through caricatural questionings of the boundaries between the human and things: in *Dream Song 16* Henry's pelt is mounted as though he is a trophy animal so that he is reduced to a 'molten yellow & moonless bag'. In the same way that the human is reified, so things can become human, and 'Two daiquiris / withdrew into a corner of the gorgeous room / and one told the other a lie'. This is more conventionally camp. The cocktails are not only humanised but made bitchily feminine and seem to gloat over the terminal taming of the male animal.

What underlies Berryman's black comedy is most urgently his conviction of masculine guilt. It is most often his response to a deep anxiety about the drives that constitute masculine identity and which are most vividly expressed in the imagery of his nightmares of dismembered women. When he confesses these nightmares to Anne Bradstreet he is doing explicitly and directly what he does, implicitly and indirectly, throughout much of his work – he is warning her to beware something deeply sinister and specifically gendered in his character, refusing to have it dismissed as trivial and insisting instead on its disquietingly representative significance. What is compelling in Berryman's work is how starkly he confesses to some of the worst gender responses and how the sharpness of his own knowledge of his gender malaise leads him to such a radical and often explicit questioning of gender. The black comedy that is such a powerful feature of his work is most often his expression of the gap of incongruity that opens between what masculinity is supposed to be – rational, powerful, authoritative – and what masculinity and its personification, Henry, actually is: baffled, sad, lustful, weak, absurd, merely pretentious.

Blackly comic incongruity arises perhaps most obviously in Berryman's ambivalent attitudes towards heroism. On the one hand he does want to believe that traditionally masculine qualities of courage and endurance can be applied to the existential endeavour that is required for his 'extremist' poetic project:

My idea is this: the artist is extremely lucky who is presented with the worst possible ordeal which will not actually kill him. At that point he's in business. Beethoven's deafness, Goya's deafness, Milton's blindness, that kind of thing. And I think that what happens in my poetic work in the future will probably largely depend not on my sitting calmly on my ass as I think, 'Hmm, hmm, a long poem again? Hmm', but on being knocked in the face, and thrown flat, and given cancer, and all kinds of other things short of senile dementia. At that point, I'm out, but short of that I don't know. I hope to be nearly crucified.[21]

A similar kind of attitude is implied in Berryman's choice of epigraphs for *His Toy, His Dream, His Rest*. He quotes Sir Francis Chichester ('No interesting project can be embarked on without fear. I shall be scared to death half the time.') and General Gordon ('For my part I am always frightened, and very much so. I fear the future of all engagements.'). So he wants to invoke notions of conspicuous courage as evidenced by men of action as an analogue for his more subjective quest into the darkest ontological corners. This indicates the macho component in the American version of existentialism adopted by many important writers – Mailer, Lowell, Bellow, for example, as well as Berryman – in the 60s, how it glamorised the notion of toughing it out without any transcendent comfort, of a muscular fashioning of meaning in the face of meaninglessness.

What is unusual about Berryman, however – and this is the direct result of his gender scepticism whose sources I have been locating – is how he parodies these ideas of heroism at the same time as he endorses them. John Haffenden has pointed out Berryman's attempts to impose an epic structure on the *Dream Songs*, how the major influence on that structure was the *Iliad* and how the 'hero, like a type of Achilles or King Lear, is cast out by real enemies, but he is also cast out by himself' (Critical Commentary, 54). He may have failed to impose this structure but that failure leads to (or is the result of) one of his greatest successes. For the *Dream Songs* cannot truly be an epic because its philosophical premises are at odds with an epic world-view – where epic is monologic in the Bakhtinian sense that it uniformly expresses a single totalising vision, the *Dream Songs* are polyphonic, they are a 'dialogised hybrid'. Its voices are many and conspicuously various:

> It includes baby-talk, childish spite-talk, black talk, Indian talk, Scottish talk, lower-class talk, drunk-talk, archaism and anachronism, megalomaniacal self-aggrandizing images, hysteria and hallucination, spell-casting, superstition, paranoid suspiciousness, slang, and primitive syntactic structures of all sorts – sentence fragments, incorrect grammar, babble and so on. (Vendler, 41)

The effect of this is to drain all of the individual voices of any final authority and to make epic and heroic ambitions seem archaic.

Amidst this polyphony what emerges most consistently is a self-consciously masculine voice and one that often, as both John Bayley (68) and Robert Pinsky[22] have remarked, can be characterised as a 'bar-room' voice. More specifically, the bar-room involved dates from when bar-rooms were more thoroughly male preserves than they are now, and the conversations enacted involve confidences divulged man to man. Perhaps the most famous feature of the *Dream Songs* – their deployment of a black-face minstrel dialogue between two 'end-men', Mr. Bones and Tambo (though Berryman does not actually use that name) – is best characterised in this way. Henry confesses to his interlocutor who responds gruffly, often dismissively: the two males share understanding but this provides only limited comfort, if any.

This bar-room sensibility has a representative significance in indicating why the epic and heroic are no longer possible, in depicting a masculinity reduced to inaction, comic but anxious and defensive banter, and self-pity. One of its most recurrent motifs is sexual desire both frustrated and fulfilled but always characterised more by lust than love, and as an experience ruefully, wishfully or boastfully confided by one man to another. Frustration is depicted in the present, as in *Dream Song 4* where Henry lusts after one of the 'feeding girls' the world is stuffed with; fulfilment happened in the past, his loins were the 'scene of stupendous achievement' (26) and he was moved 'by delicate ladies / with ripped-off panties, mouths open to kiss' (373). In 'Damned', published in *Love and Fame* – where

Berryman has dropped the Henry persona and speaks directly as himself – the confessional element is much more sharply present and all the more disquieting for that reason:

> She came again & again, twice ejecting me
> over her heaving. I turned my head aside
> to avoid her goddamned tears,
> getting in my beard.[23]

What makes the *Dream Songs* more complex and important than the merely personal poems in *Love and Fame* is their dialogic nature, and part of this is their intertextuality which contrasts the epic heroism of the *Iliad* with bar-room anti-heroism, and expresses Henry's hungering in *Dream Song 4* partly with 'metaphors out of the love-tradition' (Vendler, 38) calling the woman 'Brilliance' and referring to her 'jewelled eyes'. Similar references are made more expansively in *Dream Songs 315* and *316* where Henry is a Spenserian knight doing battle on behalf of his lady, and against lust.

The references to idealised love and heroism throughout the *Dream Songs* represent an aspiration towards an ideal version of the masculine but they are always undermined by their self-consciously textual nature which reveals their dubious constructedness and their contrast with the actual events of Henry's life. What this textuality and intertextuality also do is to draw attention to Berryman himself as a male author, and to mock and parody him as such:

> I studied my weapons system.
> Grenades, the portable rack, the yellow-spout
> of the anthrax-ray: in order. Yes, and most
> of my pencils were sharp.

Macho camp is again in evidence here, in *Dream Song 50*, where Berryman parodies science fiction writing and deconstructs it as the fantasy of a male author who imagines himself menaced (again) by mysterious alien forces and prepares to face them with a 'stiff' defence. The comic timing which is one of Berryman's great strengths is deployed in these lines to let the stanza fizzle out into that characteristic bathos which indicates the gap between heroism and its opposite (elsewhere between Achilles or the Red Cross Knight or Roy Earle, and Henry) but here more specifically stresses the distance between heroic action and merely writing about it.

A similar reflection on the maleness of male authors is made in *Dream Song 77* where Henry 'shaved & swung his barbells, duded Henry up' and then 'Wif a book of his in either hand / he is stript to move on'. His books acquire a similar status to barbells, or guns, and certainly they are mocked for asserting his 'authority'. The phallic aspect of this is even more explicit in *Dream Song 75* where Henry's book becomes a 'flashing & bursting tree', an 'unshedding bulky bole-proud blue-green moist / thing'. Authorship as an assertion of maleness is a recurrent preoccupation and is also apparent in Berryman's explorations of his relationship with other authors, his awe for Yeats and Frost as authorial father figures, his rivalry with and love for Robert Lowell, Delmore Schwartz and Randall Jarrell:

> Lowell and Berryman, both barefoot, were climbing up the big sycamore tree which shaded the small, stone Revolutionary house. Lowell was perched at the very top of the tree, in the uppermost branches. Just beneath him, trying to get higher, higher than Lowell, was Berryman ... in retrospect, it seemed a nice image of the intense rivalry between these two poets. (William Arrowsmith quoted in *Life*, 173)

Berryman strove for phallic mastery as an author. What is much more remarkable about him is how sharply he knew that this was what he was up to, especially for a male author writing in the 1960s, and how knowingly he could analyse and mock this striving. This is linked to his exceptionally precise knowledge, elsewhere, of the gendered nature of his experience, a knowledge which arises from his profound gender disturbance, and how mistrustful this makes him of his own masculinity. It may have been because she sensed this element in him that led Adrienne Rich to befriend Berryman, to call him 'the master poet of this half-century',[24] and to refer to how

> *The Dream Songs* are open everywhere; open, at the risk of total breakdown, to nothing less than the life that breathed them: its black vistas, grotesque fantasies, errant affections, memories, lucid indignations, true loves. (127)

This openness allows Berryman to explore his gender malaise and also to learn from it so that the *Dream Songs* are enormously sophisticated in their gender self-consciousness and understanding.

It is not an accident that Berryman learned his mature manner during the writing of 'Homage to Mistress Bradstreet' – learned it, that is, in the process of exploring what it was to be a *female* author. In order to become the author of the *Dream Songs* Berryman needed to learn to write dialogically, which requires the ability to imagine and evoke radically other perspectives. The 'Homage', 'with its fresh amalgam of styles ranging from the seventeenth century to the mid-twentieth, was a farewell and a new birth' (Mariani, 256) and in order to write it Berryman had to participate imaginatively in 'feminine' experience, to feel as though with a 'feminine' sensibility. He did extensive research, in particular, into the experience of childbirth, asking many of his woman friends who had undergone it to describe it to him. Brenda Engel responded to Berryman's

> 'very specific and intense questions: how long did the strong labor pains last: what kinds of thoughts went through my head during labor; how [did] the pains change … as labor progressed'. She could see Berryman straining to understand *exactly* what a woman went through, both physically and psychologically, in the course of giving birth.' (Mariani, 256)

When he had finished the stanzas on childbirth Berryman said 'Well, I'm exhausted … I've been going through the couvade. The little monster nearly killed me!'[25] That is, he had been going through the process which men in some primitive tribes go through of a kind of empathetic pregnancy and parturition.

The importance of this is that it shows how, in writing the Bradstreet poem, Berryman invented a dialogue of genders. His painstakingly naturalistic account of childbirth represents his determined attempt to understand a thoroughly female experience and its impact on feminine psychology. What is more broadly significant is how this is constructed as a part of the poem in a self-conscious relationship to other parts where the two poets, male and female, lovingly interact with each other. The effect of this is very different from those moments where Wordsworth and Yeats incorporate 'feminine' material contributed, respectively, by their sister and wife. The dialogic element resists mere incorporation and makes the 'feminine' and the 'masculine' interrogate each other. Berryman's openness crucially assists this by introducing that material which most troubles his own sense of himself as a man – his nightmares of murdered women. The question that arises, then, of the association of the feminine with the creative, and masculinity with the destructive, is deliberately raised and so allowed to infiltrate the poem's central theme of Bradstreet's role as mother, and, as it were, founding mother of American poetry. Having absorbed or created this model of female and feminine creativity, Berryman was able in the *Dream Songs* to invent a male character who displays, with thorough openness, a self-conscious, brazen and at the same time ruefully abashed masculinity.

3
Ted Hughes and the Goddess of Complete Being

The most important clue to Ted Hughes' gender attitudes is provided by his *Shakespeare the Goddess of Complete Being*, where he says for instance that

> The peculiar division of the sexes, which bestows on woman the miraculous power to create man out of her blood, while it deprives man of any such ability, and which deposits the infant male, through his helpless, formative years, into the possessive control of the Female, injects a peculiar conflict into the situation.[1]

The struggle, against this background, to establish a masculine identity is evoked repeatedly in Hughes's work and the reference here to conflict is symptomatic of the belligerence that continually characterises that struggle. I want to show the extent to which Hughes's development involved his increasing awareness of the gender issue; how he moved from shaping his own forms of masculine expression to questioning gender and to regretting what he diagnosed as a masculine drive to repudiate the feminine. The latter is again most explicit in Hughes's bizarre book on Shakespeare but it is implicit everywhere in his middle and later poetry. In this context I will address myself to Jacqueline Rose's critique of Hughes in her brilliant book *The Haunting of Sylvia Plath*.[2]

The outline of this development is evident in Hughes's 1992 essay 'Poetry and Violence'[3] where he defines the concern of his early poems as being with 'a strong, positive mode of violence'

> since behind it presses the revelation of all that enables human beings to experience – with mystical clarity and certainty – what we call truth, reality, beauty, redemption and the kind of fundamental love that is at least equal to the fundamental evil. (255)

He argues here that his notorious early preoccupation with violence was actually an insistence on enforcing a 'recognition of the operation of divine law in the created things of the natural world' (259) in which the predatory instinct plays an inevitable, and therefore 'positive' and creative part. It is possible that, as he wrote the poems, the early Hughes was moving towards this position: however, these are not the terms in which poems like 'Hawk Roosting' and 'Thrushes'[4] are written, and their readers at the time would have been surprised, to say the least, by the stress that Hughes placed, towards the end of his life, on mystical love. I'll be arguing that his interest in violence was closely linked to his struggle with masculinity – it is all the more relevant, then, that having retrospectively justified his early poems in mystical terms, Hughes concludes 'Poetry and Violence' with an optimistic statement of his own version of eco-feminism. Cheered by 'New Age' interest in occult religions – which he relates to his own interests since the late fifties – and the popularity of natural history broadcasts, he discerns a profound change which he sees, crucially, as feminising the culture:

> Along with this, maybe more visible in the US, countless changes have slowly but surely returned the Paleolithic world, the 'sacred' status, bringing with it, in the most curious fashion, the natural world's first and foremost representative – woman. ... It is the massive resurgence of something as archaic and yet as up to date – as timeless, and as global – as the 'sacred' biology of woman. ... And the universal movement in which all these different currents make one tide is the movement to save the earth by a reformed good sense and sensitivity. (267)

This later harping on the feminine contrasts sharply with its absence in Hughes's early work. It is telling that in his 1967 creative writing handbook for schoolchildren *Poetry in the Making*[5] Hughes has a chapter where he gives advice on writing about relatives but finds himself writing only about *male* relatives – a brother, an uncle, his father. In particular he finds it impossible to write about a mother, and is himself struck and nonplussed by this:

> Our feelings about some of our relatives, particularly about our mother and father, are so complicated and so deeply rooted that they may be just too much for a writer to manage, and he finds he cannot say a thing about them. In writing these poems of mine

about relatives, I found it almost impossible to write about the mother. Now these people in my poems are not my real relatives, they are members of a family I was inventing. Nevertheless, when it came to inventing a mother, I found it impossible to write about such a person in the style in which the poems are written. I was stuck. My feelings about my mother, you see, must be too complicated to flow easily into words. I ended up writing a poem that left me quite unsatisfied. Now in contrast to this, I found it very easy indeed to write about the brother I invented. (102)

Even up to his death in 1998, Hughes had written very little about his mother, and this is itself significant given the terms in which he describes the mother–son relationship in my first quotation, his emphasis on the helplessness of the infant male, and the 'possessive control' of the 'Female', which suggests a continuing resentment of women's power and a continuing fear of falling under the spell of that power. It is true there is 'Anniversary'[6] but this is a dream vision of his mother after her death and the poem's surrealism creates a calculated coolness unusual in Hughes's work. His mother and her sister Miriam (who died aged 18) have been transformed into firebirds and stroll listening to the larks. The one clear feeling that emerges is resentment. The mother resents the sacrifices she made for her sons, especially the poet who she claims to have assisted in the sacred business of writing, galloping through a wall and over the moors to bring him a new pen and lay it on the altar. Yet the poet also resents his mother for preferring his brother and using him 'to tune finer / Her weeping love' for that brother.

'Anniversary' confirms the point the younger Hughes made about himself – that his feelings about his mother are 'too complicated to flow easily into words'. Some of his reluctant awe of her is conveyed in her posthumous acquisition of fiery feathers and her association with cosmic cycles of generation ('Creation and destruction of matter') which perhaps confirms his uneasy point in his book on Shakespeare about woman's 'miraculous power to create man out of her blood'. The poem also hints at the issue of how the son acquires his sense of self partly by seeing himself reflected in his mother's eyes – and also at Hughes's disturbance that what he sees reflected there is himself as his brother's shadow. But 'Anniversary' above all seems to oscillate around its subject, and to remain unfocused while leaving the baffled impression of the most important things not being said.

By contrast Hughes wrote three poems about his father which are characteristically direct and energetic. All three focus on his father's war experiences and their impact on the Hughes household, especially on the poet himself. The first section of the earliest, 'Out',[7] depicts his father as an alien presence in the home who seems to belong instead with the English war dead. As such, moreover, he brings hallucinatory war images with him into the home, and transforms the firelight into a 'blood-flicker / On biscuit-bowl and piano and table-leg'. A double process is at work. The father, and the war associations he brings with him, take 'strong and stronger possession' of this domestic scene, but this scene is at the same time helping to heal him and distance him from the war. The gender implications of this are only just beneath the surface. The link between men and war and therefore between masculinity and murderous destructiveness is further confirmed by the binary opposition this scene presents that, by contrast with this, links women and domesticity and therefore femininity and healing.

What is disquieting in this passage, however, is that the ever stronger possession that the war exerts is shown being most thoroughly felt by the four-year-old Ted Hughes, who is depicted as his father's 'luckless double'. Hughes senior is recovering but Hughes junior is learning what it is to be a man through identifying with his father's suffering as a soldier, and in a later poem 'Dust as we Are'[8] becomes a sort of scapegoat for that suffering, or what Hughes calls a 'supplementary convalescent', having 'to use up a lot of spirit / Getting over it'. These poems dwell on the imagery of war and represent it very much as *imagery* – they are self-consciously not the poet's own experience but something learned orally – from soldiers' accounts – and textually through First World War poems. 'Dust as we Are' makes this most explicit in referring to 'an after-image of the incessant / Mowing passage of machine-gun effects' – lines that distinguish themselves by sounding unusually postmodernist for Hughes and so indicating that he is uncharacteristically concerned here with the issue of representation. This is because he wants to draw attention to the second-hand nature of this experience, to how he absorbed it in its particularly mediated form as the experience of others but with its own exemplary significance for him.

The gender implications of this are important because they show how, to use Hughes's terms, the helpless infant male who is in the possessive control of the Female, nonetheless hears about 'masculine' activities that conventionally take place outside the 'feminine' domestic setting, but hears about them as things largely to be imagined and speculated about. 'Dust as we Are' refers to war as a guilty secret which men keep from women:

> Naked men
> Slithered staring where their mothers and sisters
> Would never have to meet their eyes, or see
> Exactly how they sprawled and were trodden.

It refers also to how Hughes 'filled / With his [father's] knowledge'. In writing these poems Hughes is influenced by the confessional poems of Robert Lowell – he is describing experiences which have formed his identity: so when he goes on to say 'After mother's milk / This was the soul's food' he is explicitly (and psychoanalytically) referring to how he detached himself from his mother by identifying with his father. The two poems I have quoted, and 'For the Duration' (Wolfwatching, 22–3) all dwell on this and insist on how becoming his father's 'luckless double' and 'supplementary convalescent' was his most crucially influential early experience.

What the two later poems dwell on most, however, is his father's silence. These crucial early experiences are not only mediated, they are problematically mediated – the man who lived through them is unable, or refuses, to speak about them. In 'Dust as we Are' he is described as so silent that he appears to be listening on a telephone, while the poet eavesdrops on the line. His silence in 'For the Duration' is a daytime 'coma' which contrasts with the dreams of war that make him shout during the night. Hughes says it was this silence that alarmed him most, the 'refusal to tell', the fact he had to 'hear from others' what his father survived and did. What Hughes is describing here exemplifies a masculine tendency to refuse to communicate powerful feelings, a tendency described and lamented by Peter Middleton:

Relationships need emotional labour, yet men have apparently been trained not to express emotion. Men are largely absent from the lives of young children, who therefore grow up emotionally supported by women. Because boys learn to separate from their mothers without finding a father ready to pass on emotional skills, unlike their sisters, they are not given much opportunity to learn them. Men's absence, and inexperience, perpetuate the situation, so that boys grow up unable to provide intramasculine

emotional support (except perhaps in sport and war, which
therefore become particularly attractive).[9]

So Hughes shows his four-year-old self being burdened with feel-
ings precisely because those feelings remain unexpressed, and
giving draining emotional support to a father who is unable to give
it back. In 'Out' his father is described as having had his 'Body buf-
feted wordless', and his silence means that it is only the maleness of
that body that allows the son to identify with the father and to learn
at the same time that males are warriors who do not speak about
what they do or feel. They fight and protect their families: 'For the
Duration' imagines the father climbing out of a trench and ends by
worrying he 'Might still not manage to reach us / And carry us to
safety'.

Hughes is clear that he was caused severe psychic damage by
these early experiences. In 'Out' he takes over his father's memory,
so that he lies on the carpet 'Among jawbones and blown-off boots,
tree-stumps, shell-cases and craters', and that memory is a 'buried,
immovable anchor' suggesting both that it is hidden and that it
stays embedded in the growing boy. In 'Dust as we Are', his father's
silence 'Mangled me, in secret', and Hughes' soul, nourished by the
food of his father's war knowledge, grows as a 'strange thing, with
rickets – a hyena'. The damage he suffered is accounted for partly in
Blakeian terms – it is caused by powerful feelings which mangled
him because they were not allowed free expression. The conse-
quences of the damage, though, are referred to a Wordsworthian
model in their effect on the organic growth of the poet's soul – the
Hughes organism grows, but in a diseased form.

This is important because Hughes's diagnosis is confirmed by the
evidence of his poems, especially the early ones which repeatedly
enact and try to shed a masculine sickness which obsessively dwells
on the twin themes of war and Nature red in tooth and claw and
revealingly discuss each in terms of the other. The assumption
behind this twinning of the themes is that which lies behind
Hughes's work as a whole: the assumption that human behaviour is
biologically driven, that it is shaped by instincts which are merely
obscured by a veneer of civilisation. Tom Paulin seems to get it the
wrong way around when he says that 'it is impossible not to view
Hughes's fascination with elemental energy as expressing an impa-
tience with the post-war consensus'[10] because the fascination with
elemental energy always has so much more priority in his work.

Paulin is nonetheless right about the impatience and about its leading to the 'rage against peace and civility [that] erupts in "A Motorbike"' (270). What is most disturbing about that poem,[11] however, is its assumption that war itself is a manifestation of elemental energy and in particular of masculine drives, so that peace can only be described negatively as not-war, and as a state which emasculates and paradoxically takes the men prisoner. So he says 'The shrunk-back war ached in their testicles' as though it were a suppressed desire, and that when the soldiers handed over their weapons they 'hung around limply' as though fighting were a kind of erection and not-fighting were a kind of detumescence. The motorbike itself has spent six years 'outclassed' by the weapons of war, as though it were one of their kind but of a lower order, but it has also been 'Cramped in rust, under washing' so that it resembles one of Hughes's caged animals and represents the suppression of elemental energy, of 'thunder, flight, disruption'. A week after a young man bought it and kicked it into life he 'escaped / Into a telegraph pole' while riding it. Taken together all this imagery works to insists that war is a 'natural' activity for men who, deprived of it, will find compensatory outlets for their desire for it; a related implication is that the society of 'post-war consensus' is experienced by masculinity like bars around a jaguar or washing on a motorbike.

It is in this context that the priority Hughes gave to biology is revealed at its most damaging and this is missed by Tom Paulin whose essay, otherwise, is the best writing there is on Hughes. Paulin's leftist outlook makes him focus on the social implications of Hughes's work: as he says, 'nature poetry is always a form of disguised social comment' (252). This is generally revealing and valuable, especially given the tendency of commentators on Hughes, like Ekbert Faas and Keith Sagar,[12] to talk about him purely in his own anthropological and mythic terms. What Paulin ignores, however, is the extent to which Hughes's own terms are deployed specifically to privilege biology. To say 'The shrunk-back war ached in their testicles' is to make the larger point Hughes was always making through his insistence on that register – it is deliberately to soft-pedal the social (rhythmically the line is organised so that 'war' gets only a muted stress compared with the bodily words) and harp on the biological. Hughes's characteristic register is deployed against the privileging of 'social comment' (and, thereby, also, against the poetry of the Movement). Paulin wants the references to Nature in Hughes to be read analogically like those in Engels when he 'argues that active social forces work "exactly like natural forces"' (272). In fact, however, Hughes does not distinguish between them: for him social forces *are* natural forces, or at least are the direct product of natural forces.

It is difficult fully to understand Hughes's view of war as a natural force without placing it in the context of the opposite view, and this is especially valuable because that opposite view inevitably also has entirely different gender assumptions. Cynthia Enloe's *The Morning After* is an account of sexual politics after the Cold War which analyses the relationship between gender and militarism and which refers to the 'cultural groundwork for waging war':

> Militarizing gender before the first shot is fired is necessary for governments preparing for war. Men have to be socialized from boyhood to see their masculine identities tied to protecting women while tolerating violence. Women have to be prepared from girl-hood to admire men in uniforms and to see themselves as bandaging the wounds inflicted by violence rather than wielding it.

Enloe's emphasis on the social constructedness of these gender responses contrasts starkly with Hughes' belief in their naturalness and with the essentialist outlook that accompanies that belief. What is deeply disturbing in Hughes is that his linking of war with biological roles appears to make war inevitable, and the gender attitudes which Enloe shows to be politically engineered are treated by Hughes as eternally linked to male and female bodies.

The psychic wound that Hughes identified in himself through his identification with his father's war experiences is evident in his work in the form of a simultaneously aggressive and defensive masculinity. Repeatedly he expresses the fear that the self is scattered in pieces and the hope of a new wholeness resembling rebirth. Later in his work he links this preoccupation with archetypal patterns discernible in Egyptian mythology, as Keith Sagar points out:

> The reassembling of the bits and pieces of disintegrated man which takes place in these poems is, of course, a version of the Osiris story. The process also redeems nature itself, by, as it were, sewing it together, reintegrating it as a harmonious unity.[14]

Earlier, however, it is much more closely related to his personal experience. The second section of 'Out' imagines an infantryman 'blasted to bits' and then 'reassembled' (Wodwo, 156). In the children's story *The Iron Man*[15] – probably Hughes's most widely-known publication – the hero is pictured at the start falling apart and all his pieces tumbling down a cliff onto the beach below. Then, bit by bit, he puts himself together again all except for one ear which has been taken by a gull and lies on a ledge of the cliff. Then he walks into the sea, but when he returns he causes havoc and eats all the farm machinery until he is lured into a pit and buried underground. But the following Spring he bursts out of the ground and this time he is placated by being given a whole scrapyard to eat. In this way his potentially destructive power is harnessed so that when the planet is threatened by a giant space-being he challenges it to a test of strength in which the two of them must lie down in a blazing fire. The Iron Man suffers horribly and grows terribly afraid but eventually wins and saves the earth.

This powerful story is directly focused on the idea of the damage caused by the suppression of violent energies. The Iron Man bursting out of the ground relates him very closely to the interpretation of King Kong as representing the 'return of the repressed'. As a fable, *The Iron Man* suggests the social importance of energies conventionally regarded as male being channelled so that they protect rather than destroy. What is noticeable, too, is that the Iron Man is dismantled and reassembled twice: firstly, at the start, as a prelude to destructiveness and secondly, after he has been tamed, as a prelude to protectiveness (he is too big to be flown in one piece to his battleground). This symmetry insists that it is the same energies which lie behind these opposite social outcomes but also that to be male is both to suffer and inflict suffering and, partly as a consequence, to feel the coherence of your self to be constantly under threat. The giant iron-ness of the hero is invented defensively against this anxiety: he is a fantasy of invulnerable maleness.

In his role as both destroyer and protector, sadist and masochist,[16] the Iron Man represents soldierliness. However, in his drive to dominate and eat he is linked to the predators that obsess Hughes's early poetry, and whose single-mindedness has been explained by Michael Schmidt as an interest in 'nature incapable of doubt' because it is thereby 'undeflected'.[17] This quality is itself figured by Hughes as a kind of armour: it makes his thrushes 'More coiled steel than living' (Lupercal, 52); they become like automatic weapons, their legs may be 'delicate' but they are 'Triggered to stirrings beyond sense'. The poem goes on to claim that what Hughes

calls the 'Bullet and automatic / Purpose' of the thrushes is shared
by Mozart's brain, which illustrates the point that Hughes is not
really an animal poet, that his animals are 'emblems, analogues,
images, the quintessence of the poetic fallacy' (Schmidt, 385). More
specifically, this indicates how the thrushes are admired because
they exemplify being as pure, hard action. Their ontological coher-
ence is assured because they are not threatened by 'indolent
procrastinations' or 'yawning stares' which might lead to the
raggedness of passivity. They are linked in this to Mozart so that
the poem can insist that human genius must be a version of instinct
and therefore also driven by non-stop purpose. All of these qualities
combine to represent an aspiration towards a supercharged and
entirely secure masculinity characterised by iron hardness and
unwavering unstoppable activity. To use Lynne Segal's terms, they
represent an attempt to replace the fragility of the penis with the
invulnerability of the phallus:

> Masculinity is never the undivided, seamless construction it
> becomes in its symbolic manifestation. The promise of phallic
> power is precisely this guarantee of total inner coherence, of an
> unbroken and unbreakable, an unquestioned and unquestionable
> masculinity. Deprived of it, how can men be assured of 'natural'
> dominance? The antagonisms of gender coalesce with the strains
> of affirming and maintaining sexual polarities.[18]

The Hughes poem most preoccupied with 'natural' dominance is
'Hawk Roosting' (Lupercal, 26) which has been called a 'dramatic
monologue' (Schmidt, 387) – but, as such, it is conspicuous for its
lack of irony. Browning's dramatic monologues work in the gap
between the world view of the speaker and that of the implied
author; Browning is especially concerned to emphasise the gap
where the speaker (like that in 'Porphyria's Lover', 'My Last
Duchess' and Guido in *The Ring and the Book*) is dwelling on his own
power over women which is finally expressed in murder. By con-
trast, Hughes's poem suggests wishful identification: the gap is not
ironic but aspirational, it arises from human frustration at not pos-
sessing such absolute power. The hawk is defined partly by his dif-
ference from humans: 'There is no sophistry in my body: / My
manners are tearing off heads'. When Hughes later says that these
poems are concerned with a 'strong, positive mode of violence'

(Winter Pollen, 255) he indicates his desire to disparage sophistry and even manners in comparison with instinct, and indicates also his own aspiration to the phallic power of the speaking raptor surveying 'the earth's face upward for my inspection'.

The extent to which these poems from *Lupercal* present an extremely gendered view of Nature becomes even clearer when they are compared with poems written by Sylvia Plath which date from a similar period in their marriage. Hughes is influenced by D.H. Lawrence in wanting a realignment of the human towards the natural and directs an angry satire against complacently 'civilised' ignorance of the natural processes which he sees as actually underlying human behaviour. As a result Nature is treated by him with purposeful awe. Sylvia Plath also expresses awe but of a fearful rather than a wishful kind. Nature for her always involves the fear of being engulfed in processes of generation that lead to self-annihilation. In 'Morning Song'[19] the relationship between mother and baby is compared to that between a cloud and the pool of water it generates, which then mirrors the cloud's 'effacement' by the wind. Where Hughes's natural images express rigid and steely self-containment, Plath's express leakage and liquefaction: the 'spindling rivulets' in 'Parliament Hill Fields' (152–3) suggest that her miscarriage makes her feel as though part of herself is draining away. Where Hughes chooses a hawk as a dramatic monologuist, Plath chooses an elm (192–3): the man/ predator is a masterful monolith, the woman/ tree is at the same time anxiously multiple and fragmented. She is 'inhabited by a cry' which metaphorically evokes pregnancy as a horrifying invasion of the self, and the wind makes her 'break up in pieces that fly about like clubs'.

* * *

Tom Paulin says that Hughes's 'aesthetic primitivism embodies [a] wounded search for a primordial wholeness' (254): in early Hughes, though, this takes the form of seizing Nature as a vehicle for compensatory fantasies which turn it, obsessively, into a phallic battleground. His ghost crabs (Wodwo, 21–2) emerge from the dark depths in order to assert their primitive truths. They are 'Like a packed trench of helmets' because the First World War colours most of what the young Hughes sees, but also because his primitivism insists a hidden battle is being endlessly fought to preserve civilisation from instinctive drives that want to subvert it and assert their blood consciousness:

> They are the turmoil of history, the convulsion
> In the roots of blood, in the cycles of concurrence.
> To them, our cluttered countries are empty battleground.
>
> (22)

'Thistles' (Wodwo, 17) imagines these unwanted plants fighting an endless battle against pastureland. They oppose the softness of cows' tongues and cultivating human hands; like the Iron Man they are the repressed returning but this time as barbed phalluses, the penis becoming armoured:

> Every one a revengeful burst
> Of resurrection, a grasped fistful
> Of splintered weapons and Icelandic frost thrust up
>
> From the underground stain of a decayed Viking.

The Viking reference links this poem to 'The Warriors of the North' (Wodwo, 159) and so, with revealing tenuousness, to fantasies of rape and pillage and a vengeful primitivism asserting itself against 'soft' civilisation which gets associated with femininity. The Vikings' penetration southward is described in sexual terms as their 'frozen swords' thaw in the presence of 'The bountiful cleft casks, / The fluttered bowels of the women of dead burghers'. This is creepy. And what is curious about it is how it reverses the usual gender binary where culture is linked with masculinity and nature with femininity and manages to take a swipe at the feminine for reasons opposite to the conventional ones.

This is important because it hints at a larger pattern in early Hughes where the focus is so exclusively on defining a 'masculine' vision that the 'feminine' is always at best felt to be missing and at worst implicitly or even explicitly disparaged. War and Nature become almost interchangeable so that any notions of Nature as 'Mother' are erased – references to nurturing and instinctively altru- istic behaviour are chillingly absent as Hughes refines his vision of the relentless dominating of the weak by the strong in what seems most accurately described as a version of social Darwinism pro- jected back onto Nature. The image of devouring is recurrent in the animal poems, and the mutual interpenetration of war and Nature is again signalled when Hughes refers to his father's 'four-year mastication by gunfire and mud' (Wodwo, 155). As Michael Schmidt says:

> Hughes is a manly poet, and his attitude to women in the poems – infrequently voiced – is often tinged with fear and revulsion. Isolation seems synonymous with independence. The poet avoids ensnaring relationships. (386)

So his radio play *The Wound* (Wodwo, 104–6) dramatises the troubled hallucinations of a soldier with a head wound as he walks nine miles to safety. These involve his arrival at a chateau which turns out to be, in part at least, a glorified brothel with, for example, someone dressed as a duchess of whom the soldier says:

> Under all that mass of glittering stuff, she's nothing. Look at her sweating under that load of lousy hair – the lengths they'll go to! Easier just to hang a flag out. Just an old very used up tart under it all. Her eyes go off sideways. Her mouth doesn't fit her face, she can't keep it shaped. She has a neck like a stuffed lizard. Her fingernails are black. (125)

This soldier's misogynistic nightmare, combined with the obsession with phallic power I described earlier, take Hughes's vision worryingly close at times to the psychic outlook of Freicorps soldiers explored by Klaus Theweleit in his book *Male Fantasies*, an outlook succinctly summarised by Jessica Benjamin and Anson Rabinbach in their 'Foreword' to the second volume:

> *Male Fantasies* is interested in how the body both organises and expresses the politics of division between gender as a totalising framework. Fascism, in Theweleit's view, is an extreme example of the political polarization of gender (not restricted to any biological division of the sexes). Feminized men are as repellent to the fascist mentality as masculine women. But, Theweleit goes further: for the male it is the woman within that constitutes the most radical threat to his own integrity. Two basic types of bodies exemplify the corporal metaphysics at the heart of fascist perception. On the one side there is the soft, fluid, and ultimately liquid female body which is a quintessentially negative 'Other' lurking

inside the male body. It is the subversive source of pleasure or pain which must be expurgated or sealed off. On the other there is the hard, organized phallic body devoid of all internal viscera which finds its apotheosis in the machine. The body-machine is the acknowledged 'utopia' of the fascist warrior.[20]

Hughes's Iron Man, his thrushes and hawk and even his thistles emerge from something very close to this psychological formation, and his early work achieves much of its coherence and power from how thoroughly polarised it is in gender terms. However, what crucially differentiates him from the men Theweleit anatomises is his self-consciousness which allows him to analyse these symptoms for himself, and increasingly to distance himself from them. 'The Warriors of the North' voyeuristically enjoys the spectacle of the Vikings asserting their primitive male will: but it also hints at the beginning of Hughes's own critique of the masculinist psychological imbalance of the Protestant ethic and capitalism, referring to the Vikings' 'cash-down, beforehand revenge', and the 'iron arteries of Calvin'.

***

Wodwo as a volume expresses profound gender disturbance. It mingles an extreme masculine assertiveness with an alarmed and bewildered critique of the masculine. It was written after the three-year writing block that Hughes suffered after Plath's suicide in 1963. The extent to which this crucial event in Hughes's life caused the shift in his gender attitudes and his increasing consciousness of gender issues is impossible to judge. What is clear, though, is that *Wodwo*, as well as expressing the disturbance I have described, contains 'Song of a Rat', which Margaret Dickie Uroff calls 'Hughes' immediate poetic reaction to Plath's death ... a painful effort to confront the agony of her life and poetry, the misery of his own suffering and guilt, the source of song in pain'.[21]

However, what the references at the end of 'The Warriors of the North' indicate is that Hughes, very early on, invests his new self-consciousness about gender with more than a personal dimension. The last lines of that poem already refer to the key idea of his work from this point on: that Protestantism represents a systemic rejection of the feminine which inflicts dire psychic consequences on

Western culture. Hughes saw this as the constitutive theme of Shakespeare's work, and the central thesis of his *Shakespeare and the Goddess of Complete Being* is that his whole oeuvre is shaped around a core myth which elaborately grieves over this loss:

> Since Shakespeare only ever chose one mythic subject – Venus and Adonis – and since he chose it for his first and (considering *Lucrece* as an automatic sequel) only long poem, one can believe that the image of the beautiful young Adonis, rejecting the voluptuous, besotted Goddess, then being bloodily, sumptuously slain by the Boar, before being restored as a flower between the breasts of the Goddess as she flies to heaven, was an obsessive nexus of images to which he was drawn by irresistible fascination. (Shakespeare, 39–40)

Hughes was convinced that Shakespeare spent his creative life writing variations on this theme, and he traces its presence with obsessive energy through most of his plays – though not, tellingly, in the history plays. What this whole endeavour does, repeatedly, is to transform political concerns into mythic ones and even Hughes seems unable to work this transformation where the politics are most conspicuous. (This, again, makes Paulin's emphasis on Hughes as a social commentator look misplaced). This book certainly says far more about Hughes than it does about Shakespeare and what it suggests above all is the extent to which, during and after the writing of *Wodwo*, he realigned his gender views. When he says, for example, that 'the man who rejects the female, in moral, sexual revulsion, becomes in a moment the man who assaults and tries to destroy her' (170) he is accounting for much of the violence that preoccupies his poems. When, too, he translates the Adonis myth into what he sees as its 'psychobiological' meaning it takes him (via a reference to 'the light and dark of the womb's lunar cycle' and *The Wise Wound* by Penelope Shuttle and Peter Redgrove) to his preoccupation with the phallic mother expressed in my first quotation. Here he wants to show how the Adonis myth expresses a rejection of the feminine caused by boyhood resentment and fear of the mother's 'possessive control'. This leads him to see this rejection as the root explanation of the overly masculine, rationalist culture of Protestantism and capitalism, and to insist that Shakespeare 'divines the psycho-biological consequences of that Marduk/Jehovah/Puritan innovation'

> and shows how Adonis' attempt to consolidate his adolescent, precarious independence from the Mother Goddess in a once-and-for-all act of severing violence against the occult power of her paralysing love is simultaneously commandeered and redirected by the uncontrollable new sexual energy which is searching for union with the unknown Female: the act of ultimate suppressive violence becomes inextricably fused with the act of supreme sexual union. (327)

The emphasis of both the Shakespeare book and Hughes's later poetry is to heal the violent divisiveness that arises from the 'peculiar division of the sexes' and their 'peculiar conflict'. But it is in *Crow*[22] that Hughes diagnoses the sickness and it is in that volume that the words 'division', 'conflict' and maybe, above all, 'peculiar' seem most relevant. *Crow* is a brilliant examination of the damage caused by the attempts of masculinity to define itself against, and establish its independence from femininity. The anthropomorphic element in the early animal poems is implicit: by contrast *Crow* draws upon the long tradition of caricature which satirises human shortcomings by depicting human / animal hybrids – in order to dwell on male incorrigibleness and destructiveness. This is partly explained by the fact that the poems were written, at Leonard Baskin's invitation, to accompany that American artist's drawings. But this leads Hughes to draw upon the sort of dark caricatural comedy that is evident throughout this tradition: for instance, the masks of Classical Greece, the gargoyles on Gothic cathedrals, the drawings of Rowlandson and Daumier and, more recently, of Grosz. This is reflected, too, in the anti-humanist spirit of works like Ben Jonson's *Volpone* and Swift's *Gulliver's Travels*. In *Crow*, as everywhere else in this tradition, the stress is on a form of reduction which has the stark energy of single-mindedness. There is crucially a sense of something missing, of the confrontational lack of the richness and complexity which humanism associates with the self – but the sense, also, that this very lack produces, paradoxically, a larger than life impact.

What is most importantly missing is the creative and regenerative spirit of the feminine: *Crow* everywhere explores the consequences of the repudiation of the Goddess, who is referred to directly in 'Crow's Undersong' (56). This poem evokes her vestigial under-presence which is a cause for at least *some* celebration (this makes it the most optimistic poem in the sequence). The Goddess is depicted constantly trying to travel towards us but not quite arriving, so that she is literally subliminal, just under our threshold of apprehension. She makes it only to 'the fringe of voice'. Even so, she brings 'petals', 'nectar fruits', 'a cloak of feathers', 'an animal rainbow', and she would not have journeyed at all 'If there had been no hope'.

This attenuated optimism looks forward to the increasing emphasis on hope in later Hughes. *Crow* is mostly concerned, however, with its attenuatedness. Repeatedly the sequence refers to how the rejection of the Goddess has its 'psycho-biological' aspect, in the form of the 'growing boy's attitudes towards his mother' (Shakespeare, 327). In *Wodwo* his focus is on the difficulty of the masculine struggle this involves, so that he fantasises about the strength the male foetus needs to exit from the womb, describing this as though it were an heroic quest, as he follows 'his weapons towards the light' (152). This struggle is also depicted in *Crow*, but with the emphasis on its wrongheadedness so that Hughes seems to be facing up to the complicated inhibitions about motherhood which he refers to in *Poetry in the Making*. 'Crow and Mama' suggests that the masculine drive towards staying busy is an attempt to maintain distance from motherly/feminine entanglement or engulfment: as soon as Crow rests his mother closes on him 'like a book / On a bookmark'. All of Crow's activities inflict pain on his mother as though she is hurt by any sign of his separateness from her – this pain, too, it is implied, threatens to engulf him. So he tries to get away: first in a car but finds the towrope is around her neck; then in a plane but finds her body 'jammed in the jet'; then in a rocket which is described like an alternative, and superior womb which is 'cosy' but where he can peer out at 'Creation' and 'the future and the universe / Opening and opening'. But when he lands on the moon he crawls out 'Under his mother's buttocks'. Crow has been engaged in something again resembling a heroic quest whose imagery stresses expansiveness, but at its end he finds only his claustrophobic beginnings. 'Revenge Fable' (70) again refers to an inability to 'get rid of' the mother but here her phallic power is stressed as she is described as a tree of which the male child is merely 'her topmost twig'. (This interestingly reverses the power relations evoked by the cloud/pool image in Plath's 'Morning Song' which I referred to earlier – there the child reflects the mother's erasure).

These 'psycho-biological' aspects are translated, however, into larger mythic concerns by the sequence as a whole. Most obviously they are linked to the Oedipus theme which, as Annie Schofield[23] has pointed out, is recurrent in Hughes' work from *Wodwo* onwards, and in which for him

> Jocasta is the Mother – Nature – the blood root – love; Oedipus is the opposite pole: the Spirit – intellect – reason – rigid moral law: the opponent and suppressor of that which, in many, and especially in the poet answers the call of the White Goddess. (199)

However, what the Oedipus poems insist is that the spirit of Jocasta cannot be erased so that 'Song for a Phallus' (75–7) follows the same circular pattern as 'Crow and Mama' and Oedipus begins and ends curled up inside the womb, despite all the frantic vengeful violence he commits in between. This poem's nursery rhyme form suggests it should be read in dialogue with 'Daddy' as a masculine response to Plath's poem about her struggle to get rid of her father. Where the poems agree is in indicting patriarchy – though in Hughes's case this is largely for what he considers its rationalism which is represented in 'Oedipus Crow' (43) by a wrist watch that is associated with Crow's flight from a 'water-spirit' who 'Twined his brains with primroses'. That watch represents the same culture of rational progress which 'Revenge Fable' sees represented in 'numbers and equations and laws' (70) which are weapons used in vengeance against the phallic mother.

The crucial idea behind *Crow* is that this masculinist rationalism has diminished human potential so far that humanity has reduced itself to a monstrous caricature. When Crow runs from the water-spirit he is mutilated, he is 'One-legged, gutless and brainless, the rag of himself' (43), when he attacks his mother with technology his head falls off 'like a leaf' (70). Similarly, 'A Bedtime Story' (71–2) describes a man who is 'intermittent', has 'only half a face', his hands are 'funny hooves', 'Half his head was jellyfish'.

These physical reductions are best read as equivalents of the reductions of the spirit such as those described in 'The Contender' (41–2) where a man indulges in a 'senseless trial of strength' which consumes his whole being. The distance Hughes has travelled from his earlier work is particularly obvious here because the man is being disparaged for qualities of single-mindeness and self-conscious power which are not far from those admired by the young poet in the hawk and the pike. Moreover, the central figure's obsessiveness is explicitly diagnosed as a masculine sickness, as an insistence on proving himself even when it is self-destructive. This is partly a matter of masculine self-insulation which also characterises the man in 'Criminal Ballad' (38–9) who is so detached when 'belly to belly' with his first love that he seems to stare at the experience

> Through an anaesthetized mask
> And felt the cardboard of his body
> And when he walked in his garden and saw his children
> Bouncing among the dogs and balls
> He could not hear their silly songs and the barking
> For machine guns

This man finds his hands suddenly covered with blood and runs away, holding them 'clear of everything', into a wood where he weeps 'Till he began to laugh'.

That last line provides an important clue to the preoccupation with humour in *Crow* which is remarkable for being, at times, so funny and at the same time more or less unique in Hughes's work in this respect. *Crow* is comic but disapproves of its own comedy, which seems of a piece with its hero's laddishness in representing a spirit of resilient energy and knowingly bad attitudes and behaviour. The humour is at the same time shocked at, and perversely proud of itself:

> In laughter, in laughter
> The meteorite crashes
> With extraordinarily ill-luck on the pram
>> (48)

'A Grin' (29), 'In Laughter' (48–9) and 'The Smile' (62–3) all explore the idea of the cruel comedy that arises from caricature, that derives entertainment from the spectacle of humiliating diminishment and disintegration. These human responses are imagined leading lives independent of human beings, a little like expressionist personifications, but deployed like this to suggest an inhuman detachment of the sort that leads the man with blood on his hands from weeping to laughing. They represent the spirit of irony which

makes Hughes uncomfortable and which he associates with a coolly
masculine rationality.

Crow's role as black joker is linked to his role as trickster, the
figure to whom Hughes refers as a 'demon of phallic energy' and
whose activities he relates to 'the immortal enterprise of the sperm'
(Winter Pollen, 241 and 240). However, the psychic problem which
Crow diagnoses arises from this male biology operating with disas-
trous unilateralness, so that, as Jarold Ramsey says, 'by the stan-
dards of primitive myth [Crow] is too late and too little as a
Transformer'.[24] That is, that part of the trickster role which involves
remedying the defective work of an inadequate Creator is itself
defective in Crow. Lévi-Strauss has referred to the trickster as
'bricoleur', or handyman (quoted by Ramsey, 174) but because of
these fallen circumstances Hughes depicts him performing, on a
cosmic and mythic scale, nightmares of botched DIY.

So 'Crow's Playmates' (60) describes Crow creating gods who
work oppositely to how they should – the river-god, for example,
drains him dry – and he gets reduced to 'his own leftover'. In 'Crow
Improvises' (64–5) he tries to mate impossibly unsuitable partners
(the sun and a leaf, the battle of the Somme and a sleeping tablet, a
dead vole and Relativity, a girl's laugh and a seven-year honey-
moon) but they merely strike sparks that inflict terrible damage on
him. In 'Crow Blacker than ever' (69) he tries to repair the disinte-
gration caused by God and man turning away from each other by
'Nailing Heaven and earth together', but 'Then heaven and earth
creaked at the joint / Which became gangrenous and stank'.

***

The writer of *Crow* is as much involved in improvisatory bricolage
as its hero – its style is minimal and makeshift. As Hughes says in
his interview with Ekbert Faas, he wanted 'songs with no music
whatsoever, in a super-simple and a super-ugly language which
would in a way shed everything except just what he wanted to say'
(Faas, 208). This minimalism implicitly draws attention to the
medium, but Hughes also has poems which explicitly refer to lan-
guage, so that *Crow* continually draws attention to its handiwork
and materials. This deconstructiveness is uncharacteristic for
Hughes and, like the humour of *Crow*, shows how much he is
writing in this sequence against his own grain in order fully to
diagnose the sickness which his later poems will try to heal. An

important symptom of this sickness for Hughes is the dominance of mere constructedness in Crow's world – this is implicitly seen in opposition to the organic creativity which he associates with the rejected Goddess. So he vilifies language as an agent of this constructedness: 'A Disaster' (33), 'The Battle of Osfrontalis' (34), and 'Crow Goes Hunting' (54) all depict words as distortive and destructive and associate them with the masculine culture of rationalism and technology which leads to environmental catastrophe.

It is interesting, then, that Hughes's next project was a commission from Peter Brook to write a play which attempted to deploy 'primeval sounds that precede the sonorous and symbolic stability that is necessary for language as communication';[25] accordingly *Orghast* involved 'glissando shrieks, roars, hoarse whispers, and harsh, explosive laughing noises'.[26] For Hughes this amounted to an opportunity to delve under the civilised and devious surface of language to unearth its physiological roots. This represents a search for a pre-linguistic origin and, as such, is best understood by reference to Julia Kristeva's concept of the *chora* which 'precedes and underlies figuration and thus specularization, and is analogous only to vocal or kinetic rhythm'[27] The *chora* can never be stably located because it is equated with what Kristeva calls the semiotic, which precedes the law of the symbolic (the signifying system by which things can be thoroughly defined), but it is crucially associated with the mother and with the feminine generally. *Orghast* can therefore be seen as an attempt to uncover the pre-linguistic universals, the biological roots of language and so suggest the possibility of physiological modes of expression. *Orghast* is a self-consciously experimental work but, as such is best seen as standing in the poetic tradition which has most interested Kristeva (that of Mallarmé and Lautréamont) and which she sees as drawing upon the resources of the semiotic. So she describes Mallarmé calling attention to the 'semiotic rhythm within language':

> Indifferent to language, enigmatic and feminine, this space underlying the written is rhythmic, unfettered, irreducible to its intelligible verbal translation, it is musical, anterior to judgment. (29)

Kristeva's equation of the semiotic with the feminine can appear to be merely a more sophisticated version of the essentialist equation of the feminine with the natural. However, it is very suggestive when it is applied to Hughes; in particular, Kristeva's linking of the *chora* with the mother hints very powerfully at what Hughes was attempting in inventing a language *before* language, before the imposition of rationalist masculine order – he was attempting to evoke a principle of eternal motherliness. For Hughes, anyway, essentialism is a key belief: he says, for example, that 'the anabolic and catabolic phases of the egg's life ... dominate the immediate subjective being of all women' (Shakespeare, 326).

Having delved, in *Orghast*, into the feminine semiotic, Hughes moved, in the poems written after this turning-point, towards developing a poetic that adapts the symbolic to create roles for himself which are explicitly masculine but nonetheless defined as ways of serving the Goddess. *Orghast* can be regarded as an attempt to speak a thoroughly feminine language: *Cave Birds* and *Gaudete*[28] invent newly masculine forms of expression by reference to both heroic quest and shamanic song. Nonetheless these forms of expression are directed towards formulating what it is possible for a male poet to do in the urgent business of evoking the Goddess and indicating her powerful if subliminal presence.

Hughes himself spoke about shamanism as a form of heroism:

> A spirit summons him ... usually an animal or a woman. If he refuses, he dies ... or somebody near him dies. If he accepts, he then prepares himself for the job ... it may take years. Usually he apprentices himself to some other shaman, but the spirit may well teach him direct. Once fully-fledged he can enter trance at will and go to the spirit world ... he goes to get something badly needed, a cure, an answer, some sort of divine intervention in the community's affairs. Now this flight to the spirit world he experiences as a dream ... and that dream is the basis of the hero story. (Faas, 206)

The later Hughes evidently saw his role as a poet by analogy with this shamanic activity. He was a visionary who saw poetry as a form of psychic healing, and was, for this reason, preoccupied with roles – that of poet laureate was only the most conspicuous of these. He deliberately placed himself in the tradition of Blake, Yeats and the Robert Graves of *The White Goddess*, and constructed himself as a medium to spiritual truths which a materialist culture unhealthily ignores. It is in this context that the eco-feminism of the later

Hughes is best understood. He saw the worth of his own activities being confirmed by changes in the culture towards a recrudescent paganism which he relates, at the end of his essay 'Poetry and Violence', to a renewed emphasis on the feminine and the '"sacred" biology of woman' (Winter Pollen, 267). Late in his life, he adopted an optimistic posture in the belief that the masculinist culture of rationalism and materialism was disintegrating.

However, there are a number of problems arising from this. Hughes seems to encounter severe difficulties in translating this vision into convincing poems. The visionary parts of his later poetry travel so far into abstraction that it is impossible to locate them from the perspective of any actual experience. There are too many lines like

> Am I the self of some spore
> In this white of death blackness,
> This yoke of afterlife?
> (*Cave Birds*, 34)

> I heard the atoms praying
> To enter his kingdom
> To be broken like bread
> On a dark sill, and to bleed.
> (*Gaudete*, 186)

> The long Shrine of hunger. Window spectra
> Break on the retina. It is the hunger
> Humbles the eye-beam.
> (*Wolfwatching*, 45)

These tributes to the Goddess seem too willed and merely pious; and they are always implicit tributes: Hughes seems to have as many inhibitions about writing about her directly as he did earlier about writing about his mother.

Strangely, Hughes's greatest successes after *Crow* are the stylistic opposite of these visionary poems. They are the painstakingly naturalistic poems he wrote about his experiences as a farmer, and as such they are the furthest from his system-building poetic, also, because they are occasional in the sense of being rooted in particular events. These poems are notable for the detailed care they take of their materials, so that they mimic the care the poet/ farmer is taking of his livestock:

> Then I picked her calf up bodily and went in.
> Little piggy eyes, she followed me. Then I roped her,
> And drew her to the head of the stall, tightened her
> Hard to the oak pillar, with her nose in the hay-rack,
> And she choke-bellowed query comfort to herself.
> He was trying to suck – but lacked the savvy.
>
> (Moortown, 53)

At times these poems hint at the possibility of the most positive outcome of Hughes' realignment towards the feminine in suggesting a kind of male nurturing, the adoption of a role most tellingly described as 'husbandry'. Unfortunately, however, they also contain gender inflections of a more disquieting kind. Craig Robinson quotes Hughes's own account of reading 'February 17th', which describes his failed attempt to help a lamb that was stuck with its head out but its body still inside its mother. A member of the audience objected to Hughes reading 'what he called a disgusting piece of horror writing'.[29] Hughes responds by saying 'Well, we either have a will to examine what happens, or we have a will to evade it' and Robinson is on his side:

> This is a real situation into which, as is often the case in his recent work, Hughes has introduced himself as agent of his own morality. Presumably, at this point in real life, those who 'have a will to evade … what happens' would be found wanting. Hughes is not found wanting, and the rest of the poem, beginning with the sentence 'I felt inside' is an example of how the courage to face facts can result in helpful action. (Robinson, 266)

The problem comes, however, with the way that Hughes presents himself as 'agent of his own morality' – that is the extent to which he establishes himself in these poems as a figure of authority. The implication is that the poet has the courage to face up to these natural horrors and he dramatises himself in that process which is made all the more vivid through the detail with which he describes the suffering body parts and the bleak landscape. Nature in early Hughes, as I have said, is constantly associated with war: in these farming poems Hughes presents himself as though reporting back from a kind of front line and so implying the extent of his heroic endurance and skill. The effect is to bestow an enormous amount of macho power on the poet, especially in comparison with his readers who live, by implied contrast, comfortable, blithely civilised lives and are likely to have 'a will to evade … what happens'. The effect was even more marked when Hughes read these poems publicly, when their hero was physically present.

It may seem contradictory to characterise these poems by reference to both nurturing and macho posturing but both elements are present in them, and this is representative of their disturbed attempt to effect a realignment of gender roles. Hughes is fascinating in gender terms because he represents such an extreme case, and one who at the same time acquires enormously increased gender self-consciousness and performs his own kind of critique of masculinity.

However, the form that critique takes, as both Margaret Dickie Uroff and Jacqueline Rose point out, is deeply unsatisfactory and disquieting. Uroff points out that the Mother-Goddess tends to appear in Hughes's poems only as a monster giving him 'messages through which he sees all he had dreaded' (Uroff, 196) and that in evoking her, he 'evokes fears of engulfment that perhaps express his own psychic terror in the face of female power' (199). Rose very persuasively extends this argument to include the roots of this Goddess theory in Graves and Jung. She links Jung's concept of the Terrible Mother to his concept of individuation in order to suggest that all that this 'implies by way of a finally integrated identity, appears to be a way of repudiating what is most troubling about sexuality and women (the second as the terrifying and abject embodiment or projection of the first)' (Rose, 162). And she shows how for Graves this feminine principle represents the Muse, and how 'his mythic conception of poetry is set quite explicitly against politics and history' (163).

Rose is cogent in indicating the damage that this view of the feminine inflicted on Sylvia Plath in placing her in the role of Muse, which can only last a few years and involves 'the risk of her own self-inflicted death' (154). This would already sufficiently indict this outlook. What should be said, in addition, however, is that the Goddess myth also inflicts damage on men. In Hughes's case it represents a move from the extreme repudiation of the feminine which characterises his early work to the wrong kind of dependence – one that looks to an idealised femininity to regenerate and heal a

disintegrated masculinity. This development can also be charac-
terised as a move from an obsession with domination towards a
desire, too closely linked to the earlier obsession, for submission.
This means that pious eco-feminist statements can be made about
the sacredness of Woman while the monstrous frightening other-
ness of the Goddess can also be more secretly and masochistically
enjoyed. These responses, before and after Hughes's turning-point,
are both too closely tied to reactions to the disquieting power of the
phallic mother.

However, the root cause of these problems lies in Hughes's most
characteristic habit of referring all human behaviour to a biological
origin. For all his recent optimism his emphasis on instincts
inevitably leads to a belief that men will always cause wars and
women will always be left to heal the resultant damage. The poem
which expresses this most clearly, 'A Motorbike', which I discussed
earlier, dates from after Hughes's conversion to the Feminine – the
fact is that Hughes's dedication to the Goddess implicitly sanctions
some of the worst 'masculine' behaviour by regarding it as biolo-
gically driven and assuming there are equal and opposite drives in
the 'feminine'. One part of the Goddess, after all, is violent and
unites 'the world of death with the world of elemental sexuality,
animality and the daemonic' (Shakespeare, 515). What is nominally
Hughes's anti-rationalism becomes, disturbingly often, this vision
which is actually part of his relentless focus on power relationships
and, in particular, of his sado-masochistic obsession with drives
towards domination and submission which colours his view of both
natural and human behaviour, and which is also in evidence in his
fascination with 'scapegoats', from his early dwelling on soldiers to
his later exploration of the figure of Prometheus. His Shakespeare
book is coloured by this outlook too, so that the playwright's whole
oeuvre is viewed as playing endless variations on the theme of a
war between the sexes considered as inevitable: Othello, for
example, murders in a frenzy of love in which

> sexuality has commandeered the primordial (pre-heterosexual)
> instinct of killing to eat, and has sublimated and transformed and
> adapted it (in the inspired economy of biological life) into the
> equally compulsory act of reproduction. (Shakespeare, 181)

It is in this combination of biology and mysticism that Hughes is
at his weakest – this also produces his least successful poems.

However, it is important to see his system-building as one of a number of responses to the concerns which motivate his work from the start and in which it is possible to read his expression of the damage that patriarchy inflicts on men. It is true that he can find almost no place in his poems for women but this too is part of the gender malaise which his work so starkly displays. If Hughes' writings are viewed from the perspective of his poems about his father's war experiences – as I have viewed them here – it becomes clear how much they express how patriarchy wounds men at the same time as bestowing power on them. No other poet so clearly reveals the psychological impact on men of such ambiguities in their position of power. No other poet has invented images which express with such vividness the fantasies of desire and fear which accompany men's knowledge of their power, and how, like 'the shark's mouth / That hungers down the blood-smell even to the leak of its own / Side and devouring of itself' (Lupercal, 52) men damage themselves in the process of damaging others. And, however unsatisfactory Hughes's system is in the end, it did provide him the framework to write *Crow*, with its subtle, comic and incisive critique of patriarchy, and its guilty and rueful self-satire.

4

Able Semen and the Penile Canon: Derek Walcott's 'Adamic Utterance'

Derek Walcott's work is driven by the desire to question, but above all to acquire paternal authority. He has always been aware of this so that in the early autobiographical pieces 'Leaving School', which dates from 1965, and 'Meanings', from 1970, he refers to his vocation as both water-colourist and poet as having been inspired by the example of his father who died in his thirties when Walcott and his twin-brother were a year old. This led him to feel that the work of his father was 'unfinished' and that 'to begin as a poet was, for me, a direct inheritance. It was natural. I feel that I have simply continued where my father left off.'[1] He refers to this again in his long poem *Omeros*[2] where his father's ghost reflects on how his verse-writing had made his son's 'life's choice' for him, and how the father's and the son's calling have blended with each other (68).

However, the questions of personal and authorial identity which are raised by this are always linked, for Walcott, with colonialism. And this – largely because of that link – arouses complex responses in him. His father's ghost refers both to his upbringing in Castries in St Lucia and to how his own 'bastard father' came from Warwickshire and accordingly named him 'Warwick'. Walcott's own vocation is then elaborately associated with this ancestral link with Shakespeare's county and he is said to inherit 'that Will', a pun that seems to insist that Walcott's drive to write derives from the English part of his ancestry.

As I shall be showing, this is crucial to him and an important key to his authorial character which can be helpfully defined by contrast to many of the assumptions of 'postcolonial' writing. It is not, however, the whole story – elsewhere he lays the stress differently and does write in a more orthodox postcolonial manner. So, in the fiftieth section of 'Midsummer'[3] he also refers to his father and Warwickshire but here insists that his poems 'aren't linked to any tradition / like a mossed cairn'. By contrast with an English tradition which this line imagines as fixed and stationary and linked to the land, he says that his own poems 'lie / where stones are deep, in the sea's memory' and so form part of a new tradition which is the literary embodiment of the postcolonial history which he says, in another poem, is not represented by 'monuments', 'battles' and 'martyrs', but is 'subtle and submarine', because 'The Sea is History' (CP, 364–7).

This is the side of Derek Walcott which to some extent connects him, then, to the self-consciously oppositional aesthetic which is associated with postcolonial writing, which refers to European traditions while at the same time subverting and declaring its radical differences from them. A powerful image for this outlook is presented by his father's ghost when he remembers his visits to the town barber, in whose mirrors 'The *World's Great Classics* read backwards' (Omeros, 71). Similarly, he is described as having been 'toga'd' there in a 'pinned sheet' but this classical image is then reoriented when Warwick Walcott declares that he has bequeathed his son 'that clean sheet and an empty throne' – the son's postcolonial condition will inaugurate a new textual beginning which, by implication, will be to some extent pre-determined by what his father started when his 'curled hairs fell like commas' (71), where the classical text is re-structured by his racial identity.

However, what pre-occupies Walcott above all in these passages are questions of power and mastery. His father refers to the barber as his 'chamberlain' and offers his son an 'empty throne' (71) and later describes himself as having felt 'diminished' even by postcards from Europe which depict its monuments, and 'streets that History had made great' and so retreating to St Lucia and a circle of friends he could 'dominate' (187). The depiction of the father/son relationship in *Omeros* is part of a pre-occupation with becoming his own man both personally and poetically. As Rei Terada says, since the poem 'is, like Homer's Odyssey, a story about the genealogy of fathers and sons, it is also a parable of poetic influence'.[4] Terada later shows how Walcott reveals the inadequacy of certain contemporary assumptions about influence – especially the notion of the later poet winning a sort of battle over the earlier in order to avoid the charge of being a 'slavish' imitator (78). He points out how alarmingly unselfconscious reviewers tend to be when they use this word in relation to postcolonial literature. Walcott is unusually troubled about the charge of slavishness because he has evolved a strategy that involves evading the battle with previous 'masters' by absorbing their power and incorporating it into his own armoury. His interaction with his father in *Omeros* can be read as representing his method of dealing with poetic genealogy – instead of confronting his father's power he appears unanxiously to acknowledge it and then allow it to boost his own. It is possible, however, to underestimate the element of confrontation in this because Walcott cleverly glosses it over – he does not struggle explicitly with his father's power but pays his respects to it while coolly assessing the small extent of his father's actual achievement. A similar effect is achieved in 'Midsummer' by the subtlety of the contrast between the imagery he associates with himself and his father: his own poems are a solid achievement, they are stones that settle 'deep' in the memory, while his father is shadowy, 'wavering and faint in the midsummer sunlight' (CP, 504).

Warwick Walcott contributes in the end to his son's armoury as an artist because he simultaneously acts as a bridge with the English literary canon and confirms, by contrast, the depth and complexity of his son's colonial and postcolonial experience. This is crucial because it is Walcott's unique arbitration between these two which provides the most telling clue to his authorial character – he distinguishes himself among postcolonial writers by his insistence on paying homage to the canon, by his posture of self-conscious deference. The importance for him of the notion of paternal authority, and his own awareness of that importance, are again evident when, in 'The Muse of History', he draws on the father/son relationship as an analogy, when he says that 'revolutionary literature is a filial impulse, and ... maturity is the assimilation of the features of every ancestor' (370). The force of this analogy in this essay is to claim English literature as his father, and then, in its heatedly rhetorical last paragraph, to disown any filial relationship with colonial history. That is to say, he wills himself to become the son of English literature, and not of the colonies:

> I say to the ancestor who sold me, and to the ancestor who bought me, I have no father, I want no such father, although I can understand you, black ghost, white ghost, when you both whisper 'history', for if I attempt to forgive you both I am falling

into your idea of history which justifies and explains and expi-
ates, and it is not mine to forgive, my memory cannot summon
any filial love, since your features are erased and I have no wish
and no power to pardon. You were when you acted your roles,
your given, historical roles of slave seller and slave buyer, men
acting as men, and also you, father in the filth-ridden gut of the
slave ship, to you they were also men, acting as men, with the
cruelty of men, your fellowman and tribesman not moved or
hovering with hesitation about your common race any longer
than my other bastard ancestor hovered with his whip, but to
you inwardly forgiven grandfathers, I, like the more honest of my
race, give a strange thanks. I give the strange and bitter and yet
ennobling thanks for the monumental groaning and soldering of
two great worlds, like the halves of a fruit seamed by its own
bitter juice, that exiled from your own Edens you have placed me
in the wonder of another, and that was my inheritance and your
gift. (373–4)

What this remarkable passage does is to evoke a vivid vision of
these forefathers while apparently erasing them, a vision in which
they are generalised as men driven by generalised masculine
motives of cruel domination. Slavery as a system is diagnosed as
purely masculine in its origins, but dismissively diagnosed as such –
as a question of what men routinely and naturally do. The presence
of female slaves is quietly erased, which is strange given that
Walcott is much whiter in his male than his female ancestry (he had
two white grandfathers, one English and one Dutch). This may be
part of a general tendency in Walcott to marginalise the feminine,
and certainly to erase it from areas as active as history. It is more
importantly indicative here, however, of how thoroughly focused
he is on the question of paternity. 'The Muse of History' strenu-
ously brushes aside Walcott's actual forefathers (and does not even
engage with the issue of actual foremothers) in order to stress his
filial relationship with canonical Western literature. He acknowl-
edges the pain of colonial history but at the same time glosses it
over, dismisses the past in order to imagine a new start, an Eden in
which the bitten apple is again whole, and in which the New and
Old Worlds are joined together. So, where the dominant tendency
of most postcolonial writing is deconstructive, Walcott's is, as it
were, reconstructive: instead of dismantling the canonical text, he
wants to reassemble it for his own ends. This means affirming the

universal validity of Western textuality, as his image of the fruit suggests; he does not want to reveal the deviously political machinery behind the concealed artifice of Western textual practice, but to endorse its claims to organic coherence and to totalising and accurate naturalness.

Paradoxically, Walcott regards this affirmation and consequent assimilation of the Western canon as making possible what he calls an 'Adamic' vision (371). He regards many postcolonial writers as torturing themselves when they reject Western writing as 'the language of the master' (371) – by contrast his strategy allows him to adopt that language as his own and thereby to acquire supreme paternal authority, to write as though he were in fact the first master and father, in a 'second Eden' where the apples 'have the tartness of experience'. This Adamic vision allows him, therefore, to have his apple and to eat it: he manages to be both the first writer *and* to draw upon the accumulated experience of his writerly forefathers. This is similar to his treatment of his father in *Omeros* where he both defers to Warwick Walcott, calling him 'Sir' (68) and, in a sense, out-fathers him by engendering a poetic work on a scale his father could not have managed (which also contains and thereby poetically engenders his father), a work in which the father points out that the son is now twice his age (68). Homer, too, is present in the poem to be both respected and superceded. He is the father of Western poetry and, through his homage to him in *Omeros*, Walcott 'defines himself against a primary Western paradigm of originality and mimetic power' (Terada, 183) and thereby constructs himself as the Homer of the New World.

The strategy which Walcott outlines in 'The Muse of History' leads him to imagine history being annihilated, and to imagine his acquiring the 'elemental privilege of naming the new world' (372). The implications of this mean that Biodun Jeyifo places the emphasis wrongly in suggesting that Walcott wants to 'debunk' the 'epistemic, nomenclatural hegemony' of the West (Critical Perspectives, 378) because this strategy involves his *participation* in hegemonic naming. Jeyifo's analysis of the implications of this hegemony is accurate enough:

> 'white' domination is not only political and socio-economic, it is also, or aspires to total effectivity in the naming of things, in signifying and explanatory systems; in other words, it seeks to be an *epistemic* order of control and manipulation.

However, far from wishing to subvert this 'total effectivity', Walcott aspires to acquire it, and does so by placing himself in a 'filial' relationship to the West and, consequently, in a paternal relationship to the New World. He pictures himself, not as Caliban or Man Friday, but as Prospero and, in particular, Crusoe, who appears repeatedly in his writings as an analogue of the poet, as he himself has explained in interviews:

> The Crusoe thing is inevitable because of his two conditions. One is the elation of being 'the monarch of all he surveys'. We are Crusoes: as poets, as novelists, as playwrights, we survey islands, and we feel they belong to us – not in a bad, godlike manner, but with that sense of exhilaration, of creative possession. The other side is the despair of Crusoe, the despair of always being alone. That is our true condition as writers.[6]

Walcott here identifies solely with fellow writers, not with others who have shared – as Friday prototypically did – in the colonial experience. Moreover, by taking Crusoe as his own prototype, he associates himself with what Jeyifo calls the West's 'epistemic, nomenclatural hegemony'. He is concerned precisely to acquire Crusoe's power to speak and write universal truths so that Crusoe is always equated with Adam – thereby erasing his ideological and historical meaning in order to strengthen his epistemic meaning. The loss of Crusoe's ideological dimension is linked to Walcott's feeling that 'Race, despite what critics think, has meant nothing to me past early manhood. Race is ridiculous.' (Conversations, 81). Most importantly, however, it works so that, in identifying with Crusoe, Walcott is identifying with a powerful male figure who, with literal originality, can linguistically engender all that he experiences, and who does so with unquestionable authority. To be a writer, for Walcott, is like being a colonist, to feel that the landscape you describe 'belongs' to you, that it is your 'creative possession' (Conversations, 63). As a writer, Walcott aspires to the condition of the patriarch.

So, in 'Crusoe's Journal', Walcott speaks of how

> the intellect appraises
> objects surely, even the bare necessities
> of style are turned to use,
> like those plain iron tools he salvages

from shipwreck, hewing a prose
as odorous as raw wood to the adze;
        out of such timbers
came our first book, our profane Genesis
        whose Adam speaks that prose
which, blessing some sea-rock startles itself
        with poetry's surprise,
in a green world, one without metaphors
                            (CP, 92–3)

This is a vision in which Crusoe/Adam can perceive, understand
and evoke the phenomenal world masterfully and unmediatedly;
the language he speaks is utterly transparent. The prose he deploys
provides him with direct, unmetaphorical access to the world in its
innocent greenness, so that it can smell like 'raw wood'. This is a
language, certainly, and its artificiality is recognised because it is
compared to carpentry which is repeatedly referred to by Walcott as
a specifically masculine activity – for instance in *Omeros* when he
says that 'Men are born makers, with that primal simplicity / in
every maker since Adam' (150) and then goes on to cite carvers,
armourers and potters. But because of Crusoe's primacy, the
hewing is erased, the prose is hewn but astonishingly retains its
odorous rawness, the sea-rock is rendered poetically but is appre-
hended, through the poetry, as startlingly itself.

Walcott is describing here his own version of literary 'estrange-
ment', one which is emphatically not a question of defamiliarising
techniques but of poetry's ability to summon up, mystically, the
freshness of the phenomenal world as though for the first time, as
though inventing it. He is referring to something similar in *The
Bounty* when he says 'I saw stones that shone with stoniness, I saw
thorns / steady in their inimical patience' where he is evoking a
moment of astonishing plenitude of being, where the appre-
hension of the phenomenal world is blessedly thorough and
complete. The poetic prerequisite for this, again, is a language that
is somehow pre- or post-linguistic, signifiers that are actually
referents, words that are actually objects, 'a syntax the colour
of slate, / with glints of quartz for occasional perceptions' (The
Bounty, 55).

Walcott's aspiration to 'Adamic' vision is part of his unique strat-
egy for overcoming his 'belatedness'. This involves the paradoxical
process of his self-conscious mimicry of Western poetry, in which

he openly declares his lateness in that tradition yet simultaneously boasts his earliness in the one just starting in the New World. The later he can appear in the old, the earlier he appears in the new. That is why *Omeros* tries

> to hear the names of things and people in their own context, meaning everything named in a noun, and everything around a name. You see maybe the whole West Indian experience is not itself – it is translated. There is a film over the name, Caribbean. You can see the object, but between the object and you there is some experience, some artifice. We look through a glass in which the noun on the other side has not yet been named. It's the origin of the real Caribbean nouns that I'm after. (Conversations, 173)

His stress on the 'Adamic' element seems to be a stress on natural-ness, but this diverts attention away from the extent to which what his primal naming does is to inaugurate cultural control. This is all the more pressingly the case because his poems are obsessively con-cerned with landscape and they are obsessively formal – self-consciously deploying a wide range of poetic forms. The impression his poems give, then, is of being driven to find linguistic devices for naming and defining the natural world. That Walcott is also a water-colourist is important here because in his poems, as in his water-colours, as Edward Baugh has pointed out, 'Every view is composed and coloured and framed as for a painting' (Critical Perspectives, 240).

That these roles of naming and framing are assumed by Walcott to be masculine is clear enough from how he associates them with Adam, as the ultimate forefather, and with Crusoe, as the adven-turer who becomes the paradigm of the patriarchal colonist. The notion of 'creative possession' is not only gendered but even insinu-atingly sexual and this lies crucially behind the figure of Helen in *Omeros* where she is both a female character and a symbolic repre-sentative of Walcott's native island because, as he has said

> In elementary school we had been taught that St Lucia was 'The Helen of the West' because she was fought for so often by the French and British. She had changed hands thirteen times. She had been regularly violated. In fact, her final capture by the British had the quality of a cuckold's surrender, since she re-mained faithful to her French colonial past. (Critical Perspectives, 24)

This leads to a widespread feminising of the landscape in Walcott's poems, and an implicit sexualising of the poetic act, in which the male poet's poem 'possesses' the landscape. In 'Sainte Lucie' (CP, 309–23) the place is both an island and a woman, 'her smile like the whole country'. Her fertility is stressed – 'her armpits / a reaping, her arms / saplings', – and is achieved through the flow of streams which mimic animal sexuality, 'as spring water eases / over shelves of rock / in some green ferny hole' (313).

Similarly, 'Walcott represents St Lucia at large by means of the female figures in "The Light of the World"' (Terada, 218). This process of representation seems all the more obvious in that poem[8] because Walcott starts out there seeming, for once, very much concerned with a literal woman who is described humming along to a Bob Marley song on the stereo of a bus. However, almost immediately, Walcott is imagining her as a portrait and comparing her to a 'still panther', a comparison he uses also for Helen in *Omeros* (39). By line 10 her head has become 'nothing else but heraldic'. Walcott can be shockingly naive on the gender issue – here, in a book published in 1988, he blithely erases the woman's literal identity and translates her into the terms of a mediaeval image, all symbol and artifice. That 'nothing else', if it were not merely naive, would seem like fighting talk from a man determined to insist on his right to allow his male gaze to reify a woman. Turning her, as he does next, into a statue, seems inevitable and completes the predictable pattern of dehumanising the woman in order to idealise her – she becomes 'like a black Delacroix's / *Liberty Leading the People*' and then, 'the light of the world'. What Walcott is up to generally in this poem is finding the 'poetic' amongst the humdrum and in this opening verse paragraph he is working to establish his right to identify clues to transcendence in the midst of the everyday. The beauty on the bus is meant to be perceived as epiphanic, and to be understood both by contrast with her context and as symbolising the potential of that context to transcend itself, to become a site of spiritual beauty. The poem's realist notation introduces metonymies ('the sixteen-seater transport', 'grit of charcoal / and the litter of vegetables', 'the roaring rum shops', etc.) out of which the eponymous metaphor arises to suggest how, nonetheless, St Lucia arouses baffled feelings of regret and longing.

Those feelings are aroused partly because he associates the island with his mother, 'her white hair tinted by the dyeing dusk' (49) and this also to some extent justifies why he thinks of St Lucia as a

woman. His anxiety that he has 'abandoned' the island (50) there-
fore also seems linked to the masculine process of distancing from
the mother which is necessary but nonetheless disorienting. The
ontological disturbances involved in this are subtly evoked when
Walcott, having referred to the men of the island 'hunched in
canoes', says 'I, who could never solidify my shadow / to be one of
their shadows, had left them their earth' (50). The 'abandonment' of
the island, and his mother, turns him into a shadow whose lack
of solidity is contrasted with the solidity of earth. It is telling, then,
that immediately after this, he declares 'I was deeply in love with
the woman by the window' (50) as though this is aroused in him as
a substitute for the previous loss.

There is much that is potentially powerful in this association of
ideas. However, the sexual fantasy that follows the declaration of
love is bathetically banal – 'I wanted her to change / into a smooth
white nightie that would pour like water / over the black rocks of
her breasts' (50) – and the construction of the epiphanic moment
seems terribly self-conscious and laboured. More disturbingly, that
construction is achieved by imposing a set of Western references on
the St Lucian setting, references which introduce a hierarchy of
materials into the poem. The insistence that the woman's head 'was
nothing else but heraldic' (48) seems geared self-consciously towards
ennobling her by associating her with literal nobility, and a rigid
system of precedence. However, while the poem's epiphanic project
may be meant to ennoble St Lucia, through this strategy it tends
actually to patronise it by backfiring and working mock-heroically
because the metaphor protests St Lucia's nobility too much.

What this does, in the end, is to highlight the dangers of this sort
of 'Adamic' utterance, and its implicitly gendered nature provides
the most important clue to those dangers. The Adamic voice speaks
at the same time with an avowedly original authority (no-one has
described this place and its native experiences before) but at the
same time with all the patriarchal weight of accumulated
Eurocentric wisdom (the techniques deployed and the references
made are derived from two thousand years of aesthetic practice).
Walcott's insistence that these elements are entirely reconcilable
means that he endlessly erases differences by painting over the
epistemological cracks. Where there was division there is harmony.
Except that this harmony is produced by imposing a set of 'univer-
sal' truths that actually originate in the West. By these universal
standards it appears, not a cultural construct, but 'natural' that

St Lucia should be regarded as a woman who is both your mother and (in fantasy) your lover. Instead of deconstructing these cultural assumptions, the 'Adamic' vision endorses them.

Kadiatu Kanneh has said that 'The feminising of colonised territory is, of course, a trope in colonial thought':[9] the trouble is that it is also very much a trope in Derek Walcott's thought. The equation of St Lucia with Helen in *Omeros* is first attributed to the colonial figure Major Plunkett so that it looks, at that point, as though the poem may distance itself from that equation, may present it and then deconstruct it as a colonial trope. Instead, however, that equation is clearly endorsed by its larger context in the poem and by its relationship to metaphors deployed elsewhere in Walcott's work:

> As the fever of History began to pass
> like the vision of the island's luminous saint,
> he saw, through the Cyclops eye of the gliding glass,
>
> over wooden waves of a naval aquatint,
> a penile cannon emerge from its embrochure.
> Able semen, he smiled. He had gone far enough.
>
> He leant back, frowning, on the studded swivel chair;
> then, with one hand, he spun the crested paper-knife
> that stopped dead as a compass, making an old point –
>
> that the harder he worked, the more he betrayed his wife.
> So he edged the glass over the historic print,
> but it magnified the peaks of the island's breasts
>
> and it buried stiff factions. He had come that far
> to learn that History earns its own tenderness
> in time; not from a navel victory, but for
>
> the V of a velvet back in a yellow dress.
> A moth hung from the beam, reversed, and the Major
> watched the eyed wing: watching him, a silent witness.
>
> He remembered the flash of illumination
> in the empty bar – that the island was Helen,
> and how it darkened the deep humiliation
>
> he suffered for her and the lemon frock.

(102–3)

Rather than casting doubt on Plunkett's 'illumination' this passage enacts the process by which he has finally learnt this truth. He is a military man and has assumed that the most significant events are large-scale and public. Now, however, he can see that what matter are not battles at sea but intimate moments focused on a yellow dress. This means that battles at sea are most accurately regarded as mere displacements of masculine energy, they translate sexual drives into the military sphere, deploying penile cannons to take possession of an island's breasts (all this envisaged through the controlling and framing device of the aquatint). The imagery of light and vision which is repeated throughout stresses that Plunkett's 'illumination' should be regarded as genuine, and the reference at the start to the island's 'luminous saint' combines the two proleptically and suggests their epiphanic link with the feminising of St Lucia, which is thus personified not only as Helen but as a saint associated with light. This also connects this passage with 'The Light of the World' where the vision is very much Walcott's own and so further endorses the equation of St Lucia and Helen. Plunkett, anyway, is not the only character to go lusting after this simile. It is implicit in the rivalry over Helen between Achilles and Hector, the two principal black characters in *Omeros*. Castries, the main town on the island, is said to be Hector's 'common-law wife / who, like Helen, he had longed for from a distance' (231). Most importantly, it is the key premise behind the poem's palimpsestic relationship with the Homeric original, the foundation on which the whole edifice is built.

The metaphorical fusing of Helen and the island is the source of much poetic power in *Omeros*. The desire that torments Plunkett, Hector and Achilles is shown also to baffle them, through this fusing, with its complexity. The fusing suggests that the object of their desire is enigmatically diffuse, disorientingly multiple, not simply a question of the drive to attain a single objective. What appears to be a desire for one object can at any moment shift and show itself to be a desire for another object. It suggests also how desire can be linked in men to the drive to dominate and possess but how that drive can paradoxically make men weak and vulnerable. Plunkett's obsession with Helen is evoked with vivid sharpness, his experience of the 'terror / of age before beauty' (97), so that she achieves a kind of 'victory' (96). Walcott also manages to use this to characterise an aspect of colonial relationships when he has Plunkett insisting to himself on the purity of his own thoughts about Helen, about how they are really 'meant to help her people, ignorant and poor' (97) – how imperialism can excuse itself as not about possession but benevolence. Moreover, the different responses to Helen of Plunkett (as colonial) and Achilles and Hector (as colonised) work to define much, by contrast and comparison, of their different backgrounds and experiences. It is telling that Helen becomes pregnant by Plunkett – the young woman who represents the New World, the old man who represents the colonial powers, the baby that is the hybrid product of the interpenetration. It is telling, too, that when Hector finds he now possesses both Helen and Castries / St Lucia, he experiences a 'frightening discontent' and a renewed longing for the sea which would take him away from both (231).

The metaphor does manage to say important things about masculine responses. Even this is limited in the end, though, by the assumptions it contains about the feminine. Late on in *Omeros* Walcott depicts himself and Plunkett discussing how they had both conflated Helen and the island, though from different points of view, and asks why they could not see Helen 'as the sun saw her, with no Homeric shadow' (271). The answer is that such objectivity would be impossible anyway, but what makes *Omeros* so incapable of even approaching this is that it is such a thoroughly masculine text with largely unexamined masculinist assumptions. This means that even when the poem is merely describing Helen's behaviour it frames it so that she appears as a feminine stereotype. She is so much the 'femme fatale' – vain, volatile, tempting but disdainful – that she is impossible to imagine as more than the sum of various masculine reactions to her. Her metaphorical treatment adds further to the gender stereotype. That she is a piece of territory implies that she is a passive site of struggle for masculine aggression. That she is linked, as an island, to a 'luminous saint' mixes in another set of masculine fantasies, so that she manages to combine the associations of whore and madonna.

The feminine is stereotyped by a masculine perspective when it is made to reflect masculine fantasies. This also means that this perspective inevitably ends up stereotyping the masculine. The focus in the poem on the struggle over a passive object of desire implies that it is an inevitable masculine drive to struggle in this way. The assumption is that history is actually the product of biological imperatives writ large and this explains why Walcott thinks that Plunkett's view of 'History' needs to be corrected in the direction of 'penile cannons' and 'able semen' (102) and why his essay 'The Muse of History' advocates amnesia. Walcott there dismisses empire-building as the routine product of masculine instincts which, in *Omeros*, necessarily defile Helen – 'What was it in men that made such beauty evil?' (124).

This is another important clue to Walcott's gender attitudes, and all the more important because it is present as an assumption rather than being directly addressed. Views of masculinity, after all, are most often present as assumptions, as taken for granted and obvious, which is why they have such devious and subtle power. The view that there is something 'in men' that inevitably struggles over Helen/St Lucia, and that this is the real origin of human conflict, has similar roots to Ted Hughes's attitudes to war. Walcott does not give this view the extensive and full psychobiological and anthropological expression that Hughes gives it. However, his view that masculine drives are the principal engine of history is similar to the view of war expressed by Hughes in poems like 'A Motorbike' where it is seen as satisfying male desires which are cognate with the sex drive, so that men in peace-time are depicted as aimless and frustrated because 'The shrunk-back war ached in their testicles'.[10]

Walcott strikes a much more moral pose than Hughes in response to this view of maleness. In the eleventh section of 'Midsummer' he sees masculinity from a perspective best described as vestigially theological, connecting it to what he calls 'the sense of sin / while shaving' (CP, 475). The context is the aftermath of a relationship though this is only referred to in an aside, represented by the absence of his lover's dresses. Jaundiced and exhausted, Walcott regards the act of shaving as a symptom of that maleness which also fuels his participation in the sexual act, but in this mood associates both shaving and sex with death and bodily waste. His sense of alienation from the whole process is signalled by how it is said to be his 'double' (his image in the mirror) who performs the shaving but even so 'refuses to acknowledge' the man he shaves. This is linked to his sense of alienation from his own maleness which he seems to want to escape – so that he can lay aside his razor – because it makes him think of the product of his veins 'as filth floating down-river / after the dolorous industries of sex' and his identity as too closely bound up with phallic drives, as having too much affinity with a cockerel 'treading his hens'.

However, the malaise that Walcott is diagnosing here arises not from anything that is inevitable about masculinity but from his own set of assumptions about it. His equation of sexuality with abject waste arises from a form of masculinity that is Crusoe-like in its self-containment, that isolates itself too much from femininity. Similarly, his view of Crusoe as simultaneously 'monarch of all he surveys' and 'always ... alone' (Conversations, 63) is symptomatic of how the form of expression he wishes to construct imagines the writer as both toweringly masterful and thoroughly isolated. The reference to absent dresses in this poem acknowledges the feminine element in the (hetero)sexual act, but so fleetingly that it marginalises it at the same time – as though it were only there to show he's not talking about masturbation, the way that the men in male 'buddy' films have girlfriends only to prove they're not gay.

Masculinity and femininity as categories can only be understood in interaction with each other. The world Walcott presents is so thoroughly masculine that its view even of masculinity is necessarily distorted and limited. Walcott himself does not see this as a limitation and has rejoiced, for example, in how thoroughly masculine his play *Makak on Monkey Mountain* is – enthusing, in particular, about the wake dance called the 'bongo' which is performed in it, and in which

> there is all the male strength that I think has been absent for a long time in Western theatre. The emphasis is on virility. This ancient idea of the actor in a theatre where women are not allowed to take part or are uninterested was true of colonial society in the West Indies and in Africa, whether in Soyinka's Company or in mine. Very few women took part in our theatre when we began, so initially all of our plays had more male characters than women. Still, it's good. I think that in a theatre where you have a strong male principle, or where women aren't involved at the beginning, a kind of style will happen; there will be violence, there will be direct conflict, there will be more physical theatre and there will be less interest in sexual psychology. (Critical Perspectives, 48–9)

That last phrase is interesting because it suggests that women are more involved in sexual psychology than men: taken as a whole, the last sentence associates men with violence and women with sex. However, the idea of a male theatre which is less concerned with sexual psychology is self-contradictory, since what motivates it is almost morbidly sexual, and the terms in which Walcott describes it are suffused with sexual psychology: 'male strength', 'virility', 'strong male principle', 'violence'. The fact that Walcott can think of this as not sexual shows how capable men are of not thinking of themselves as members of a sex, let alone a gender – of unthink-ingly attributing all that to women and distancing themselves from it.

When I say that Walcott appears sexually aroused in that passage I don't mean to imply anything gay in that arousal, which occurs because of his own identification with these male roles. The arousal is very much a heterosexual one because it involves a fantasy of powerful and dangerous maleness with which Walcott clearly feels a close affinity. It is hard to imagine any inclusive set of images of masculinity that would not include this fantasy. What is problem-atic about it in Walcott's case, however, is its place in his set of general attitudes to gender, how much it is a part of a tendency towards a masculine separatism in which poetry expresses a Crusoe-like isolation and drama expresses a purely male (and there-fore conflictual) collectivity.

Considering how extensive Walcott's canon now is it is shocking how little part women play in it. The most important exception to this is Chapter XXXII of *Omeros* where Walcott writes about his mother, and which I'll discuss later. Elsewhere, however, the women in his poems have hardly any lives of their own at all. Walcott's elegy for his mother 'The Bounty' conveys no sense of her as an individual and is instead the occasion for a suave but ulti-mately banal celebration of nature and fertility (The Bounty, 3–16). The poems in *The Arkansas Testament* that describe a relationship that takes place in Los Angeles reduce the woman involved to a lit-erary cipher and at the same time suggest that a further problem with Walcott's 'Adamic' utterance is that its newness is much less in evidence than its oldness, that what it often ends up expressing are archaic attitudes. Though Walcott does not speak explicitly in 'The Muse of History' about the theological aspects of the Adamic sens-ibility they do have a residual presence in it, especially where gender is concerned. Walcott is incapable of thinking of sex without thinking of sin and regards the association of the two as obvious. The first section of 'Summer Elegies' describes their love-making quite attractively (93), but then ends:

> The snake hangs its old question
> on almond or apple tree;
> I had her breast to rest on
> the rest was History.
>
> (94)

Walcott seems unaware that the snake plays no part in the thoughts of most contemporary lovers. When he goes on, in 'A Propertius Quartet' to associate himself with Sextus Propertius and his lover with Propertius' 'Cynthia' he seems merely self-dramatising, adopting a mode which would embarrass most contemporary poets, and expressing a sexual guilt very few people currently feel:

> This is the price we pay, Sextus, for the ridges
> of shoulder blades under a sheet, for crevices rendered, necks
> curled with seraphic hair. The cock cries with the tearing
> sound of a sheet and it picks at stitches
> with its beak. She paid for it with a lost earring,
> she whose first syllable was Sin, as yours was Sex.

> (97)

Walcott wants, nonetheless, to say that it is 'in bed, where we are / most ourselves' (99) and to declare a preference for these intimate moments compared with the large-scale events of public History. The problem with this is that it sounds like a poetic formula, especially when the example of Shakespeare's Antony is invoked to back it up, an invocation Walcott also makes, and at greater length, in 'Egypt, Tobago' (CP, 368–71). However much Walcott protests that love is pre-eminent, the persistence of this contrasting of the two worlds, public and intimate, keeps indicating his suspicion that sex is not only sinful but frivolous and that too much of this sort of thing will unman you, will make you, like Antony, lose your sword, or become a 'fallen column' (CP, 369). If sex is as important as Walcott claims, why is there so little of it in his work? By invoking Antony, Walcott invokes the notion of an heroic masculinity rendered vulnerable by a woman, but by doing so he immunises his own poetic self against this vulnerability by cladding it in the armour of the Western literary tradition. The dangerous uncertainties of actual interpersonal experience are thoroughly translated into traditional forms and metaphors. As a result, his sword and column remain unthreatened, and his Adamic utterance helps to reinforce the canon.

That Walcott regards that canon as reassuringly phallocentric is clear from the terms in which he discusses it. 'Volcano' (CP, 324–5) associates literary genius (Joyce and Conrad) with symbols of power (thunder and lions roaring) and then with a series of phallic images – flares on oil derricks, a cigar, a volcano. It wonders if it would not be better to give up writing and simply to read, but even this is described in terms of competitiveness and power – writing is an attempt to 'repeat or outdo' 'masterpieces', the alternative is to be 'the greatest reader in the world'. Certainly, the posture Walcott adopts here is some distance from postcolonial subversion of the canon and more closely resembles the identification he makes and consequent arousal he feels when describing the 'male strength' of the actors in his theatre company.

However, his posture is also filial in the sense of being another avowal of Walcott's 'Adamic' project. The writers Walcott refers to are European but the landscape is Caribbean: once again the hidden message is that Walcott can acquire patriarchal authority by deriving an empowering example from the one and an original subject from the other. In 'Eulogy to W.H. Auden' (Arkansas Testament, 61–5) his posture towards the English poet is similar, calling him 'Master' and imitating his (later) voice even to the extent of sounding complacent and supercilious, declaring that Auden 'knew war, like free verse, is a sign / of awful manners' (62). This is the lowest point in Walcott's mimicry of a canonical voice because it exaggerates an English upper-middle class attitude derived from over-protected privilege – and then endorses it! This seems all the more sycophantic because it implies a betrayal of other postcolonial writers; its implied equation of formal poetry and good manners suggests that unEnglish writing is the product of barbarians, and compounds this by suggesting that such behaviour is similar to that which produces vulgar conflict. The good manners in this sense are like universal values that guarantee we do not fall into chaos and war.

To dwell on this, though, would be unfair to Walcott because his position is usually more ambiguous, like the one described later in this eulogy:

> Once, past a wooden vestry,
> down still colonial streets,
> the hoisted chords of Wesley
> were strong as miners' throats;
>
> in treachery and in union,
> despite your Empire's wrong,
> I made my first communion
> there, with the English tongue.

> It was such dispossession
> that made possession joy,
> when, strict as Psalm or Lesson,
> I learnt your poetry.
>
> (63–4)

Where the lines about manners imply Walcott's complete identification with the English, 'treachery and union' represent ambiguous responses to both England and St Lucia, to both the colonisers and the colonised – he sympathises with, and betrays both sides. The difficulties of this position are even clearer when he insists, again, on a paradoxically celebratory response to 'dispossession', when he insists that it was the very experience of being colonised that made the colonisers' culture such a worthwhile 'possession'. It is here, in Walcott's strategy as a writer, that he is most pushed towards adopting the English posture in order to acquire the coloniser's privilege of authoritative naming. Walcott's authorial identity is constructed through this identification which, at the same time as placing him in the English position towards St Lucia, places him in a 'masculine' position towards colonised territory, which 'possession' renders feminine. That the 'Adam' who has the right to name is regarded by Walcott as both necessarily a coloniser and exemplarily male is clear from the terms in which he talks about this issue:

> I think the condition of colonialism, or of any first migration of people who were given another language, means the erosion of identity and the desperation to preserve their identity, which can sometimes be punished or banned. But even deeper than that, in adjusting names, somebody from Europe comes over here and changes his name. ... What happens in the process of that naming? If someone is called Achille, what is he? You have to go through a whole process of becoming a name that you have been given. It's the process and technique of removing identity and altering identity so you can rule or can dominate. There must be a moment in a woman's life when she changes her name, like in marriage – if women are supposed to change their names – when that person becomes Mrs. X, who is Mrs. X? (Conversations, 192)

To name is to be masculine: to be named or, in particular, to be renamed is to be feminine – this is the linguistic equivalent of the feminising of colonised territory. In *Omeros*, Achille, suffering from sunstroke, makes a hallucinatory journey back in time to pre-colonial Africa: there he meets and talks with his father, Afolabe (136–9), who is preoccupied with the fact that Achille no longer has the name he gave him. Afolabe 'finds the idea of arbitrary language unbearable. … To understand the meaning of one's own existence, one understands one's name' (Terada, 29–30). However, what is also clearly evoked here is the rupture of a purely masculine geneal-ogy and the assumption that Achille should grow to be the man his father has determined he shall grow to be. Afolabe is referred to as Achille's 'life-giver' (136) and 'breath-giver' (139) as though he did not merely name him on his own but actually make him on his own (Achille's mother is nowhere mentioned). That Achille no longer has the name his father gave him means that he is un-fathered and consequently, according to Afolabe, his self is erased. Afolabe says that, in naming Achille, he was expressing 'the hope' he had for him as a child: 'Unless the sound means nothing. Then you would be nothing. / Did they think you were nothing in the other kingdom?' (137). Similarly, the arbitrariness of language is regarded by Afolabe as calamitous because it thoroughly undermines a man's ability to name his world. What Afolabe sees as vital, in other words, is the tribal equivalent of the poetic role Walcott imagines when he speaks about 'Adamic' utterance. For him the colonial experience, which is represented by the loss of his son's original name, involves the shattering of the link between the self and the world, in the loss of that masterful naming that comprehends both. If Afolabe cannot point and say 'There / is the name of that man, that tree, and this father' then every sound is merely 'a shadow that crossed your ear / without the shape of a man or a tree' (138) and he is 'not Afolabe, your father' and 'you, nameless son, are only the ghost / of a name' (138–9).

This loss of a coherent identity is also the subject of 'Names' (CP, 305–8) though this poem suggests that naming is a European activ-ity and that European names were imposed on objects and places because 'My race began as the sea began, / with no nouns, and with no horizon'. Revealingly, Walcott then says that the colonisers 'Being men … could not live / except they first presumed / the right of every thing to be a noun' (307). The ironic tone is deceptive here – the irony is genuine enough to the extent that Walcott does iden-tify, up to a point, with the colonised, but it is misleading because, as I have been showing, he identifies *more*, and more deliberately, in this context of naming, with the colonisers. That phrase 'Being men' may also sound ironic and detached but in fact it carries the endorsement of the rest of Walcott's work – naming is inevitable for males and their natural right. The ironic aura of a related passage in 'The Schooner, *Flight*' can be similarly explained:

> we live like our names and you would have
> to be colonial to know the difference,
> to know the pain of history words contain,
> to love those trees with an inferior love,
> and to believe: 'Those casuarinas bend
> like cypresses, their hair hangs down in rain
> like sailors' wives. They're classic trees, and we,
> if we live like the names our masters please,
> by careful mimicry might become men.'
>
> (CP, 353–4)

There is irony here to the extent that Walcott does want to insist on the vigorous and individual life of everything in the New World and so to insist that 'casuarinas' have as much right to their own name as cypresses. There is much less irony than there appears to be, however, because he wants also to insist that it is not only poetic to compare them to cypresses but inevitable and both trees inevitably come to represent grief. The New World cannot help mimicking the old, and just as casuarinas become interchangeable with cypresses, the colonised mimic the colonisers because 'we live like our names'. The last line of the passage sounds ironic but if it is read in the context of Walcott's other writing the irony emerges as a cover for something sincerely meant: the colonised are in a filial relationship with the colonisers and will acquire the masterfulness that is required of men by imitating their masters. This reading is further supported by the metaphorical feminising of the trees, whose 'bending bodies wail like women' (353) and whose 'hair hangs down in rain / like sailors' wives' (354). Once again the ability to name is masculine and being re-named is feminine.

***

Walcott's writings, then, are continually marked by signs of the gender insecurity which is aroused in him by the colonial experience. This produces, in response, a defensive masculinity that exaggerates itself and which is analogous, in its poetic manifestation, to the political response identified by Elleke Boehmer:

> The feminization of the male colonized under Empire had produced, as a kind of reflex, an aggressive masculinity in the men who opposed colonialism. Nationalist movements encouraged their members, who were mostly male, to assert themselves as agents of their own history, as self-fashioning and in control. Women were not so encouraged.[11]

The consistency of Walcott's gendered response to colonialism reveals with surprising clarity how thoroughly he wants to establish a masculine role in all his dealings with it: his 'Adamic' strategy guarantees his manliness in both technique (derived from a tradition which he himself regards, approvingly, as patriarchal) and subject-matter (where he faces the rawness of the New World with fatherly authority). He is almost fanatical in immunising himself against anything that could be regarded as feminine in the colonial experience, and in refusing any role that is contaminated with feminine associations.

That the feminine should be perceived as a threat, therefore, is inevitable. Having adopted the role of Adamic naming he uses it as best he can to tame that threat, and contain it: Walcott's Adam is endlessly suspicious of his Eve and what she might be up to with snakes and apples. The feminine must, as a priority, be definitively named so that the threat can be thoroughly policed. As a result, there is a tendency throughout Walcott's work to push the feminine towards allegory, to name it and then re-name it as standing for an abstract quality which can more completely define it within a hierarchy of values. Even as she enters 'The Light of the World' (Arkansas Testament, 48–51) the woman is 'the beauty' and she is soon a portrait, then heraldic and then 'the light of the world', receding further and further into self-conscious artifice and representativeness. Similarly, Helen in *Omeros* represents St Lucia and personifies what men strive for and what sparks conflict between them.

Even more symptomatically, in Walcott's play 'Dream on Monkey Mountain'[12] the dangerous delusion of the central character Makak is transmitted to him through a female apparition, who tells him that he comes 'from the family of lions and kings' (236) encouraging him to believe that he 'will walk like he used to in Africa, when his name was lion!' (240). She is later defined by the Corporal as 'the wife of the devil, the white witch' (319):

> What you beheld, my prince, was but an image of your longing. As inaccessible as snow, as fatal as leprosy. Nun, virgin, Venus, you must violate, humiliate, destroy her; otherwise, humility will infect you. You will come out in blotches, you will be what I was, neither one thing nor the other. Kill her! Kill her! (318–9)

The central action of this play, which is Walcott's most famous drama and widely regarded as his most successful, involves personifying a postcolonial menace as feminine and then literally extinguishing it. As Tejumola Olaniyan says,

> racism and Eurocentrism, unfulfillable and recalcitrant desires – in short, everything the black *man* should run away from – are mapped onto the white *woman*, who is then *justifiably* beheaded[13]

Olaniyan is here pursuing an argument started by Elaine Savory in an incisive essay[14] where she says that Walcott's 'treatment of women is full of clichés, stereotypes and negativity' (246) and then persuasively demonstrates how his weakest writing is linked to his most misogynistic moments. The tendency of her essay, though, is to suggest that these moments are isolated and not to focus enough on the impact they have on Walcott's work as a whole. She regards it as fortunate, 'given his attitudes to women', that his

> creative world is a predominantly male one, in which men have close and important understanding of one another. He also deals with racism, colonialism and the situation of the poor masses with intelligence, anger and originality. (246)

What this ignores is the extent to which no thoroughly accurate understanding of men is possible from a perspective which seriously misunderstands and marginalises women.

I would argue that this also damages Walcott as a political writer because, as I have demonstrated, his attitude to colonialism is inseparable from his gender assumptions. A telling example of this is in 'The Star-Apple Kingdom' (CP, 383–95) which is in my view his best poem and has strong claims to being one of the great poems of the twentieth century. It brilliantly mingles satirical writing about colonial predatoriness with a panoramic evocation of old and new worlds and their interpenetrations, and a nightmarish magic realism. It is that last quality that significantly extends the poem's ability to evoke the horrors of colonial experience beyond what is possible for a realist depiction of places and events. Yet inextricably involved in this element of the poem are the gender attitudes I have been discussing, as Walcott has the allegorical figure of 'the Revolution' enter as a 'black woman, shawled like a buzzard' (CP, 387):

> She was as beautiful as a stone in the sunrise,
> her voice had the gutturals of machine guns
> across khaki deserts where the cactus flower
> detonates like grenades, her sex was the slit throat
> of an Indian, her hair had the blue-black sheen of the crow.
> She was a black umbrella blown inside out
> by the wind of revolution, La Madre Dolorosa,
> a black rose of sorrow, a black mine of silence,
> raped wife, empty mother, Aztec virgin
> transfixed by arrows from a thousand guitars,
> a stone full of silence, which, if it gave tongue
> to the tortures done in the name of the Father,
> would curdle the blood of the marauding wolf
>
> (CP, 388)

Walcott's more characteristic Anglo-American idiom could not have encapsulated experiences as scattered historically and geographically as this, and could not have turned them into such exotic and surreal metaphors. It is impressive to see him writing with such combined precision and adventure, especially mingled with the more realist, metonymic writing elsewhere in 'The Star-Apple Kingdom'. It is all the more disquieting, then, that here, where he is most powerful, he is also subtly undermined by the recognition that he is once again presenting the feminine in an allegorical form and that there is a link between this and the gender anxiety that is expressed elsewhere in his work. What might be read, therefore, as a telling expression of political anger is also read as a much more personal nightmare of feminine threat. This has the effect of damaging the authority that Walcott so obsessively strives for – precisely because the obsessiveness of that striving too clearly discloses the anxieties that underlie it.

That Walcott strives so conspicuously for authority, straining at every poetic muscle and sinew, is all the more regrettable because he is often at his best when he strives the least. It is revealing that this is also, on at least two occasions, where he most allows the feminine a say. The portrait of his mother in Chapter XXXII of *Omeros* (165–8) observes the scene in the 'Marian Home' with careful but relaxed detail and evokes her amnesia wistfully but economically and then rejoices briefly as she recognises him as her son. This scene is so unusual in Walcott's poems that it draws attention to the lack of humanity elsewhere in his work, how lacking it is in simple human emotions and responses of this kind. Again, it is hard not to think that this is largely the result of how anxiously masculine Walcott is as a poet.

The other uncharacteristic moment is telling in an altogether different way and so exceptional it proves the Walcott rule I have been defining and suggests an altogether different route he might have taken. This is the scene in *Omeros* where Achille dresses as a woman:

> Those elbows like anchors, those huge cannonball fists
> wriggled through the armholes of the tight lemon dress.
> Helen helped him stuff the rags and align his breasts.
>
> (275)

It is important that this carnivalesque subverting of gender occurs very close to a scene in which Walcott makes his own authority problematic by describing Maud Plunkett's funeral, then declaring 'the fiction of her life needed a good ending' (266), and then deconstructing the fiction-making process by revealing the link between the fiction of Maud and the reality of his mother, 'whose death would be real, real as our knowing' (266). In both these cases the feminine is allowed to enter the text and subvert the masculinist control which Walcott elsewhere insists on imposing on it.

This effect is fascinating but all too rare in his work. Far more often readers of Walcott encounter an author who identifies with Shabine, the poet hero of 'The Schooner *Flight*', a sailor who, like Walcott, has 'Dutch, nigger and English' (CP, 346) in him, and who leads a ruggedly adventurous life (Walcott's love of Conrad and Hemingway is in evidence here). When the cook on the ship snatches Shabine's poetry from his hand and starts throwing it about among the crew, and 'mincing me like I was some hen /

because of the poems' (355) Shabine throws a knife at him which
hits him in his calf:

> I suppose among men
> you need that sort of thing. It ain't right
> but that's how it is. There wasn't much pain,
> just plenty blood, and Vinnie and me best friend,
> but none of them go fuck with my poetry again.
>
> (355)

This is all too obviously a defensive reaction to the charge that
poetry is a sissy activity – to fuck with his poems is to make them
feminine by placing them in a feminine sexual role. More obviously,
though, it is a fantasy of the poet as Clint Eastwood or Arnold
Schwartzenegger, the poet saying 'Make my day' or 'Hasta la vista,
baby'.

5

Sons of Mother Ireland: Seamus Heaney and Paul Muldoon

It is remarkable that two men with such similar backgrounds as Seamus Heaney and Paul Muldoon (Northern Irish, rural and Catholic) should have become such radically different poets. What has been most important in determining this difference has been the difference in their ages (Heaney was born in 1939, Muldoon in 1951) so that they passed through their most formative periods at very different times in post-war culture. Muldoon experienced the 1960s at a crucial stage in his development and has therefore been shaped by all the most important cultural effects of the postmodern. Heaney by contrast, although he is only twelve years older, is very much a pre-1960's figure and seems more than a generation older. Heaney has far more in common with poets of an older generation like Ted Hughes and Derek Walcott than he has with Muldoon whose sensibility links him with younger poets like Simon Armitage and Carol Ann Duffy. Some of the difference, of course, is simply a question of temperament. At times Heaney can seem a generation older than Edwin Morgan who is his senior by 19 years but who has made it his business to understand and absorb the far-reaching cultural changes that have taken place over the past 30 years.

It is in his assumptions about gender that Heaney's affinity with Hughes and Walcott is most conspicuous. His conception of what constitutes the masculine and the feminine powerfully determines his conception of poetic expression: these are rigid categories for him and they are obsessively deployed in his discussion of the poets who have most influenced him. It is telling how in two essays, 'The Makings of a Music' and 'The Fire I' the Flint'[1] he links Hopkins and

Yeats and makes the same point about what constitutes masculine poetic expression:

> I wish to make one final comparison with another poet in order to clarify this 'masculine' element in his approach. W.B. Yeats is also a poet in whom we are offered the arched back of English in place of its copious lap; and again in Yeats we are constantly aware of the intentness on structure, and the affirmative drive of thought running under the music, of which the music is the clear-tongued pealing. Like Hopkins, he was impatient of 'poetical literature, that is monotonous in its structure and effeminate in its insistence upon certain moments of strained lyricism' and he was possessed of 'the certainty that all the old writers, the masculine writers of the world, wrote to be spoken or to be sung, and in a later age to be read aloud for hearers who had to understand quickly or not at all'. (Preoccupations, 87–8)

The gender polarities in this passage recur throughout Heaney's early criticism. The 'copious lap' which is rejected with such distaste has associations with a disturbingly enveloping feminine sexuality. To be fair to Heaney its off-handed misogyny is uncharacteristic and suggests how much his eye is on the contrasted 'arched back' which defines exactly the hard strenuousness he wants poetry to aspire to. For readers of early Heaney it is evidently linked to the idea of digging as an analogue for poetry, the idea of a poetry that is like manual labour, and this passage can therefore be used to gloss that analogue. Just as the arched back is linked here to 'intentness on structure' and 'the affirmative drive of thought', so the idea of digging with a pen which is the most important one in 'Digging'[2] is also linked to the prescription of those poetic qualities. What is disturbing, however, is how these qualities can be so automatically assumed to be masculine and then linked – with self-congratulation by these male poets – to oral rendition of (presumably) epic, heroic poetry. Precisely because these are assumptions they have to be focused upon before their implications become clear. If these are uniquely masculine qualities then the feminine must involve mental softness and slackness: lack of intentness on structure, a negative lack of drive in thought.

Heaney goes on to try to distance himself from these assumptions but actually digs himself in deeper:

> So I am setting up two modes and calling them masculine and feminine – but without the Victorian sexist overtones to be found in Hopkins's and Yeats's employment of the terms. In the masculine mode, the language functions as a form of address, of assertion or command, and the poetic effort has to do with conscious quelling and control of the materials, a labour of shaping; words are not music before they are anything else, nor are they drowsy from their slumber in the unconscious, but athletic, capable, displaying the muscle of sense. Whereas in the feminine mode the language functions more as evocation than address, and the poetic effort is not so much a labour of design as it is an act of divination and revelation; words in the feminine mode behave with the lover's come-hither instead of the athlete's display, they constitute a poetry that is delicious as texture before it is recognised as architectonic. (Preoccupations, 88)

What Heaney manages to do here, far from immunising himself against the charge of sexism, is to draw out the sexist implications in these polarities and then endorse them in that sexist form. For what he does above all is to draw attention to how much they contain assumptions about power relations between men and women: that to be masculine is to command, quell and control, and that these exercises of power are linked to masculine 'labour'. It is this poetic drive to power which lies behind all of Heaney's work, and while his views of language and identity have grown enormously in sophistication, his gender attitudes have changed very little. In his most recent volume *Seeing Things* he still sees masculine activities like fishing and ploughing as analogues for poetry, and 'The Pitchfork' has travelled little distance in this respect from 'Digging':

> Of all implements, the pitchfork was the one
> That came near to an imagined perfection:
> When he tightened his raised hand and aimed with it,
> It felt like a javelin, accurate and light.
>
> So whether he played the warrior or the athlete
> Or worked in earnest in the chaff and sweat,
> He loved its grain of tapering, dark-flecked ash
> Grown satiny from its own natural polish.[3]

The one change that has taken place in this volume is away from a determined concentration on the assertion of 'masculine' power towards an embracing of what by Heaney's account in these early critical essays is 'feminine'. 'Pitchfork' is standard Heaney, being explicitly concerned with the 'conscious quelling and control of the materials', with a form of labour that is explicitly 'athletic, capable, displaying the muscle of sense'. Elsewhere, however, the increasing display of a mystical sensibility links *Seeing Things* to modes of 'evocation' and to acts of 'divination and revelation' recounted in a texture best described as 'delicious':

> All the time
> As we went sailing evenly across
> The deep, still, seeable-down-into water,
> It was as if I looked from another boat
> Sailing through air, far up, and could see
> How riskily we fared into the morning,
> And loved in vain our bare, bowed, numbered heads.
>   (16)

To this extent, Heaney's development parallels Ted Hughes's in the move towards attempting to accommodate what a self-consciously masculine sensibility characterises as feminine.

In Heaney's case, however, this accommodation is much more local, it has not had the structural effect on his career that is evident in Hughes. Heaney has been more consistently concerned to prescribe a manly form of expression and then to follow his prescriptions to the poetic letter. This was partly a response to his own early sense of himself as worryingly unmasterful. When he wrote his earliest pieces imitating Hopkins he called himself

> *Incertus*, uncertain, a shy soul fretting and all that. I was in love with words themselves, but had no sense of a poem as a whole structure and no experience of how the successful achievement of a poem could be a stepping-stone in your life. Those verses were what we might call 'trial pieces', little stiff inept designs in imitation of the master's fluent interlacing patterns, heavy-handed clues to the whole craft. (Preoccupations, 45)

Not being the master here is like sexual failure. It is to be in love, but 'shy' – to write a successful poem is to make it successfully through a rite of passage but he is so far frustrated because his poems are 'little stiff inept designs'. I may seem to be making too much of the sexual analogy here but it is confirmed by Heaney's imagery when he discusses successful poetic performance. In Heaney's reading of Yeats' 'Long-Legged Fly', the fly 'has a masculine gender' and the poem involves an 'intent siring'; Hopkins' posture in his mature work is 'one of mastery, of penetration', the crucial element in Hopkins' creativity is the 'penetrative, masculine spur of flame'; more comically, Hopkins' technique involves 'ram-rodding the climax rhyme by rhyme' (Preoccupations, 78, 87, 94, 76). Most explicitly of all:

> If the act of mind in the artist has all the intentness and amorousness and every bit as much of the submerged aggression of the act of love, then it can be maintained that Yeats' artistic imagination was often in a condition that can only be properly described as priapic. (Preoccupations, 100)

A successful poem by these accounts is the product of an act in which biological maleness receives its most thorough expression, an act which is powerful, aggressive, penetrative and thoroughly in control. At times this is joined by the mysticism which becomes increasingly explicit as Heaney's career progresses: then this masculine expression will achieve literal apotheosis. So, by Heaney's account, Hopkins' ideas (especially sprung rhythm) were brought to fulfilment by the suggestion of his rector that he write a poem about the wreck of the Deutschland:

> The new rhythm that was haunting his ear had the status of dark embryo, but it needed to be penetrated, fertilized by the dark descending will; the rector's suggestion had the status of an annunciation in what Stephen Dedalus, that other scholastic artist, called 'the virgin womb of the imagination'. (Preoccupations, 95)

So the 'intent siring' that forges the poem mirrors the original act of divine creation. Yeats' image of the long-legged fly recalls, for Heaney, Genesis 'where God the Father's mind moves upon chaos'; and 'the poetic act itself is a love-act' which is analogous to 'Christ's mastering descent into the soul' (Preoccupations, 78 and 97).

From the start of his career, then, Heaney endows the poetic act with associations of male sexuality and power in which the two are thoroughly mingled, and charges these associations with spiritual meaning. He defines the masculine and feminine as rigid polarities and then imposes them as such systematically on his subject-matter. Most crucial here is the consistency with which he feminises the Irish landscape. He describes himself as 'betrothed' to 'green, wet corners, flooded wastes, soft rushy bottoms'; discussing Patrick Kavanagh he is taken with 'the notion that the curve of the hill is the curve of a loved one's beauty, its contour the contour of a woman with child' (Preoccupations, 19, 143). This means that digging and ploughing are regarded as masculine acts performed on the passive body of the earth. Heaney considers 'Digging' a rite of passage poem where he ceased to be 'Incertus', it was an 'initiation' into the poeticosexual act, in which 'digging becomes a sexual metaphor, an emblem of initiation, like putting your hand into the bush or robbing the nest, one of the various natural analogies for uncovering and touching the hidden thing' (Preoccupations, 42).

This means that the ideology that lies behind Heaney's nature poems is very similar to that behind Hughes's early work, and in fact made more systematically explicit. The assumptions of this ideology are that human psychology is above all biologically driven, and that there are human instincts which do not essentially differ from animal instincts. As male poets both Hughes and Heaney experience a *frisson* of masculine identification when they describe 'natural', and what they consider characteristically male acts and forms of expression.

The potency which Heaney acquires by writing 'Digging' is reflected in its curt, hard-boiled idiom, especially when he asserts, speaking of his pen, 'I'll dig with it'. This potency is the explicit subject of 'Follower' (6) where Heaney's father is depicted as the complete master of the craft of ploughing, and the young Heaney as ambitious to acquire that mastery but being instead merely 'a nuisance, tripping, falling, / Yapping always'. The boy's loquaciousness is itself a sufficient indicator of his lack of full manly status which requires competent action, like adept ploughing, and concomitant taciturnity. As Blake Morrison has pointed out[4] Heaney's emphasis on reticence is linked to the political circumstances in which he grew up and is echoed in his own early style. The boy's 'yapping' indicates that this is another initiation he has not yet achieved – he has not yet learned that Northern Irish politics insist that 'Whatever You Say Say Nothing' (78). When 'Digging' initiates him it defines him as a poet who will make poetry as much like unfussy labour, as little like 'yapping', as possible, and the terms in which he retrospectively talks about it are thoroughly gendered. He is slightly rueful about a couple of its lines which he thinks have the 'theatricality of the gunslinger', but he is surely not speaking 'deprecatingly' of it, as Michael Parker suggests,[5] when he refers to it as 'a big coarse-grained navvy of a poem' (Preoccupations, 41, 43) – for this description clearly enjoys the sense that it is tough and strong and Irish.

The ending of 'Follower' moves into the present and reverses the hierarchy which all but the last two lines describe – now the baton of potency has been passed on to the son and it is the father who is in the weaker position. Now the son has passed through his initiation, as the poem's own skill self-reflexively demonstrates – the poetic skill it displays is the textual 'follower' of the father's ploughing, with an analogous facility and exactness. However, the passage of time required for the son to achieve this is also that in which the father must necessarily decline, so that now it is the father who stumbles behind the son, 'and will not go away'. This succinctly – that is, as close to reticently as it can manage – summarises complex feelings in the father–son relationship. The symmetry which is established by reference to the idea of following, and which defines the reversal of roles, is almost chilling. This symmetry also displays the poet's writerly potency and is the equivalent of the father's economy of ploughing effort. It seems heartlessly dismissive of the father's loss of potency, impatient that he has become the irritating equivalent of what the son used to be, and exults in how the father's decline makes the son's rise all the more conspicuous. At the same time, however, these lines hint at guilt on the son's part about his feelings of having triumphed over his father, anxious identification with his father's vulnerability, and sadness at his decline.

The more general importance of the symmetry in 'Follower', however, is how it introduces the idea of a male lineage which is defined largely by its active relationship to the Irish landscape. The father's ploughing and the son's writing are analogues for each other and both involve controlling and shaping materials associated with the land, which Heaney's imagery consistently feminises. These associations are explored further in 'Glanmore Sonnets':

> Vowels ploughed into other, opened ground,
> Each verse returning like the plough turned round.
>
> (110)

This feminising of the landscape in Heaney is systematic. So Michael Parker, who of all Heaney's critics is the one who can be most relied upon to talk about him in the poet's own terms, refers to how in the third and fourth stanzas of 'At a Potato Digging', 'the poet draws a parallel between this contemporary scene of bowing, bending and stooping and the ancient obeisance paid to the Earth Mother, the source of all fertility' (Parker, 70). What has been insufficiently realised is the extent to which this gender ideology links Heaney to certain other male poets. Heaney's critics tend to be too focused on Ireland to recognise how much he has continued to share, in particular, with Ted Hughes. Terry Gifford and Neil Roberts are exceptions to this and indicate how Hughes, Heaney and Peter Redgrove share a number of preoccupations:

> The association of the female, mud or earth, and some form of rebirth, is common to all three ... all of them embody, in varying degrees and proportions, a pervading critique of the masculine intellect, of the Platonic-Christian division between soul and body, and the rape of Nature by Western civilisation.[6]

What is most important, though, is how this ideology leads to a belief in what Hughes calls a Goddess of Complete Being: as I show in my chapter on Hughes, he draws on the Adonis myth to suggest that capitalist Protestant culture represents a rejection of the feminine and a reaction into a masculinist emphasis on rationalism which leads to the worst psychic disorders in Western civilisation:

> At a definite moment, rationality acquires prestige (according to some celebrated examples, this happens where the Goddess-destroying god begins to get the upper hand). Rational philosophy proceeds by swift or groping steps to objective science. That is by the way. What matters inside the head, evidently, is that under the new dispensation of rationality, words (and rationality itself) nurture their innate tendencies – to abstraction and logic – in formulations that are increasingly exclusive of all other factors[7]

Heaney has a very similarly mythic model of history deployed in his case to account for a moment of change which initiates colonialism:

> the enmity can be viewed as a struggle between the cults and devotees of a god and a goddess. There is an indigenous territorial

numen, a tutelar of the whole island, call her Mother Ireland, Kathleen ni Houlihan, the poor old woman, the Shan Van Vocht, whatever; and her sovereignty has been temporarily usurped or infringed by a new male cult whose founding fathers were Cromwell, William of Orange and Edward Carson, and whose godhead is incarnate in a rex or caesar resident in a palace in London. (*Preoccupations*, 57)

Critics have paid insufficient attention to the extent to which this political vision is coloured by gender assumptions. This is crucial because the idea of the Goddess is linked to the imposition of rigid gender categories which I was describing earlier. So when Heaney comes to write his 'bog people' poems he does so with assumptions very similar to those in the Hughes of *Crow* and after, assumptions derived from Carl Jung and Robert Graves' *White Goddess*, based on a belief in a transcendent feminine principle which must be attended to if psychic divisions are to be healed. Heaney has described how these poems were inspired by P.V. Glob's *The Bog People* which argues that the bodies that were exhumed, having been preserved by peat,

> were ritual sacrifices to the Mother Goddess, the goddess of the ground who needed new bridegrooms each winter to bed with her in her sacred place, in the bog, to ensure the renewal and fertility of the territory in the spring. Taken in relation to the tradition of Irish political martyrdom for that cause whose icon is Kathleen ni Houlihan, this is more than an archaic barbarous rite: it is an archetypal pattern. And the unforgettable photographs of these victims blended in my mind with photographs of atrocities, past and present, in the long rites of Irish political and religious struggles. (*Preoccupations*, 57–8)

It is precisely the insistence that this is an 'archetypal pattern' that reveals how much it is premised on an unexamined gender essentialism. What is most disturbing about that premise is how it leads from a labelling of the land as feminine and a linked belief in a fertility goddess to an insistence on 'archetypally' masculine responses to that archetypal femininity, especially when they are associated with atrocities, with a tradition of violence. This problem is compounded by the profoundly ambiguous status of the Goddess who is simultaneously revered and feared, whose demands can also make her the object of loathing, and who therefore can represent a masculine view of a stereotypical femininity writ large. So Margaret Dickie Uroff says that when 'Hughes evokes the goddess, he evokes fears of engulfment that perhaps express his own psychic terror in the face of female power'.[8] For this reason she 'appears always as a monster, giving him … answers he dare not write, messages through which he sees all he had dreaded' (Uroff, 196).

The aesthetic assumptions behind the bog people poems arise from how they embody Heaney's masculine response to the goddess, his own tribute to her. This has to be understood by reference to his own construction of the poet's role as I have described it, a role which thoroughly expresses biological maleness and which is analogous to the male sex role as that is traditionally constructed. The bog people poems are constructed out of the relationship between the poet and the goddess who endorses the poet's masculinity but at the same time threatens it with her own power. It is this ambiguity which arouses the poet's creativity and links the goddess to the figure of the Muse as she is described by Robert Graves and whose meaning for Ted Hughes is described by Jacqueline Rose:

> we can recognise in this threatening, all-devouring female principle the imago of the phallic woman who, because she contains all things, threatens the man at the very core. According to this analysis, the idealisation of the woman is not contrary to the image of her as violent … the idealisation and the aggression are the fully interdependent and reverse sides of the same coin.[9]

Rose goes on powerfully to indict the damage that this fantasy of the feminine causes to women. However, as I point out in my chapter on Hughes, it is also damaging to men because of the obsessive dynamic of domination and submission which it imposes and its sadomasochistic linking of sexuality with violence. Its deployment by Heaney to account for political atrocities is especially disturbing because it implies that those atrocities arise from a form of sexual compulsion. The assumptions here are again ones shared by Hughes – that history is psychobiologically driven, that it is essentially the product of instincts. What makes Heaney seem a much less dangerous poet than Hughes is that he characteristically dwells on sex rather than violence, but the bog people poems are memorable because they make a primordial peaty cocktail of the two.

The relationship between the poet and the goddess is sexual, but so too is the relationship between the poet and the bog people. As always when reading Heaney, there is a strong sense of the implied author: one of his most remarkable achievements has been to construct a version of himself as a poet which his readers recognise. This is partly a matter of his public persona, the 50-ish year old public smiling man with the opulent Irish accent speaking opulent English, old-fashioned as a poet should be, and above all actually a very nice man. This is reassuring and works better as a persona because more or less true, and partly explains why Heaney has been so readily taught in schools. But it tends to draw attention away from the bizarreness of what is going on in these poems. Michael Parker is characteristically bland in his defence of them:

> underneath the sexual topsoil allegorical material lies buried. Their subject is the Republican tradition, and how the cruelties inflicted upon 'dark-bowered queen', Mother Ireland, Kathleen ni Houlihan, Shan van Vocht, have brutalised her sons, engendering a love of territory and ancestry that can carry them to appalling extremes. (134)

This attempt to disinfect the poems ignores the extent to which the poet's maleness is inextricably involved in them at every point, how much they construct that maleness – partly through the precedent of earlier Heaney poems and partly through the controlling metaphor of the fertility goddess – and then implicate it in their exploration of the roots of political violence.

The sexual element in them is the most important key to their ambiguous effect on how the poet's maleness is perceived to respond. That is, the sexual element suggests that the male poet is masterful and in control but at the same time threatens that control. The poet is in control because he is constructed in the act of looking at the exhumed bodies:

> you were flaxen-haired,
> undernourished and your
> tar-black face was beautiful.
> My poor scapegoat,
>
> I almost love you
> but would have cast, I know,

the stones of silence.
I am the artful voyeur

of your brain's exposed
and darkened combs,

(72)

The gaze is poeticosexual. The poet is a self-confessed 'voyeur', which means that he can hold exciting material at arm's length and enjoy it while masterfully gauging and controlling his own response. The object of the gaze is hyperbolically the object of a male gaze – hyperbolically passive (being dead), hyperbolically reified (being turned into tar), hyperbolically submissive (being a 'scapegoat'), hyperbolically 'exposed' (because her brain is literally open). More than this, though, the poet is a voyeur who is 'artful'. His poem mimics an act of voyeurism, which is itself controlling, and controls it further by rendering it aesthetic. The sacrificial victim becomes an artifact to be contemplated; she is imagistically static, and her status as 'scapegoat' relates her to the controlling metaphor, derived from Jessie L. Weston, of *The Waste Land*.

On this controlling side Heaney's maleness is implicated with that of the 'men of violence'. However, the sexual element that threatens his control identifies him more with the victims of that violence. The poet 'almost' loves the little adulteress. According to Heaney, 'the poetic act itself is a love-act', it has 'all the intentness and amorousness and every bit as much of the submerged aggression of the act of love' (Preoccupations 78, 100). This unsettles the cool detachment of the gaze. Where elsewhere the love-act is analogous to 'Christ's mastering descent into the soul' (Preoccupations, 97) in other words to an idea of transcendence, here the attendant deity is female and pagan and the sexuality is accordingly, from a male perspective, contrastingly subverting and wild.

It is here that Heaney shares much in common with Derek Walcott; the figure of Kathleen ni Houlihan has similar associations in Heaney's work to that of Helen (personification of St Lucia) in Walcott's. The idea that colonised territory becomes feminised obsesses both poets. As Clair Wills has said

the representation of the Irish land as a woman stolen, raped, possessed by the alien invader is not merely one mythic narrative among many, but, in a literary context, is *the* myth. ... The trope functions not only as the means by which the poet can lament the loss of the land, but also, through his linguistic embodiment of it, the means by which he may repossess it.[11]

Heaney's addition of associations of the Goddess/Muse to this specifically Irish myth further sexualises and destabilises his relationship with it so that his need to bolster the maleness of his own role in relation to this myth is all the more marked, and all the more insecure. The bog people poems are powerful precisely because they contain all these complex responses:

> The feminization of the male colonised under Empire had produced, as a kind of reflex, an aggressive masculinity in the men who opposed colonialism. Nationalist movements encouraged their members, who were mostly male, to assert themselves as agents of their own history, as self-fashioning and in control.[12]

This element in Heaney is there most notably in 'Act of Union' (74–5) which depicts England's act of colonising Ireland in graphic sexual terms, and in which, most tellingly, Heaney adopts the male (and therefore paradoxically the English) role:

> And I am still imperially
> Male, leaving you with the pain,
> The rending process in the colony,
> The battering ram, the boom burst from within.
>   (74)

This links Heaney to Walcott whose gender insecurity in the face of colonialism makes him habitually associate himself with the colonisers rather than the colonised. It can be explained further by reference to Heaney's allegiance to English literature, which he sees as his 'masculine strain' by contrast with his 'feminine element' which relates to 'the matter of Ireland' (Preoccupations, 34). There is a contrast with Walcott, though, in the readiness with which Heaney owns up to that feminine identification. Heaney has far less swagger than Walcott, less defensiveness, and far more self-knowledge, and this allows the bog people poems to be edged with vulnerability. Their ambiguity powerfully evokes psychic conflict and gender disturbance about the experience of colonialism: they allow these elements to surface and trouble the poet's mastery. They are creepily sexual, but they also constantly deconstruct that creepiness.

***

Heaney's most characteristic image is of digging and unearthing: his poems assume a surface versus depth polarity and delve under the present moment to discover pure origins. In Muldoon, by contrast, the hierarchy of surface versus depth, like all other hierarchies, is collapsed and questions of origin remain questions. His poems constantly interrogate the idea of origins alongside those of gender identity because, as Clair Wills has pointed out, the father figure more than any other figure in his work, is 'associated with a lost truth' (Wills, 200). The crucial difference between Heaney and Muldoon is that the younger poet is convinced that this truth is irretrievable. At times it seems as though Muldoon wants to do endless playful rewrites of 'Follower' to explode its symmetry and cast doubt on the certainties it expresses about the father–son relationship.

'Mules'[13] follows 'Follower' with these motives and also parodies Heaney's poeticosexual theorising. Heaney's view that a poem is a product of 'intent siring' charges it with fatherly authority, and a sexual energy that is thoroughly legitimated. For this reason, the poem comes thoroughly sanctioned by patriarchy, all the more so because it is fathered with impressive forefathers – Wordsworth, Hopkins, Yeats – in mind; at the same time the poem's desire for this sanction also implicitly endorses patriarchy. By contrast, 'Mules' calls paternal and thereby authorial authority radically into question by depicting Muldoon's father assisting at an act of siring that produces, not a legitimate human baby, but a 'gaunt sexless foal'. The poet treats his father with carnivalesque disrespect by showing him in an act of male identification with a copulating jackass. He and the jackass's owner Sam Parsons 'Tense for the punch below their belts': this becomes a collective male experience but one in which the penis is referred to reductively as a mechanical instrument but also punningly associated (by reference to a blow disallowed by the rules of boxing) to vulnerability and illegitimacy. Later they are said to have 'shuddered / To think' of the foal's birth, the line-ending dismantling the colloquial idiom so that it mimics a Freudian slip that implies a masturbatory fantasy and also mocks poeticosexual conception, and other forms of intellectual creativity that are compared to parturition.

Muldoon's sly suggestion that this is all wanking is characteristic. 'Mules' jeers at theories of poetic conception that draw on assumptions of phallic power and patriarchal lineage, and also takes a swipe at such assumptions being sanctioned by reference to ideas of divine creativity. What Heaney calls 'Christ's mastering descent into the soul' (*Preoccupations*, 97) is parodied here by the comic implication that the foal has dropped from heaven and that its afterbirth is a 'fine silk parachute'. The poem had already drawn upon the Biblical associations of donkeys: by the end it is clear that it parodies the idea of 'epiphany', of moments of transcendent insight deployed by writers (most explicitly James Joyce) to provide manifestations of larger patterns of meaning. Muldoon's scepticism about this key idea in modernism indicates the extent to which he can be regarded literally as postmodernist. His reference to epiphany is an example of how, according to Fredric Jameson, 'Modernist styles ... become postmodernist codes'[14] and this further suggests that a helpful way, up to a point, of defining what 'Mules' does is by reference to Jameson's definition of pastiche as a specifically postmodern version of parody

> without any of parody's ulterior motives, amputated of the satiric impulse, devoid of laughter and of any conviction that alongside the abnormal tongue you have momentarily borrowed, some healthy linguistic normality still exists. Pastiche is thus blank parody, a statue with blind eyeballs: it is to parody what that other interesting and historically original modern thing, the practice of a kind of blank irony, is to what Wayne Booth calls the 'stable ironies' of the eighteenth century. (17)

Muldoon's pastiche of 'intent siring' and 'epiphany' as models of writerly conception does not satirise them in the sense of advocating viable other modes of poeticosexual conception. The foal that is conceived in 'Mules' is 'sexless', and the poetic father is depicted in a quasi-masturbatory fantasy. The poem wants to relinquish all models of meaning based on patriarchal authority. However, it does suggest a different model of textual production (to this extent its irony is not entirely blank and Muldoon is not as thorough a postmodernist as, for example, John Ashbery – see Chapter 7).

The model I am referring to here is that of the hybrid. This is the key metaphor in Muldoon's work, and opposes Heaney's metaphor of the poem as male heir with an emphasis on a bastard mingling of textual materials, on subversive miscegenation. So 'Mules' provides a brief paradigm of Muldoon's canon which also wants 'the best of both worlds', evolves texts which are designedly 'neither one thing or the other', multiplies discourses and genres and hesitates between registers. The form of 'Mules' is also paradigmatic in this sense in its deployment of half-rhymes in a scheme that refuses to settle. The conjoining of 'foal' and, right at the end, 'fell' is especially telling and produces an unnerving, rather than a clinching effect.

However, the most significant rhyming pair are 'father' and 'other'. This is where Muldoon comes closest to a satirical intention and hints that, in general, Muldoon's irony is often much less 'blank' than it appears to be. This, too, is where 'Mules' is linked to 'Immram' whose speaker's father is referred to as a 'mule' (66) and which can be regarded as 'a quest for a precursor, a poetic father' but which 'does as much to destroy as to nourish any potential father figures' (Wills, 40). The primary meaning of 'mule' in this case is a carrier of drugs, but the word also refers to Muldoon's earlier poem and to how 'Immram' subverts notions of secure male lineage. Once again Muldoon can be said to achieve this in a sense most importantly through the poem's form, which is itself a kind of 'mule' drawing upon references both to epic and to the prose style of Raymond Chandler. However, the hybridness of the form is also explicitly reflected in the content, and the speaker's search for fatherly origins is subverted from the start as he is informed that his father was an 'ass-hole' and that this makes an ass-hole out of him. His mockery of his father in 'Mules' is inevitably also self-mockery, especially because it is aimed at his father's sexuality, but here the point is made more clearly:

> My grandfather hailed from New York State.
> My grandmother was part Cree.
> This must be some new strain in my pedigree.
>
> (58)

The turning of the father into the other is taken one postmodern step further in 'Cauliflowers'[15] where Muldoon senior is metaphorically linked to a process of gene-splicing that makes vegetables glow in the dark. This takes the idea of the hybrid and adds a further layer of artificiality – like 'Mules' it stresses impurity, but it also casts doubt on the whole idea of naturalness. This is important

because traditional masculinity defines itself by reference to patriar-
chal precedent backed by biological necessity. The otherness with
which Muldoon insistently riddles the father figure calls all this into
question. The association of the father/ poetic predecessor with this
bizarre gene-splicing comically turns the poet into a luminous
cauliflower. What this stresses is the constructedness of masculinity,
that it has less to do with psychobiological drives than with social
and cultural roles and expectations. In 'Incantata',[16] Muldoon's
elegy for Mary Farl Powers, he quotes her referring to a tendency in
him

> to put
> on too much artificiality, both as man and poet,
> which is why you called me 'Polyester' or 'Polyurethane'.
>
> (17)

Some of Muldoon's recent work has shown too much of a tendency
towards baroque elaboration but generally his polyurethane aspect
can be read as making its own points about the constructedness of
the poem and authorial identity. This can be understood with espe-
cial clarity by contrast with the bog element in Heaney whose roots
are in a Romantic ideology of organicism.

The male poet and his poem as polyester, as luminous cauliflower
– this is Muldoon's most important contribution to poetic represen-
tations of gender and identity. Formally this point is enacted by his
carnivalesque conjoining of comically diverse materials, his dialogic
mingling of apparently irreconcilable idioms, and his form is
anyway his most important point. This contrasts with Heaney's
view of the poem as the product of a literally seminal and therefore
unitary moment. It stresses, above all, illegitimacy. The emphasis on
style and form may seem to be 'blank' in Jameson's sense, and is
certainly blank to the extent that it denies any belief that a 'healthy
linguistic normality' exists by contrast with this impurity. But it is
precisely this stress on impurity which is not blank but exemplary
and even political. This presents masculinity as disorientingly
without its traditional sanction and so enacts a late twentieth
century bafflement about what it means to possess a masculine
identity.

In 'Immram' the disorientation is literal. Where Hughes and
Heaney look northwards to the origin of a male cult which simulta-
neously shocks and arouses them, 'Immram' is obsessed with the

idea of westwardness as the direction once taken by pioneering purpose but now symptomatically defunct in a Californian terminus. Young men can no longer go west to assert their youthful manliness. 'Immram' links this loss to the idea of the heroic quest which is a key idea in epic: this too is a form of masculine expression that is no longer available. A nostalgia for this is similarly expressed in the more recent 'Yarrow' (The Annals of Chile, 39–189) with its references to boy's adventure stories. Muldoon's treatment of these ideas is systematically playful but they do accumulate meaningfully alongside the other gender elements I have discussed to suggest a specifically masculine directionlessness.

Muldoon's parodic references to texts – epic, Chandler, adventure stories – which draw attention to their textuality, to their elaborate construction of heroic images, are linked to his depiction of masculine self-construction, of the self-conscious adoption of personal styles and postures. Heaney's organicism implies the naturalness of the roles he depicts – ploughman, digger, etc – and their analogical relationship to the poet: Muldoon's deconstructive strategies insist on artifice. What is remarkable is how little there is in him of the *frisson* of masculine identification that is so conspicuous in Hughes and Walcott and, to a lesser extent, in Heaney. The characters in 'Immram' are mocked as macho narcissists like the lifeguard from Big Sur

> Who made an exhibition
> Of his dorsals and his pectorals
> While one by one his disciples took up the chant
> *The Lord is my surf-board. I shall not want.*
>
> (65)

The deadpan or comic style of 'Immram' may suggest blankness but the focus on debasement of the heroic ideal, culminating at the end of the quest with the discovery of the Howard Hughes figure as a human wreck, suggests moral revulsion. There is similar debasement depicted in 'The More a Man Has the More a Man Wants' (85–109) which is characterised by a shocking loss of affect in its response to terrorist outrages. This particular blankness, however, is related, not to authorial responses but to those of the poem's presiding spirit Gallogly. He is constructed as a character by reference to the mythic figure of the trickster, who is described by Ted Hughes as a 'demon of phallic energy' whose activities are linked to 'the immortal enterprise of the sperm'.[17] Traditionally, although the trickster is playful on a cosmic scale his role is essentially positive, but Gallogly like Hughes's Crow (but with less of his comedy) is a postmodern trickster who has become thoroughly destructive. His black humour is psychotic. He uses a condom in the construction of a bomb and a girlie mag as bait to attract its victim and so mingles murder and sex.

This is all much more disquieting than the male posturing that is depicted in 'Immram', with its focus on the travestying of traditional manliness of the frontier sort. What both poems imply, however, is that an atavistic masculinity is having a deeply destructive impact on contemporary culture, and that a new construction of masculinity is required to match current conditions.

Elsewhere, Muldoon implies that this new construction is anyway already being insinuated into existence, especially by shifts in gender relationships brought about by changes in sexual behaviour. There are numerous passing references in Muldoon's work to casual sexual encounters. 'Truce' (55), in particular, welcomes these encounters not so much in themselves but more as a sign of new attitudes to each other of men and women. It depicts an armistice starting gradually and then gathering momentum and then declares at the end that the fraternising soldiers draw on their last cigarettes

> As Friday-night lovers, when it's over,
> Might get up from their mattresses
> To congratulate each other
> And exchange names and addresses.

The references to war and sex interpenetrate each other so that it is impossible to tell in the end which is the tenor and which the vehicle, and this too is part of the point. Both are gendered activities and will affect each other much as the 60's slogan 'Make love not war' implied: the ending of a masculinity viewed as inevitably belligerent will also encourage different arrangements between the sexes, and individual truces in the 'war between the sexes'. What the note of enjoyment and even celebration of equality and mutual pleasure in the last stanza certainly suggests is a shift away from stereotypical sex roles and concomitantly rigid gender identities (masculine aggression, feminine coyness) assumed in Heaney's opposition between the 'athlete's display' and the 'lover's come-hither' (Preoccupations, 88).

Muldoon's view of postcolonial identities can also be most tellingly understood from this perspective. Unlike Heaney he has no feelings of secret gender complicity with the drive to 'possess' which colonialism represents, no identification with its patriarchal imposition of its own values. 'Meeting the British'[18] is a contemptuous indictment of the damage caused to native cultures:

> They gave us six fishhooks
> and two blankets embroidered with smallpox.

But it focuses most on the bizarre troubling of identity that results from the intermingling of cultures: the native American speaker of the poem finds himself 'calling out in French'.

Because Muldoon finds his own masculinity unperturbed by the colonial experience he is left free to look away from the point of origin (having evoked it) towards the hybrid multiplying of cultural identities that are produced by colonialism. His poem 'Whim'[19] parodies Heaney's 'Act of Union' but makes the sex, as it were, significantly casual so that it does not glorify male potency, as Heaney does, as a side-effect of depicting colonial power. Instead the man is said to have 'got stuck into her' and then to have 'got stuck / Full stop'. Then, much later, an ambulance is called and 'They were manhandled on to a stretcher / Like the last of an endangered species'. That last image is *post* – colonial to an extent Heaney never quite manages – this kind of colonial union is dying out everywhere. Because Muldoon is not at all secretly impressed by drives to territorial possession he can be dismissive about both men and England, and moreover evoke how power can also inflict damage on those who possess it. The couple stuck together is a much more positive image than Heaney's act of union. This is partly because it is carnivalesque rather than heavy-breathing, but also because it takes for granted that the woman, Ireland, is the equal of the man, England. And, taken alongside Muldoon's other depictions of gender relations, it hints that both postcolonial and postmodern gender identities have come unstuck, and will be increasingly multiple and open to interrogation.

6

'Insofar as they are embodiments of the patriarchal idea': Women Representing Men

Adrienne Rich has been the most important political poet writing in English in the past 30 years. By 'political poet' I mean one who expresses a committed position and who deploys poetic strategies to reveal how structures of power impose themselves on the emotional lives of individuals. To understand the extent of her achievement it is necessary to read her essays alongside her poems – even aside from her stature as a poet she is an important feminist theorist. Moreover, because in each genre she largely tackles a similar range of issues, reading her as both an essayist and a poet reveals how much she has struggled with the generic boundaries of poetry in order to make it say what she wants it to say. This has made her an experimental poet, unusually, *because* she is a political poet: because, that is, she has pushed and pulled at the edges of the poetic in order to charge it with political meaning, and to surprise political meaning with the vivid energy of the poetic. So at one extreme, as in 'Snapshots of a Daughter-in-Law',[1] she has bombarded the poem with all the resources available to her – imagery, allusion, irony, parody – while at the other she has chosen a minimalism in which the boundary between poetry and discursive prose is perilously in question, as, for example, in 'Heroines' (292–5), which discusses with deliberately prosaic starkness the social and economic position of nineteenth-century women.

Most of the difference between these two poems results from Rich's development away from self-conscious modernist textuality and irony to a plainer idiom of her own. 'Snapshots of a Daughter-in-Law' is indebted to modernist long poems like Ezra Pound's *Cantos* and William Carlos Williams' *Paterson* which incorporate quotations from diverse sources as part of their techniques of collage and montage which interrogate how texts structure their linguistic materials. Rich adopts this mode but, crucially, re-directs it so that language and textuality are held up for inspection now from an explicitly gendered perspective. Therefore, what had been merely an aesthetic strategy in male modernists becomes political when it is used by Rich. As she has said:

> Poetry is, among other things, a criticism of language. In setting words together in new configurations, in the mere, immense shift from male to female pronouns, in the relationship between words created through echo, repetition, rhythm, rhyme, it lets us hear and see our words in a new dimension.[2]

In co-opting deconstructive montage for feminist ends, Rich explores the extent to which patriarchal values are, usually invisibly, written into the everyday relationships of words. By re-ordering those relationships ('through echo, repetition, rhythm, rhyme') she exposes those values and defamiliarises them.

As a result, more than any poet before her or even in her own time, Rich has questioned – in the process of constructing the poem – the extent to which poetry writing is a gender performance, how much the language and poetic form are shaped by the poet's gender. The impact of this questioning is felt with special acuteness because Rich has never doubted the ability of poetry to take on the most important, complex and abstract issues – the ones, that is, that are least poetry-friendly, that are the most intractable to translation into poems. When she deals, in her essays, with the ramifying debates over gender essentialism, or the extensive psychological impact on women of what has been regarded as their appropriate work, the form copes easily. When she deals with the same subjects in her poems, the form balks. It is because of this that the form is called into question, and the nature of Rich's concerns ensures that the question asked is about gender. Does the form balk because it has been overwhelmingly a masculine form, and therefore does not want these questions asked?

In 'Shooting Script' (137–46) questions about poetry as a genre are joined by questions about film, so that the focus is particularly on the deployment of imagery. The pun on 'shooting' links the idea of masculine art with war and implies that it may be similarly obsessed with violent possession; its collocation with 'script' implies that masculine texts deploy language also as an instrument of territorial possessiveness, as well as wondering whether war is inevitably written into the masculine psyche. The twin concerns with the poetic and the filmic focus on the selection of isolated phenomena and their framing as images, and the poem suggests that this may be a deathly process. In the last section, Rich produces a series of brilliant images that deconstructs imagery:

> Whatever it was: the grains of the glacier caked in the boot-cleats; ashes spilled on white formica.
>   The death-col viewed through power-glasses; the cube of ice melting on stainless steel.

These images might well appear as an arty montage in a film, or equally as examples, in twentieth-century poetry, of the kind of Imagist effect theorised by Ezra Pound, where each object is defined by being placed alongside another with contrasting colour, shape or texture, and where Pound's term for it, 'super-position',[3] unlike mere juxtaposition, gratuitously implies a kind of hierarchy (or objects performing missionary sex). However, the emphasis, in the images, on the draining of colour, and on dispersal and coldness hint at numb sterility, at 'still life', in French called 'nature morte'. This isolating of phenomenal fragments is diagnosed as morbidly analytical, as driven by a need to murder to dissect.

What is crucial here is how these images are made to suggest a specifically masculine way of both perceiving and ordering perceptions, and how such apparently harmless processes are linked to much more sinister drives. 'Shooting Script' is concerned both with the Vietnam War and its media representation and concerned above all to draw attention to the alarming symmetry between them. Therefore, by defamiliarising the masculine symbolic that orders the poem's poetic and filmic imagery, 'Shooting Script' explores how the same sensibility is responsible for systemic violence. This exploration is already political but it is joined by another feature of the poem which is more so in being linked to Rich's larger programme for supplanting patriarchy: for 'Shooting Script' establishes a pattern of imagery which is designed to subvert its imagistic, eponymous hard news.

So the shooting script is associated with an analytical hardness that is linked to a form of voyeurism in its drive to use the gaze both to fix its object and control it. This inevitably distorts what it sees and reports: section 9 is a monologue spoken by a soldier who says that the newsreel footage appears to represent a different war from the one he experienced, which cannot be contained in this way:

> Someone has that war stored up in metal canisters, a memory he cannot use, somewhere my innocence is proven with my guilt, but this would not be the war I fought in. (142)

By contrast with the defining and containing imagery most thoroughly represented by these metal canisters, the poem introduces imagery of openness and fluidity. In fact it does this in its first section in order to subvert the phallogocentric in advance. The first line complains, 'We were bound on the wheel of an endless conversation' (137) and so introduces the poem's central concern with language as a prison-house. This idea is elaborated in the lines that follow but also opposed as the poem's alternative pattern of imagery is also introduced, with references to the sea, 'A tide that ebbs and flows against a deserted continent', and, more explicitly, to 'A cycle whose rhythm begins to change the meaning of words' (138).

Taken together, these contrasting patterns of imagery suggest interplay and the possibility of change, and the image of the shell mediates between them. This is to some extent an image of containment but as such suggests an alternative to the image of the canisters which represent a complete enclosedness that is deathly. By contrast, the shell represents protectiveness which is also open-ended. Much of the message of the whole poem is epitomised in the contrasting gender associations of the two: the phallic hardness of the canisters versus the nurturing rotundity of the shell. Where the canisters represent armoured and static inwardness, the shell suggests the possibility of movement inwards and outwards, and the threshold of change. Most importantly, Rich uses it to imagine the potential for an altered language whose emphasis is on the provisional, on questioning rather than definition, referring to 'A shell waiting for you to listen', and 'The meaning that searches for its word like a hermit crab' (138).

For similar reasons, at the end of section 10 Rich presents a series of images that insist on the refusal of the feminine to be seized and contained:

> You are spilt here like mercury on a marble counter, liquefying into many globes, each silvered like a planet caught in a lens.
> You are a mirror lost in a brook, an eye reflecting a torrent of reflections.

> You are a letter written, folded, burnt to ash, and mailed in an
> envelope to another continent. (143)

These images again oppose the canister; they represent the opposite
sensibility to those in section 14, the glacier grains in the boot-cleats
and so on. They are the response to men who attempt to possess
women with crudely romantic strategies, and they oppose that
attempt with a baffling elusiveness. Where the section 14 images are
hard and fixed, the mercury is neither solid nor liquid, and its
changeableness suggests that its possible meanings will not be con-
tained or stilled. Similarly the burnt but posted letter suggests
subversive eschewal of, and playful terrorism aimed against con-
ventional communication. Most importantly, the drowned mirror
and the bombarded eye oppose the fixedness of the camera, and
the imagist poet, with a proliferation of shifting images; they be-
wilder voyeuristic control with movement and multiplicity.
Therefore, what the shell does to language, these images do to the
territorial ambitions of the framing gaze.

'Shooting Script' exemplifies what has been most important in
Rich's achievement. Her poetic career has coincided with crucial
advances made by feminism in terms of legislation for women's
rights in Western countries, and in terms of much increased aware-
ness of gender. She herself has played a large part in the latter and
has been more influential than anyone else in promoting this
awareness in the poetry world. 'Shooting Script' is only one
example among many of how ambitiously and at the same time
meticulously she explores cultural events and their media or
aesthetic representation to expose how much they are specifically
masculine forms of expression. From 1963 onwards, with the publi-
cation of *Snapshots of a Daughter-in-Law*, her poems always implicitly
question poetry itself – down to its minutest generic details – for
signs of what is gendered in its assumptions. Frequently, too, she
makes these questions explicit, and they must always be read along-
side her essays, especially those on women poets like Emily
Dickinson and Elizabeth Bishop, where Rich's creative and polemi-
cal talents reinforce each other.

Rich is at her most convincing when she is asking such questions
about gender, rather than attempting to make definitive statements
about it. In this interrogative mode, for example, she can make a
political point by deftly invoking a register which reveals how patri-
archal assumptions are interwoven in the texture of language itself.

So in 'Heroines' (292–5) she uses phrases such as 'without recourse' and 'bequeath property' like a form of free indirect speech to subvert this language and its users simultaneously. Such parodying of register is one of her most effective devices for interrogating masculine discourse, and introduces a dialogic effect for subtly political ends and thereby reveals how oppressively monologic that discourse has historically been.

Similarly, 'Trying to Talk with a Man' (149–50) unsettles an apparent consensus by introducing perspectives that are subversively alien to it. Its use of pronouns for this purpose is especially telling. So in the first line 'Out in this desert we are testing bombs', the use of the first person plural implies a collectively sanctioned activity, but one which is also unsettled by its linking with sterility and destructiveness. The abrupt shift to the singular immediately then disrupts the claim to consensus, especially because it contrasts with the manly no-nonsense register by insinuating a metaphor that suggests that the alternative is both disturbing and marvellous:

> Sometimes I feel an underground river
> forcing its way between deformed cliffs
> an acute angle of understanding

The 'acute angle' refers self-reflexively to the poem's dialogic method of contrasting perspectives. The equating of 'understanding' with the 'underground river' draws attention to its etymology, suggesting a knowledge underlying the surface consensus, one associated with fertility rather than the desert, and one which is literally 'subversive'.

The shift to 'you' at the end of the poem carries associations of the traditional love poem but, unlike in that idiom, there is here a genuine attempt to communicate with the addressee. The traditional male love poet, moreover, may well complain that his mistress makes him feel 'helpless' but in this context the helplessness, and the failure of dialogue, are altogether graver. When she says 'Your dry heat feels like power / your eyes are stars of a different magnitude' she disorientingly mingles the registers of love poem and science. This is Rich at her most effective because these lines do carry their own charge of shocked sexiness mingled with their horror. They do suggest why women might find this dangerousness attractive while also recoiling from a charisma fuelled by destructiveness.

All of the available pronouns are used in this poem with the significant exception of the gendered ones. This is part of what I have called Rich's interrogative mode in the sense that the poem is concerned above all to question what is gendered in the poem's described activities and its self-consciously diverse responses to them. The exploratory quality of this is taken further in 'Diving into the Wreck' (162–4) which investigates the 'under' part, as it were, of 'understanding' with the assumed premise that there are modes of being and knowing that lie below the surface of ordinary experience. The power this image has for Rich is made especially clear by how it rears up again in an impassioned paragraph in her essay 'Compulsory Heterosexuality and Lesbian Existence' where she is arguing that there have been very elaborate and numerous measures imposed to ensure that women are sexually available to men, and that these measures in particular involve the 'rendering invisible of the lesbian possibility' which therefore becomes 'an engulfed continent which rises fragmentarily into view from time to time only to become submerged again'.[4] The drowned mirror, the underground river, the drowned ship, the engulfed continent: these are all images of latent understanding which is related – especially because of the symbolic linking, traditionally, of women and water – to suppressed femininity.

'Diving into the Wreck' is Rich's most famous poem and deploys its great technical facility in order to imagine a mythical place where gender divisions are healed. The poem's speaker becomes both a mermaid and a merman and all the pronouns start to overlap, 'I am she: I am he', and 'We are, I am, you are / ... the one who find our way' (164). Its fame may well have been aided by its apparent lack of Rich's characteristic anger. The theme of masculine destructiveness is muted (though it is part of the poem's premise, in the ship being wrecked in the first place: this implies that what the ship represents has historically been suppressed). The emphasis, however, is on utopian recovery: 'I came to see the damage that was done / and the treasures that prevail' (163). This makes the poem far more than usually emollient and its fame may well distort the way Rich is perceived, especially because its emphasis on androgyny suggests that she is far more willing to compromise than usual. In fact, she rejects androgyny, alongside humanism, in 'Natural Resources' (262). According to Wendy Martin she turns against it

> because she feels it is grounded in opposition and does not adequately express the fluidity and variety of experience; she argues

that the word *lesbian* more accurately describes a woman who commands her own energy.[5]

'Diving into the Wreck' assumes that civilisation has wrecked a potential mode of being that would be far superior to what we have, that there has been a 'disaster' (164). While this is muted in this poem, however, it is the main focus elsewhere in her work. Increasingly, this leads her to meditate on nature and the damage inflicted on it. Increasingly, too, her work implies that nature is feminine and that which has corrupted it is masculine. 'Waking in the Dark' (152–5) suggests that the primordial forest has been despoliated by male drives, that the 'frontier' spirit resembles masculine acts of sexual possession. The consequences of this are tragic both for the virgin land and for human sexuality. The pioneering sensibility therefore reduces what was natural to

> scenes of masturbation
> and dirty jokes.
> A man's world. But finished.
> They themselves have sold it to the machines.
> (153)

This leaves the woman speaker to wander about dazed in the 'unconscious forest', grieving over what might have been. The poem ends with a contrasting vision of lesbian sexuality which is depicted as open and fluid like a natural process, and where the movements of the lovers are like those of 'underwater plants' (155).

Similarly, 'The Phenomenology of Anger' (165–9) characterises the masculine as obsessed with computing facts, building factories and committing atrocities. It lists these in a cumulative indictment that assumes they are related drives and which culminates, again, in a depiction of the assault on nature with the implication that all these other misdemeanours find their fullest expression there, in an attack on the fertility of the land which threatens its continuing viability. By contrast with this it imagines a world that might have been where people would have lived 'in collusion with green leaves', and in coexistence with 'the Crab Nebula' (168).

What this amounts to is an increasing adoption by Rich of a kind of eco-feminism. The first principal assumption of this ideology is that men are responsible for a systemic perversion of the natural. 'Meditations for a Savage Child' (179–83) is most revealingly read as a metaphoric account of how this process takes place. It deals with how a boy who has grown up, away from human society, in the forest is experimented upon by a scientist, and has civilisation inflicted upon him against his will. This is made to function as an analogue for how patriarchy imposes its structures – linguistic, institutional, political – on the raw materials, human and natural, which it must transform and order.

The second principal assumption of Rich's eco-feminism is that women must look to each other to oppose these processes. They must do this, as Wendy Martin says, by actively working 'to create a vision that captures their organic connection to the deepest forms of life' (221). It is this organicist ideology, whose roots are in Romanticism, that increasingly dominates her work. She still thinks of poetry, intermittently, as a construct, but she is more and more drawn to wanting it to resemble something natural, so that 'the truth' can rear out of spoken language like something 'moist and green' (236). For this reason, too, she is drawn to 'the image of the spider to describe her poetic process' (Martin, 224). This also has its origins in Romantic organicism, suggesting as it does that the poet draws her material – spontaneously, self-expressively – like a natural product out of her own mind. She uses the analogy in 'Natural Resources' (261) and in 'Integrity' (274) referring to 'the spider's genius' that both spins and weaves 'from her own body'.

It is here that Rich's gender attitudes become problematic and disturbing. Her political message becomes increasingly dominated by the idea of a female principle which must be wielded against the depredations of male culture; these polarities (obscured though they often are by the complexities of Rich's metaphors) underlie most of what she writes, and they are unhelpfully crude and alarmingly based on traditional assumptions about men and women. Most shockingly, they are occasionally touched by mystical assumptions that resemble those of Robert Graves and Ted Hughes and which can be used to reinforce a form of male sexism (albeit of a sophisticated and poetic kind). That is, there are times when this idea of a female principle linked to nature is associated with the idea of a fertility goddess, as for example in 'The Images', where the poet encounters a powerful mythical female figure on the streets of Manhattan:

> When I saw her face, she of the several faces
> Staring, indrawn,   in judgment,   laughing for joy
> her serpents twisting,   her arms raised

> her breasts gazing
>   when I looked into her world
> I wished to cry to loose my soul
>   into her, to become
>   free of language   at last[6]

Wendy Martin describes this passage as concerned with 'the sentience and many-aspected power of the Great Mother' (220) and so makes explicit – perhaps more explicit than Rich herself would like – its link with a belief in archetypes and therefore to something close to a Jungian account of gender.

Liz Yorke has been concerned to defend Rich against charges of essentialism, insisting, for example, that

> Rich's arguments imply that the maternal body is lived: it is bound up in its specificity with the realms of the social and the political and is a crucial site of struggle in which psychoanalytic, sexual, technological, economic, medical, legal and other cultural institutions contest for power.[7]

In fact, however, her adoption of an organicist ideology combined with her occasional forays into the mythic work to create a notion of female power which is defined precisely by contrast with the social and political which, by her account, are endlessly contaminated by masculine destructiveness. According to this ideology, society contains a version of the feminine but one which has been (like her 'Savage Child') perverted by patriarchy. Despite this there exists, somehow outside society (or, to be more faithful to her imagery, *under* society) another femininity which can be invoked to struggle against this society which allows the expression only of masculinity and of falsified femininity. The role that women must aspire to then uncannily resembles that which Romantic artists imagined for themselves: to invent a world of imaginative values that could subvert capitalism, and to do this by occupying an existential territory that would be a model representing the opposite of what the social and political currently are. This model makes no sense, however, unless it is based on an idea that gender pre-exists society; unless, that is, it is invoking an idea of the feminine that is timeless and essential.

Rich's essentialism is especially problematic, moreover, because it leads her into a crude stereotyping of men and women. There is a tendency, throughout her work, to idealise women and traduce men. Liz Yorke quotes the lines from 'The Phenomenology of Anger' where Rich imagines burning up her male enemy with acetylene spreading out of her body and says that 'Many critics were disturbed by this imagery which they saw as man-hating' (43). She goes on to defend the lines by insisting that the enemy here is not an individual man but 'a mythic figure symbolising the forces of destructive domination, which she hates' (44). The problem is that this again confirms the essentialist polarities which underlie her work: this mythic 'enemy' is clearly the opposite of the Great Mother in 'The Images'. He is a masculine archetype representing destructiveness and the corruption of nature. This implies that all men are tarred with his brush, and always will be.

Given the single-mindedness with which Rich pursues her desire to describe her gender polarities in action, it is not surprising that almost every time she depicts a man he acquires mythic and symbolic associations with patriarchal power in general. As she says in her essay 'The Antifeminist Woman':

> I am a feminist because I feel endangered, psychically and physically, by this society, and because I believe that the women's movement is saying we have come to an edge of history when men – insofar as they are embodiments of the patriarchal idea – have become dangerous to children and other living things, themselves included; and that we can no longer afford to keep the female principle enclosed within the confines of the tight, little post-industrial family, or within any male-induced notion of where the female principle is valid and where it is not. (*On Lies*, 43–4)

What crucially narrows Rich's account of gender relations is that she almost never depicts men as anything other than 'embodiments of the patriarchal idea'. This admittedly means that her depictions of men who can be regarded as such embodiments without much trouble are often very vivid and convincing. For example, the policeman in 'Rape' (172–3) glories in his own power which allows him simultaneously to patronise the rape victim and to exercise his prurience over the details of her case – which his position allows him access to, and also the privilege of describing in his own terms. The sense of masculine arousal caused by the combination of sex and power in this incident is tellingly conveyed.

Even here, however, there are elements of crude lampoon as the policeman and 'his stallion clop like warlords among the trash' (172). And taking Rich's work as a whole, this focus on men as wielders of corrupt power is so unrelenting that its limitations become glaring. The few exceptions to this rule become memorable because of how exceptional they are. The depiction of her father in 'Sources'[8] is effective precisely because she starts by describing how his authoritarianism in her childhood led her later to define him as 'the face of patriarchy' (9) and allowed her to dismiss him as such, because she mocks herself for this (if briefly) and then recognises a more complex truth:

> I saw the power and arrogance of the male as your true water-mark; I did not see beneath it the suffering of the Jew, the alien stamp you bore, because you had deliberately arranged that it should be invisible to me. It is only now, under a powerful, womanly lens that I can decipher your suffering and deny no part of my own. (9)

As a male reader I'm grateful for this acknowledgement that men can suffer too, but it also draws attention to how rare such acknowledgements are in Rich, which is especially odd given that she does have an acute awareness of racial issues – these are one of the main topics of 'Sources'. Men are self-evidently powerful in gender terms, but they may equally be vulnerable in terms of race: as a Jew why isn't Rich more thoroughly aware of this?

More tellingly, this also draws attention – because it shows her, for once, aware of male vulnerability – to Rich's apparently total ignorance of the issue of class. It is only by leaving class out of her political analysis that Rich is able to invent a model of power that places men always at the top and women suffering, but learning to be subversive, underneath. This model is crude and serves to distort actual gender relationships which intersect, inevitably but complicatedly, with class relationships.

An understanding of class is mostly felt as a baffling absence in her work as a political poet, as an inability to imagine either a powerless man or a patriarchally powerful woman, where both positions may arise in particular contexts through economic positioning. Occasionally, though, this glaring blind spot impinges on what is actually there in her work, as when, in 'Natural Resources' she imagines a female miner (257). This is meant to represent potential feminine subversiveness and is linked to another image of the natural underlying the social and potentially undermining it, an image in which 'understood' and 'underwood' are made to rhyme symptomatically. But given how important miners have been in labour history, and how overwhelmingly masculine the work has been, it just seems grotesquely ignorant and insensitive on Rich's part to invent this fiction to serve her metaphor, which therefore seems precious and silly: 'slowly the mountain's dust descends / into the fibers of her lungs' (257).

This contributes to the sense that Rich often conveys that she is serving only a narrow factional interest, that she is concerned to further the cause only of middle-class lesbians. It is also part of a wider vision, that often seems merely paranoid, in which men are regarded as the source of all evil and women as the source of all good, a vision in which everything is reduced to gender. So 'Twenty-One Love Poems' (236–46) takes her lesbian relationship to epitomise everything that could transform the world for the better, and in section VI she declares that her lover's 'small hands' could right all wrongs and carry out an 'unavoidable violence' so that violence thereafter would become 'obsolete' (239). The crudity of the gender obsession is blatant here as all the questions about political violence are simplistically answered with the equivalent of a love poem as political slogan: Small Hands Good: Big Hands Bad.

I'd feel more sympathetic to Rich's sentimentalising of her lover if she weren't so dismissive elsewhere of heterosexual love. Her intolerance of heterosexual passion is just as severe as that aimed conventionally, and patriarchally, against gays. In 'When We Dead Awaken: Writing as Re-Vision (1971)' she says that when women poets wrote in the past of their love for men they were merely redirecting their anger about male power over them and that the woman poet is now overcoming the tendency

> to write of Love as the source of her suffering and to view that victimization by Love as an almost inevitable fate[9]

This victimization comes about because men require their lovers to perform kinds of nurturing that they previously received from their mothers:

> Much male fear of feminism is infantilism – the longing to remain the mother's son, to possess a woman who exists purely for him.

These infantile needs of adult men for women have been senti-
mentalised and romanticised long enough as 'love'; it is time to
recognise them as arrested development. (*On Lies*, 221)

The curious thing about this is how it ignores the fact that such an
argument could just as easily be used to characterise lesbian love –
to claim that this, too, is a failure to transfer love sufficiently from
the mother, and after all claims that gay sexuality is immature
have often been made. For a gay writer to draw on such
grotesquely crude models of psycho-sexual development, given
how much gays have been traditionally the victims of such
models, is extraordinary. Only a ferocious single-mindedness
could lead Rich to do this, and one of a similar kind to that in
'Compulsory Heterosexuality and Lesbian Existence' which dwells
to such an extent on the idea of women being forced into straight
sexuality that it implies that no woman ever found excitement or
fulfilment there.

This is a pity because the essay's anger and grief over the
numbers of women who, throughout history, have been pre-
vented from fully expressing their lesbian desires and who must
have suffered untold unfulfilments as a result, are passionately
and at times vividly conveyed. Rich is a very strange writer who
can make exceptional and unusual points with brilliant originality,
and yet miss what should be staring her in the face. She is a very
uncomfortable writer for the male reader because of both her
strengths and her weaknesses. That is, because she attacks
patriarchy with such vividness and detail but also because she
travesties much about gender relationships in the process. Because
she is so acute about the psychology of male power but seems to
know nothing about male vulnerability, and because her account
is so ferociously partial, so that she wants to tell men that their
sexuality is routinely 'focused like a burning-glass', that their
desire is 'without discrimination' and must be satisfied as though
by 'a fix' (205) – which sounds more like the desire of a psycho-
pathic rapist.

***

Contemporary women poets have tended to be far more conscious
of the gender issue, inevitably, than contemporary male poets, and
this has led them to refer to what masculinity means to them, if

only as an adjunct to their explorations of femininity. Adrienne Rich has said that in the work of Sylvia Plath and Diane Wakoski

> Man appears as, if not a dream, a fascination and a terror; and … the source of the fascination and the terror is, simply, Man's power – to dominate, tyrannize, choose, or reject the woman. The charisma of Man seems to come purely from his power over her and his control of the world by force, not from anything fertile or life-giving in him. (Gelpi, 91)

This description could certainly be applied accurately to Plath's poems about her father. 'The Colossus'[10] is haunted by his loss which is felt at the end of the poem, significantly, as more like the loss of a husband ('No longer do I listen for the scrape of a keel / On the blank stones of the landing') – specifically, perhaps, given the Classical context, as like Penelope missing Odysseus. This introduces more tenderness into the poem than Rich allows and also more sense that it can be painful to live without men, however painful it may be to live *with* them. However, fascination and terror certainly describe the poem's central metaphor in which Plath's father is likened to the eponymous gigantic, but now ruined statue. As such he suffers a similar ontological fragmentation to the one Plath attributes to herself elsewhere – though this is ascribed less to him, perhaps, than to her attempts, as his daughter, to recover him fully in her memory. His colossal size and age work metaphorically to evoke the awe her father aroused in her as a small child – but even then there is more metaphorical weight left over given the powerful surreal premise and the meticulous details that follow from this premise. She can never completely piece him together and

> Scaling little ladders with gluepots and pails of Lysol
> I crawl like an ant in mourning
> Over the weedy acres of your brow
> To mend the immense skull-plates and clear
> The bald, white tumuli of your eyes.

His stony monumentality suggests that the awe he arouses is combined with inhuman distance and authoritarianism, and this is enlarged upon (literally) in 'Daddy' (222–4) where he now stretches across America, from one ocean to the other. Where 'The Colossus' expresses some sympathy for her father, this expresses none: only furious resentment about his power over her and her inability to escape him, so that she seems to have lived her whole life inside him like a foot inside a shoe. The father figure is very much an 'embodiment of the patriarchal idea' and Plath seems closer to Rich in this poem than she normally does, though she gives its complex ideas a simple impact which Rich never achieves. 'Daddy' manages this largely through its formal references to nursery rhyme, with the repetition of its 'do', 'two', 'you' rhymes, its 'gobbledygoo' invoking of baby talk which suggests the helplessness of the speaker in relation to her father's masculine power. It is this, too, which justifies the poem's controversial references to the holocaust. The father as Nazi, the daughter as Jew need to be taken as analogues of patriarchal relationships – but self-consciously, too, through the references to nursery-rhyme, as caricatural analogues. As in the tradition of caricature (which often refers itself to the naive truthfulness of a childlike vision) this is a knowingly distorted and satirically exaggerated representation of a figure of authority. As such, however, it depicts patriarchal power with a force and economy unavailable to realism.

'Daddy' implies that the father's oppressive power creates a pattern in the daughter's life where she is drawn towards lovers who are similarly oppressive:

> Every woman adores a Fascist,
> The boot in the face, the brute
> Brute heart of a brute like you.
> (223)

Plath satirises patriarchy, but she is also concerned – much more than Rich ever is – to indicate that one of its principal strategies is to make women complicit with it. She savages her father, but mocks herself at the same time, and the nursery rhyme references even parody helplessness and work in the end to mock female masochism, however much it is shown to be an imposed response. The effect on her, as an adult, of her father's oppressiveness is a kind of compulsion to repeat, in which she makes a model of him 'with a Meinkampf look' which she then marries. She is drawn to lovers who will tyrannise and drain her, drawn to a 'vampire' who impersonates her father and drinks her blood for seven years (224).

It's impossible for readers of Plath not to think of Ted Hughes at moments like this, and it's not surprising that this infuriated him.

It's certainly unfair given that Plath, as I've said, is so obviously dealing in satirical caricature aimed at a patriarchal system, far more than she's talking about her actual father and husband. This doesn't clear Hughes of the wider charges I deal with in my chapter on him, but to feel an animosity to him based on poems like 'Daddy' is the equivalent of insulting a soap star in the street. The actual Hughes is much closer in 'The Rabbit Catcher' (193–4) where he is depicted as having set traps, and waiting for 'those little deaths / … like sweethearts. They excited him.' The sexual element in this is then expanded to implicate their relationship which is seen in the same light:

> Tight wires between us,
> Pegs too deep to uproot, and a mind like a ring
> Sliding shut on some quick thing,
> The constriction killing me also.

Even here, however, the extent of Plath's expressionist colouring must be pointed out: this is no more like a real person than the cruel landscape at the start of the poem is like a real place, the heated description there referring, for example, to the 'malignity of the gorse'.

***

The rabbit catcher's association with death and the way he brings that association with him into his relationship, so that he seems to stifle the life out of his partner, clearly mark him out less as an actual man than as another 'embodiment of the patriarchal idea'. Such embodiments have also featured in more recent women's poetry. In Jo Shapcott's 'Robert and Elizabeth'[11] poems, the relationships between two sets of writers – Robert Browning and Elizabeth Barrett, Robert Lowell and Elizabeth Hardwick, are conflated to form a paradigm of relationships between male and female artists. The emphasis is on mutual confusion caused by the masculinist assumptions on the side of the Roberts who find their Elizabeths 'nebulous' to an extent that even threatens their own self-mastery, making them 'ineffectual' (56). This is of a piece with their preference for granite landscapes and the anxiety that fenlands arouse in them, with their 'acres of confusion between land and water' (57). At the intellectual level this translates itself into an obsession with definitiveness, so that the Roberts are masters of grammar, syntax, crosswords and terminology which is punningly related to 'Terminus, rare god of boundaries' (55) and so to semantic closure. All of this defamiliarises patriarchal ideas which are then contrasted with a tentative suggestion of a feminine alternative in which definition is replaced by a relational concept of meaning. Shapcott's image for this is knitting, an Elizabeth activity which baffles the Roberts:

> I can't get my mind round knitting.
> It starts to have everything
> when you come down to it – rhythm,
> colour and slow but perceptible change.
> The meaning is all in the gaps:
> a pattern of holes marked out by woolly colour,
> a jumper made of space, division and relations.
>
> (61)

This is connected, through this poem's epigraph from Gregory Bateson, with genetics ('It will be found that DNA mentions nothing but relations') and so contrasts the Robert concern with the terminal with an Elizabeth association with a life-giving openness.

Shapcott's linking of Robert's 'Terminus' with the deathly is adumbrated at the start of the sequence with a reference to troops whose training routine is 'designed to make / men of granite' (54). This aspect of the masculine is further explored in Shapcott's 'Phrase Book',[12] which seems to me one of the most important contemporary poems, and which contrasts two kinds of bliss. One is 'terminal', being an acronym used to help fighter pilots remember strategies for evading radar: 'Blend, Low silhouette, Irregular shape, Small, / Secluded'. This is used to epitomise a macho war culture whose language the poem brilliantly mocks, and contrasted with a more usual and loving version of the word:

> Bliss is how it was in this very room
>
> when I raised my body to his mouth,
> when he even balanced me in the air,
> or at least I thought so

What is so effective about these lines is how Shapcott introduces them in a context which is very much about men as embodiments of the patriarchal idea, and how their eroticism evokes, within that context, an alternative masculinity for which it is possible to feel an excited affection. This is a view of men which is entirely lacking in Rich and Plath but which seems easily available to Shapcott, being also present, for example, in 'Love Song with a Flock of Sheep' and 'Matter' (*Phrase Book*, 12–13 and 21). What makes this poem so memorable is how it laments that what is lovable in men is damaged by what is patriarchal, and how this again causes feminine bewilderment. This is wittily conveyed by references to a phrase book register, which implies that men and women speak different languages:

> Bliss, the pilots say, is for evasion
> and escape. What's love in all this debris?
> Just one person pounding another into dust,
> into dust. I do not know the word for it yet.
>
> Where is the British Consulate? Please explain.
> What does it mean? What must I do? Where
> can I find? What have I done? I have done
> nothing. Let me pass please. I am an Englishwoman.

***

In the work of Shapcott's slightly younger British contemporary Carol Ann Duffy men are also frequently presented as embodiments of the patriarchal idea, and she is scathing about institutional male power. This sometimes leads her into her version of ecofeminism, as in 'Selling Manhattan'[13] which is spoken by a native American who expresses bewilderment at the destructive territorial possessiveness of Western men: 'Man who fears death, how many acres do you need / to lengthen your shadow under the endless sky?' Similarly 'The Dolphins' (25–6) is spoken by a dolphin which is baffled by its captured state and repeats the word 'man' as if desperately attempting to understand this strange species which mysteriously oppresses it.

Both these poems are dramatic monologues and use varieties of naive language to defamiliarise the perspective of routinely oppressive Western and, by implication, masculinist thought. Dramatic monologue is Duffy's favourite form and this is linked to her concern with language as an instrument of power, with how it can be wielded for almost invisibly political ends. In 'Poet for our Times'

(70–1) the speaker is a headline writer for the gutter press whose talent involves the systematic dumbing down of every issue, the systematic travestying of anyone outside the male white heterosexual pale:

> IMMIGRANTS FLOOD IN CLAIMS HEATHROW WATCHER.
> GREEN PARTY WOMAN IS A NIGHTCLUB TART.
> The poems of the decade. ... *Stuff 'em! Gotcha!*
> The instant tits and bottom line of art.

Duffy uses dramatic monologue self-reflexively to indicate how a person's language can be effectively colonised, how that person can be turned into a kind of ventriloquist's dummy. 'The Dummy' (36) deals with this explicitly, allowing the dummy to speak back, and there is a more complex version of ventriloquy in the brilliant 'Small Female Skull' (109–10) where the speaker looks surreally at her own detached head and takes it to the mirror 'to ask for a gottle of geer'.

This self-reflexiveness asks to what extent the self is composed of the language that it speaks, and combined with Duffy's satire against patriarchal structures it struggles against the masculine values that the language always already expresses. This is something Duffy shares with Rich but these two poets come from very different traditions. Rich develops out of modernism and evolves, through feminist revision of modernism's experimental forms and ideological assumptions, into her own version of postmodernism. Duffy, by contrast, develops out of a British tradition of poetic realism whose most important forefather is Philip Larkin, and combines this with some populist influence from the Liverpool poets (to whom Larkin also gave some limited approval).

Duffy's concern with the complexities of identity and with body politics leads her at times to adopt a surrealist or expressionist mode but these are never allowed to dominate for long. Her largely realist assumptions and her mostly conservative forms make her a much more accessible poet than Rich, but while Duffy's poetic appears mostly much less sophisticated than that of her American predecessor, her understanding of gender seems to me much *more* sophisticated. Duffy's eco-feminism is nothing like as systematic as Rich's and is not combined with anything approaching an organicist ideology. She is generally much less concerned to evolve a universalising poetic system and this leaves her free to explore the nuances that are present and the shifts that occur inside gender interactions.

'Psychopath' (43–6) is certainly driven by Duffy's desire to explore male violence against women, but it works extremely hard to evoke the sense of an actual man and actual events. Duffy, unlike Rich, is acutely conscious of class as an issue in power relationships – this is a part of her realist Britishness. This poem characterises its protagonist very much as a working-class figure operating in a series of working-class milieux, which are evoked with careful realist notation – this is especially true of the fairground, its candyfloss, goldfish, coconuts and Tunnel of Love. But it also painstakingly establishes a 50's setting – references to that period's icons (Jimmy Dean, Brando, Elvis, Ruth Ellis) and to its styles (the psychopath's 'duck's arse' hairstyle, the victim's petticoats). And it also vividly mimics the psychopath's verbal mannerisms ('A right well-knackered outragement') as well as subtly suggesting his mental oddness ('Bang in the centre of my skull, / there's a strange coolness'). Even then, it draws attention to its own artificiality, and immunises itself against that as a charge, by using mirror imagery that refers at the same time to the psychopath's narcissism and to how much the poem distorts him as it reflects him. The punning phrase 'Let me make myself crystal' suggests that the poem merely constructs him, that he is a figure of glass rather than flesh. So when he poses his 'reflection between dummies in the window at Burton's' it is clear that Duffy is making a characteristic reference to ventriloquy. Here is a male psychopath, but he is speaking through the mouth of a feminist poet.

This is a form of gender interaction in itself and already indicates that it is fully possible for males to be at a disadvantage. The sense of the female victim's innocence and helplessness is chillingly conveyed, but in terms of the poem it is the female poet and not the male psychopath who is in charge. Elsewhere, Duffy is conspicuous for the knowledge she expresses (sometimes linked to her knowledge of class) about male vulnerability – a concept which would appear almost a contradiction in terms to Adrienne Rich. 'Boy' (78) is spoken by a man who wants to regress to childhood and turns this desire into a sexual fantasy:

> There was an older woman
> who gave me a bath. She was joking, of course,
> but I wasn't. I said *Mummy* to her. Off-guard.

'Mrs.Tiresias' (137–40) reworks the myth in contemporary dress as the monologue of a transsexual's ex-partner who takes his shortcomings in the feminine role as pathetic proof of male insufficiencies:

> Then he started his period.
> One week in bed.
> Two doctors in.
> Three painkillers four times a day.
>
> And later
> a letter
> to the powers-that-be
> demanding full-paid menstrual leave twelve weeks per year
> (139)

The comic timing here is typical of Duffy and makes her a very effective reader of her work. More importantly her ability to make effective jokes about gender signals her knowledge of its paradoxes and incongruities, a knowledge conspicuously lacking in Rich, whose tunnel vision makes her humourless. Duffy, like Rich, has written lesbian love poems – 'Girlfriends' (85) can certainly be characterised in that way, while 'Warming her Pearls' (60–1) is more concerned with admiration and confused longing. But she is also acute about heterosexual responses, as in 'Correspondents' – 'Beneath my dress, my breasts / swell for your lips' (55). Elsewhere, too, she seems to draw on the tradition of gay poets writing love poems that disguise the gender of the love object, and by doing so she calls the whole issue of gender into question. 'Adultery' (119–20) may at first reading seem obviously to be about a woman having an affair with a man: but her partner's gender is never mentioned and nothing they do rules out the possibility that her partner in adultery is a woman, especially one who is enjoying playing a male role. This means that gender ambiguity becomes one of the key issues in Duffy's work, and she sometimes uses the mysterious element in dramatic monologue – the fact that readers only know what the monologuist is like by guessing from what the monologuist says – to lay gender issues deliberately open. 'Stealing' (49–50) may seem at first obviously to have a male speaker because the actions described are gratuitously violent, but the poem works, finally, by only asking the gender question – especially because whatever sex the dummy is, the ventriloquist is a woman:

> I'm a mucky ghost, leave a mess, maybe pinch a camera.
> I watch my gloved hand twisting the doorknob.
> A stranger's bedroom. Mirrors. I sigh like this – *Aah*.
>
> (49)

* * *

The gender question also obsesses Sharon Olds, but very much from a heterosexual perspective. She is fascinated by the alienness of the masculine and is unique in the exhilirated energy of her celebration of it, of the male body, its 'massive / hocks, flanks, thighs, elegant / knees, long tapered calves', and female responses to it, 'the cock / in our mouth, ah the cock in our mouth'.[14] She is the opposite of the woman poet Rich describes who thinks that the 'charisma of Man seems to come purely from his power over her and his control of the world by force, not from anything fertile or life-giving in him' (Gelpi, 91). Her poems are repeatedly excited by the idea of male potency, as when she describes what it was like to be in her first boyfriend's car:

> Your front seat had an overpowering
> male smell, as if the chrome had been
> rubbed with jism, a sharp stale
> delirious odor like the sour plated
> taste of the patina on an old watch, the
> fragrance of your sex polished till it shone in the night[15]

Olds is also to some extent woman-identified and has poems about her mother, sister and daughter, about pregnancy, abortion, a miscarriage, childbirth and motherhood – all of these poems are written with her characteristic insight and flair for detail. She expresses acute fellow feeling for other women and also, quite often, surprised gratitude, as when she refers to her older sister's 'harshness' but then realises how that sister had protected her, as a 'hostage protects the one who makes her / escape as I made my escape, with my sister's / body held in front of me'.[16] On the other hand she also tends to seem unimpressed by women in comparison with men, as in 'The Housewives Watching Morning TV' (*Satan Says*, 31) which quotes an assistant fire commissioner on a talk show contrasting male and female arsonists, the males using 'three whole bags of garbage', the females 'a pair of nylons / … or a napkin', doing it for a 'grudge' and starting delicate, less effective fires. There is an element of irony in the poem, of mocking the fireman, but what he says is still taken seriously, and the poem ends with the housewives

> listening to him calmly, smoke
> creeping from our mouths, as if under a door,
> black as Emma Bovary's bile.

The sense that men are furious fire while women are insidious smoke is characteristic, and the depiction of her son, in 'Son', partly arises from the poet having come from a 'women-only bar' when she looks at him sleeping and enjoys the sight of his face with his 'opal eyelids quivering / like insect wings' and prays that the world will make room for him, for his

> head, lips,
> throat, wrists, hips, cock,
> knees, feet. Let no part go
> unpraised. Into any new world we enter, let us
> take this man.
>
> (*The Dead*, 68)

The word 'man' there is spoken with a disquieting solemnity and reverence but it is Olds' ability to feel this way that leads to some of her most effective writing, which tends to arise out of the disturbed excitement that is aroused in her by the idea of distinctive and powerful maleness.

It is in Olds' poems about her father that this is at its clearest. She appears to be totally uninterested in men as embodiments of the patriarchal idea – except where this could be read into her literal concern with the bad father where her focus is so much on her own characteristic excitement at his badness that any political element is either deeply problematic or non-existent. To say that she feels complicit with her father's badness is an understatement. She feels part of it, she feels herself to be a part of him: 'half / me, half / mine' she says:

> Man, male, his cock that I have loved
> beyond the others, beyond goodness, so far beyond

> pleasure I have loved his hatred, coldness,
> indifference, solid blackness
>
> (*Satan Says*, 70)

These feelings lead her to see herself as a female variant of her father so that 'Why My Mother Made Me' (*The Gold Cell*, 33) says that her mother when she first saw the poet's father wanted to *be* him ('She wanted that / power. She wanted that size.'). Her way of achieving this was to have a daughter who was like herself but was actually that man. Even more bizarre is 'Poem to my Husband from my Father's Daughter' (*The Dead*, 56) where she imagines her husband being attracted to a hybrid of herself and her father:

> You are fearless, you
> enter him as a woman, my sex like a
> wound in his body

This leads to a vision of herself as a lion, which is reminiscent of some of the stories in Angela Carter's *The Bloody Chamber* but taking the notion of hybridness one step further – not just man as beast but man-as-woman-as-beast. During sex between the poet and her husband she takes her great tongue and begins to 'run the rasp delicately / along your skin, humming'.

The deeply divided feelings she has about her father – furious resentment of how he mistreated her overwhelmed by a potent sense of identification with him, a sense of a maleness in her that corresponds with him – have led Olds to write a book-long sequence of elegies about him called *The Father*.[17] Perhaps Olds' greatest talent as a poet is for a relentless literalness – her way of digging her teeth deep into a subject and refusing to let go, the steadiness of her gaze which wants to include everything, however mundane or shocking. Her focus in this volume on the physical facts of her father's death, the symptoms of his lung cancer, the tumours and mucus, combined with her relating of this to very specific past experiences of him as his daughter, mean that this volume presents itself as a kind of naturalism. This is aided by Olds' deployment of her own kind of free verse which works hard to evoke the particular and ambient flux, the jagged currency of the experience as it happened. This book is so firmly focused on a literal

father that it seems to demand that generalisations about 'patri-
archy' must be made with immense care:

> My father was not a shit. He was a man
> failing at life. He had little shits
> travelling through him while he lay there unconscious –
> sometimes I don't let myself say
> I loved him, anymore, but I feel
> I almost love those shits that move through him,
> shapely, those waste foetuses,
> my mother, my sister, my brother, and me
> in that purgatory. (73)

7

The Politics of Camp: Frank O'Hara and John Ashbery

The most important insight into gay self-representation in post-war poetry is provided by David Bergman when he refers to 'gay ego-lessness' as arising from 'the homosexual's relationship to society' and also as 'one of his tools for dealing with' that relationship.[1] His exploration of this is especially useful for my purposes because it helps to define, by contrast, the self-image of the heterosexual male. Bergman draws on Nancy Chodorow's description of straight men as possessing a 'more emphatic individuation and a more defensive firming of experienced ego boundaries' which leads to their 'denial of … connectedness and isolation of affect'.[2] This helps to explain why straight male poets are so self-assertively preoccupied with the acquisition of a 'voice', with stamping their poetic identity every-where on their language and content. Lowell and Berryman, in par-ticular, are preoccupied throughout their work with twisting the poem into a shape that mirrors them.

The most influential early experiences of gay men are entirely dif-ferent from those of straight men because no-one is raised to be gay, and as a result they have what Bergman calls, quoting Erik Erikson, a 'negative identity' which is '*not* merely an inversion of selfhood – being the opposite of what others expect one to be – but rather an absence of identity – no one can point the gay child toward a model of who he is' (45). Bergman goes on to link the homosexual and the vampire, since both 'possess a narcissism without a reflection' and so both 'fall into the abyss, not to embrace themselves, but in a vain search to grab hold of any image' (45).

The expression of egolessness has been one of the most important contributions that gay poets have made to contemporary poetry, especially because it has important links with the interrogation of notions of the unitary self which has been so central in postmod-ernist literature and theory. The still underestimated work of Edwin Morgan raises egolessness into an aesthetic principle that paradoxically structures his poetic. He deliberately deploys an astonishing range of personae and poetic forms (the sonnet, free verse, sound and concrete poetry, for example) in order to destabilise any continuity of 'voice' or identity.[3] For similar reasons, the far more widely discussed work of John Ashbery dissolves the poetic ego in the multiple fluxes of language and is much more clearly related to the project of post-structuralist theory in that respect.

Strongly linked to this sense of egolessness is the sense of gay otherness. Because the sexuality of the gay man is entirely different to that which conceived him, he is made to feel 'a categorical, perhaps even ontological otherness':

> This negativity of self mirrors the sociological fact that no homosexual is raised as such; he finds no likeness in the family circle. Thus, the homosexual misses the bonding and identification which for the heterosexual bridges the gap between himself and others. Indeed the family reminds the homosexual of his own 'unlikeness'. (Bergman, 30)

Edwin Morgan and John Ashbery have both evolved a poetic founded upon otherness, a centrifugal poetic deliberately lacking any core of sameness which could constitute aesthetic identity. Egolessness and otherness produce self-conscious dispersal and diffuseness. Morgan's multiplying of forms and voices places the emphasis on endless defamiliarising: everything his poems treat becomes radically unfamiliar. Given the sense that Bergman evokes of gay detachment from the family, Morgan's preoccupation with defamiliarising can be seen to have secretly gay origins – it is about subverting modes of perception that are constituted by the wish always to see family resemblance, to structure the world in a reassuringly 'familiar' way that satisfies the assumptions of a heterosexual and patriarchal ideology. A similar effect is produced by what Geoff Ward calls the 'breathless juxtaposition' deployed by Frank O'Hara, because it was 'so wilfully facetious and provoking to the poetic consensus of its time' and which

> may be better understood by the light of Barthes' emphasis on dispersion, friability, shimmer. Undoubtedly with both writers there is an obvious association to be made between textual deviation and sexual divergence from the sanctioned norm.[4]

The preoccupation with otherness leads Edwin Morgan most characteristically towards science fiction – his distant planets and aliens are deployed to interrogate ontological boundaries, to question what is too easily assumed about human normality. It leads Frank O'Hara and John Ashbery to the much more obviously gendered strategies of camp, which has been described by David T. Evans as 'a defensive manoeuvre by a group so oppressed that it has no other socio-cultural or political alternative'.[5] This is the element of camp which is disturbingly missed by Susan Sontag in her classic 1964 piece 'Notes on Camp' which is exhaustively thorough in its account of the aesthetic aspects of the subject but entirely lacking any sense of its implicit politics. Sontag's piece is written from the perspective of a brilliantly acute observer rather than that of someone involved so that, far from considering camp a defensive manoeuvre arising from oppression she considers it as élitist, as expressing the outlook of 'an improvised self-elected class, mainly homosexuals, who constitute themselves as aristocrats of taste' (117).

In fact it is precisely because camp manifests itself as self-consciously aesthetic but actually embodies a hidden politics that it has been crucially important in the culture of the last forty years. This has meant that it has been hugely influential in revealing and deconstructing the concealed politics of the aesthetic norms which it has subversively travestied. As David Bergman has pointed out, because gays have historically adopted the codes of heterosexual behaviour in order to conceal themselves, they have been acutely aware of the codedness of those codes. Camp is the inevitable result of this gay history because it is

> the mode in which coding is most self-consciously played with and where the apparent emptying of self-expression is most conspicuous. Of course, by making these 'culturally determined codes' self-conscious and conspicuous, gay writers destabilize them and open them to analysis and criticism. Thus the avoidance of 'self-expression' becomes paradoxically a powerful expression of gay selfhood. One might say that camp is the post-structuralist mode *par excellence*. (Bergman, 105)

Frank O'Hara was the most influential figure in postwar poetry in the deployment of camp, largely because he reinforced and substantiated its gestures with techniques derived from avant-garde

art, especially dada and surrealism, which had already decon-
structed the codes of the art establishment. These two could be
made to collaborate with each other because of their shared self-
reflexiveness. Susan Sontag says that

> Camp sees everything in quotation marks. It's not a lamp, but
> a 'lamp'; not a woman but a 'woman'. To perceive Camp in
> objects and persons is to understand Being-as-Playing-a-Role. It
> is the farthest extension, in sensibility, of the metaphor of life as
> theater. (109)

Surrealism had similarly drawn attention to the painterliness of
painting, and the textuality of texts, and, like camp, had made witty
play with the sophisticated *frisson* of recognition that this arouses.
Where the two differ is that surrealism contains the vestige of a
modernist surface versus depth model – being premised on the
concept of the unconscious – whereas camp is thoroughly postmod-
ern in its confrontational depthlessness.[7] Its Wildean preference for
style rather than sincerity (Sontag, 116), its emphasis on codes
rather than self-expression, question whether there actually exists
any 'real' self beneath the coded behaviour. O'Hara's techniques
can be described as largely derived from surrealism but his sensibil-
ity is overwhelmingly camp and this is what is finally most import-
ant, as surrealism is co-opted by him for camp ends.

To describe all this more accurately, though, it is necessary to be
more specific about the poetic influences on O'Hara. He was very
widely read in European and American modernist poetry, but the
most important influence on him was the French poet Pierre
Reverdy, who shares much in common with the surrealists Breton,
Eluard and Desnos, who were his contemporaries, but also has
crucial differences from them. As Kenneth Rexroth has said,
Reverdy's poems aim to reorder, not just verbal syntax, but that of
the mind itself and moreover, its 'restructuring of experience is
purposive, not dreamlike, and hence it possesses an uncanniness
fundamentally different in kind from the most haunted utter-
ances of the Surrealist or Symbolist unconscious'.[8] Rexroth
considers that this means that Reverdy has more in common with
cubism than with surrealism, because his work involves the
'conscious, deliberate dissociation and recombination of elements
into a new artistic entity made self-sufficient by its rigorous
architecture' (8).

The link between Reverdy and O'Hara has been frequently mentioned by critics but never thoroughly explored. Marjorie Perloff's book offers no more than hints. She does, however, quote a statement by O'Hara himself:

> When Ashbery asked O'Hara to contribute poems that might be influenced by Reverdy for the special Reverdy issue of *Mercure de France*, O'Hara responded, half-jokingly – 'I just couldn't stand the amount of work it [the Reverdy project] would seem to take, since the minute you mentioned it I decided that everything I've written except "In Memory of my Feelings" and "Dig my Grave with a Silver Spoon" has been under his influence'.[9]

Perloff's 'half-jokingly' is beside the point because the majority of O'Hara's really serious statements were made in this tone. When he says 'everything I've written' he is speaking the truth in the sense that Reverdy provided O'Hara with a particular framework within which a poem might be written – a way of structuring it. So, many of O'Hara's most characteristic poems, like Reverdy's, are constructed 'with dismembered propositions from which subject, operator and object have been wrenched free and structured into an invisible or subliminal discourse which owes its cogency to its own strict, complex and secret logic' (Rexroth, 9).

In 'Homage to Pasternak's Cape Mootch'[10] the first 'dismembered proposition' is a quotation from Pasternak and the second is a direct description of the scene on which the poem focuses. Here O'Hara has shifted from Pasternak to the idiom of William Carlos Williams:

> 'The mind is stifled.' Very little sky
> is visible through the ailanthus,
> and through the ailanthus is the red brick
> and the grey brick, and the smell of cats

While he is engaged in this direct, imagistic treatment, O'Hara seems to be stressing the pre-eminence of the objective. He seems to be saying that the mind is stifled by the ailanthus, the brick, the smell of cats, and so demonstrating Williams's insistence that there be no ideas but in things. The next lines, though, introduce a shift in technique as the poet's hand comes to rest on a teabag and the 'whole day' is said to step 'daintily' across his body. These are much larger gestures than imagism prescribes, and that camp adverb is clearly an impression rather than something experienced physically. The third verse is even more subjective:

> Yearning grasses growing from my eyes
> to this music do you lean, shallow and wet
> like a pebble?

The poem has now clearly moved from definition to suggestion and evocation, from a Williams mood to a Hart Crane mood – though this is more daring even than Crane. This signals that the mind is influencing the scene. The playfulness of 'daintily' is a kind of sarcasm in the face of adversity and registers the mind's refusal to be too easily stifled. But there is a shift beyond even this. For by the third verse the mind is clearly taking over; it is a mind more stifling than stifled. The confusion of senses, and the syntactical ambiguity stress this; the grasses, the music, the pebble are instruments of self-torture – they are not physically present. O'Hara emphasises this when he allows part of one of his similes suddenly to make an actual, and completely implausible appearance. In lines 10 and 11 he says that tea rolled into a cylinder resembles marijuana next to a pool and then in lines 15 and 16 a pool suddenly appears. This is the signal for fantasy to take over altogether as his nose drips 'slightly chlorinated' water onto his cigarette and he breathes heavily as a result of 'swimming through the wood of this parquet / which is deep brown, the tall trunk of hell'.

This indicates how his self-pity is determining what objects look like: the transforming power of interpretative bias is stressed by the gap between what the reader has been told about the scene and what that scene becomes from the perspective of a particular state of mind. To start as objectively as possible was therefore necessary. The last stanza arises from associations that are several steps away from the objects from which they sprang. The drops of water are connected with the sweat and humidity. The tall trunk is connected to the ailanthus, the grasses, and the 'delicate twigs' of an American cigarette. It also seems to spring out of the water falling onto the cigarette like a sudden jungle growth. The lines insist on subjectivity: the water has become 'slightly chlorinated' to associate it with a swimming bath and prepare for 'swimming through the wood'. The *tertium quid* of the tall trunk is the offspring of a self-consciously implausible marriage – as in Magritte's painting 'The Explanation' where a bottle and a carrot appear to be the parents of a hybrid bottle/carrot.

The initial difficulty of this poem arises from the lack of any solidly stated context in which to understand the individual observations which are made. The hand falling on the teabag is the first warning of an enigmatic context. It is a 'dismembered proposition' in Rexroth's sense because it is difficult to define its status. The movement from objective to subjective, and from literal to metaphorical and then literal/metaphorical, arouses a sense of an alogical and acausal sequence. The combination of this with an abnormally focused attention is one of the commonest experiences in reading O'Hara. The teabag is encountered in this way, and the same effect is made more explicit elsewhere when – again with a line-ending increasing the surprise – he says: 'Put out your hand / isn't there / an ashtray, suddenly, there?' (214). In O'Hara, as in Reverdy, ideas precede things, and he makes clear his opposition to Williams' stress on the precedence of things when in 'To a Poet' he says: 'when the doctor comes to / he says "No things but in ideas"' (185). O'Hara feels his New York environment to be saturated with thought and feeling, so that objects have been transformed in advance, before the poem starts. This is expressed most extremely in 'Nocturne', whose Reverdian rearrangement of reality takes a typically camp O'Haran form. 'Nocturne' is moving, once its context is understood – before that it can seem merely disorienting. In fact its speaker is a tall building:

> My eyes, like millions of
> glassy squares, merely reflect.
> Everything sees through me,
> in the daytime I'm too hot
> and at night I freeze
>
> (225)

'Nocturne' is literally self-reflexive. Having acquired a mental life the building can quietly insist that its glassy squares are eyes and are only 'like' glassy squares. And the poem parodies the poetic habit of assuming 'personae', a habit which which O'Hara's playful manifesto 'Personism' (498–9) implicitly rejects.

O'Hara's Reverdian strategy of deploying 'dismembered propositions' to construct enigmatic contexts is directed most significantly towards questioning the self. The apparent erasure of what Rexroth calls 'subject, operator and object' means that the agency of those selves is implicitly investigated. Their erasure from the poem is linked to gay egolessness but the construction of the enigmatic context hints at the presence of a specific ego whose state of mind has created that context. This is very different from Rexroth's version of the Reverdian 'subliminal discourse' in which the self is transcended in order to evoke an 'intense significance' which is evidently epiphanic or thoroughly mystical (see 10–12). O'Hara's vision, by contrast, is thoroughly secular and conflates the 'significant' and the 'trivial'. An important part of the campness of his outlook is that it celebrates the bric-à-brac of mid-twentieth century metropolitan life. The dismembered propositions in his poems very often include such bric-à-brac and endow them with poetic meaning.

O'Hara's most significant achievement is his combining of a Reverdian dismemberment of poetic materials with a camp subversiveness about ontological assumptions. He is characteristically postmodernist in this co-opting of a modernist technique which is then rendered more playful and self-reflexive. The poetic materials which are dismembered are often presented parodically, so that 'Homage to Cape Mootch' gestures towards Pasternak, Williams, Crane and a more generalised symbolist and surrealist idiom, all dismembered and restructured with quasi-Reverdian but also quasi-jokey motives. This places all of these poetic materials in camp quotation marks: more significantly it does the same for the poetic identity which the reader must conventionally assume is responsible for them.

It is this calling into question of poetic identity which is also the most significant effect of O'Hara's most famous work, his 'I do this, I do that' poems, even though it is here, too, that this identity appears to be most unproblematic:

> It's my lunch hour, so I go
> for a walk among the hum-colored
> cabs. First, down the sidewalk
> where laborers feed their dirty
> glistening torsos sandwiches
> and Coca-Cola, with yellow helmets
> on. They protect them from falling
> bricks, I guess.
>
> (257)

It is in lines like these that O'Hara most demonstrates the painterly and cinematic qualities that critics have identified in his work; Marjorie Perloff, for example, speaks of how he adapts 'the techniques of film and action painting to the verbal medium' (121). The difficulty, though, is that the minimalist placing of these visual details in poetic form registers an implicit puzzlement about their meaning. O'Hara refuses to allow them to acquire a meaning too easily, his treatment seems to be flatly untransforming. Yet the need to put such material into poems indicates a need to organise it, and, while they depict urban depthlessness, they also indicate the refusal of the observer of the urban surface to accept this lack of depth, and show him in the process of imposing a depth of his own. The form this takes in 'A Step Away From Them' (257–8) and 'The Day Lady Died' (325) is of the poet's introduction of memory into the scene, so that entirely different poetic materials are juxtaposed and emphasise their distance from each other. They face each other, within the poem, baffled and unyielding, and refuse to make the compromise which would mould them into thematic integrity. The poem thereby indicates something about the texture of experience and also questions the validity of the transformation which poetry inflicts on its material. But simply by juxtaposing such material, they force a transformation to take place:

> First
> Bunny died, then John Latouche,
> then Jackson Pollock. But is the
> earth as full as life was full, of them?
>   (258)

The context of this poem is a problem even though it appears to be all context. For the poem's centre is elsewhere, in the state of mind of the poet, in his 'subliminal discourse', which dismembers the urban scene and also the memories through which that scene is filtered. 'A Step Away From Them', as the title suggests, stresses a separateness, for the poet feels his separation from his friends who have died, and, through feeling this, is separated also from the New York scene through which he is moving. In hinging upon this the poem focuses on the isolation of the poet's thoughts from the phenomena by which they are surrounded. By placing these phenomena in all their randomness, in a poetic form, O'Hara makes them clamour for order; for this reason, they cluster around the subjective centre of the poem, its preoccupation with death. After the first reading, all the poetic materials of 'A Step Away From Them' restructure themselves around the names, and the question, 'is the / earth as full as life was full, of them?': the crowded streets O'Hara describes orient themselves towards this wondering about fullness. Similarly, all O'Hara's activities in 'The Day Lady Died', after the first reading, seem to reach towards the last-mentioned one, his purchase of a *New York Post* with a photograph of Billie Holiday on it, which leads to the poem's crucial last shift:

> and I am sweating a lot by now and thinking of
> leaning on the john door in the 5 SPOT
> while she whispered a song along the keyboard
> to Mal Waldron and everyone and I stopped breathing
> (325)

To say that these two poems centre on the deaths to which they refer is not to say that they are elegies. In fact their sketched randomness is a deliberate strategy to avoid the too obviously meditational. O'Hara describes something of this method when, in speaking of 'Second Avenue' he speculates that its obscurity arises

> in the relationship between the surface and the meaning, but I like it that way since the one is the other ... and I hope the poem to be the subject, not just about it. (497)

O'Hara is stressing here his need to give the appearance of flatness; he is clearly envying the extent to which painting can more easily immunise itself against portentousness. So, 'A Step Away From Them' is not about the deaths of his friends: it is an enactment of the confrontation between a state of mind and a scene, between ideas and things. It is important to him, however, that the poem is not *merely* flat but sets itself on the threshold between its surface and its meaning, and this is most tellingly demonstrated by the ending of 'A Step Away From Them':

> A glass of papaya juice
> and back to work. My heart is in my
> pocket, it is Poems by Pierre Reverdy.
> (258)

His heart is not on his sleeve, he is not a poet who is *all* surface, but a pocket is somewhere between the surface and a 'real' inner self. The poem's hidden meaning is a subliminal Reverdian discourse. However, the equation of the traditionally poetic 'heart', and all its associations of passionate authenticity, with both clothing and text is flagrantly camp because it transforms 'nature' into artifice. The 'pocket', then, travesties the idea of poetic depth by insisting that beneath the surface there is only another surface.

The effect of O'Hara's poems might be most accurately summarised by reference to their undermining of assumptions about the 'heart' – assumptions, that is, about a core of self and its authentic emotional depths. His work can also be contrasted, in this respect, with the assumptions of 'confessional' poetry which probes away at influential early experiences in order to establish how the poet's identity evolved. O'Hara opposes any ideas of the self as at all rigidly identifiable and presents it – especially in the 'I do this, I do that' poems – being invented moment by moment. This is a self in process, which is why cinema and action painting are accurate analogues for his poems. Camp is still crucial here as the destabilising motive force behind the open-ended, questioning presentation of the poetic materials; and the collapsing of ego boundaries, which this poetic requires, also suggests how much this is a gay achievement, how much it opposes straight male concepts of the self.

This is an identity, then, which is only defined performatively. Nonetheless, these poems do evoke in the end a memorable sense of the poet's presence in the scene walking his lunchtime walk and talking his New York talk, and so performing himself as poet. O'Hara's successor John Ashbery pushes the camp/surreal poetic much further so that the poetic self is altogether erased. O'Hara's critique of fixed notions of the self is most accurately seen, philosophically, as a critique of ontological essences which is closest in spirit to existentialism. His deployment of free verse fluidity and openness is aimed at improvising an identity and is related to 'projectivist' notions of shaping the poem as an organism that is a living representation of the poet's breath and body. His poems therefore are negotiations between this projectivist organicism and camp artifice. Ashbery, by contrast, has none of the former and extends the latter systematically, so that everything inside his text and out of it is placed between quotation marks. This is extended much more thoroughly than in O'Hara to include the sense of the poet inside his poem. O'Hara can be accurately understood by reference to

Heideggerian explorations of 'being in the world'.[11] Ashbery's work, by contrast, is post-existentialist in the sense that it is, like Derrida's, endlessly sceptical about the metaphysics of presence and wants to explore how much the sense of 'presence' is constructed by language. Perhaps the clearest example of this is how Ashbery's poem 'The Tennis Court Oath'[12] refers to David's 1781 painting of the same name in which figures were erased and replaced as they fell out of favour with the government. Ashbery has therefore written a text with a problematic relationship to its title which refers to a deeply problematic representation of history which was itself finally abandoned. All of this therefore calls thoroughly into question any sense of the 'real' and of authentic ontological continuity.

This constellation of radical concerns has made Ashbery the most challenging poet of the last 20 years, so that what is above all a gay sensibility has been profoundly influential. His use of camp's self-conscious aestheticism and theatricality has revealed the extent to which the establishment poetic has been specifically a gendered poetic, how a straight masculine perspective had imposed itself as an unquestioned norm. His work, combined with that of women poets – especially of explicit feminists like Adrienne Rich – has been of great importance because it has drawn attention not just to the aesthetic expressions of gender, but its ideological expressions. This has been one of the most important and positive achievements of postmodernist subversions of monolithic 'common-sense' attitudes. Its impact has been to help towards a changing understanding of how the wide range of masculinities and femininities shape each person's experience and view of the world.

'Self-Portrait in a Convex Mirror' (*Selected Poems*, 196–212) applies this critique to the beginnings of modern masculine self-fashioning in the Renaissance. It centres on the self-portrait by the Mannerist Francesco Parmigianino and deconstructs it as a thoroughly gendered rendering of the self, a rendering which is about what Chodorow describes as masculine defensiveness in the bolstering of ego boundaries. It describes how the painter cut in half a ball of wood and then copied his reflection onto it: the result is that his image is 'Glazed, embalmed' and above all 'sequestered' (196). Ashbery then goes on to explore how this masculine occludedness imposes its vision on the world:

Actually
The skin of the bubble-chamber's as tough as

> Reptile eggs; everything gets 'programmed' there
> In due course: more keeps getting included
> Without adding to the sum, and just as one
> Gets accustomed to a noise that
> Kept one awake but now no longer does,
> So the room contains this flow like an hourglass
> Without varying in climate or quality
>
> (201)

So the poem demonstrates how this particular kind of self-regard gets thoroughly enmeshed with an ideological system which makes its vision seem 'natural'. Ashbery draws on discursive modes derived from Wallace Stevens and W.H. Auden to explore the implications of this, and then on his own characteristic imagery (which is edged with surrealism) to contrast this hard enclosedness with an alternative emphasis on openness and fluidity. Deployed together, these modes produce a camp mastery that deconstructs mastery and advocates an improvisatory responsiveness, and this does seem to me one of the great achievements in postwar poetry.

Another of Ashbery's greatest achievements has been his reassessment of poetic modernism through camp parody. Some of his finest recent moments have also done this, as in his long poem in quatrains, 'Tuesday Evening':

> Such are the passwords that tired Aeneas
> wept for outside the potting shed,
> when, face pressed to the pane, he sought Linnaeus'
> sage advice. And the farm turned over a new leaf instead.[13]

This reads a bit like Pound's 'Hugh Selwyn Mauberley' – the satirical juxtaposing, in a twentieth-century setting, of an epic hero and a giant of the Enlightenment (conveniently half-rhyming with each other) suggests a wry anti-humanist ruefulness about the loss of such potential in the modern period. But the textual references are pushed parodically too far, so that the stanza seems to try also to make a point about pastoral and/or Romantic nature poetry culminating in a pun that links nature and text ('new leaf'). Then again 'passwords' suggests a thriller – or, more likely, because of the potting shed, Enid Blyton – and 'sage' is a very silly pun indeed.

What Ashbery has learned most importantly from modernism is its defamiliarising strategies and it is his co-opting of these for camp motives that accounts for much of what he does. This amounts to the systematic turning around of the charge of otherness which is made against gays, so that it is turned against straight ideology. That is to say, Ashbery's camp renders the straight world other. In his poems, the 'normal' is relentlessly defamiliarised so that it becomes 'strange'. This means that his poems have been doing for decades what Gregory W. Bredbeck calls on gay writing to do:

> We might find a way to assert gay men and lesbians as more than simply different by establishing the difference of everything. We might find a way of speaking the truth by recognizing that truth is false. We might find a way to our own essences by demonstrating that there is nothing essential.[14]

The trouble is that Ashbery has deployed these strategies so often and so repetitively that, at least over the last ten years, they have become stale. What started by stressing difference and otherness has come to be characterised disturbingly by sameness. This is connected to the postmodernist collapsing of hierarchies which at first seemed liberating and exciting but has led, textually, to a bland undifferentiated flux. Ashbery was especially good at subverting the poetry of 'angst' by surreally introducing trivial, or merely aesthetic things to be anxious about. He is still good at this, as in the first stanza of 'A Day at the Gate':

> A loose and dispiriting
> wind took over from the grinding of traffic.
> Clouds from the distillery
> blotted out the sky. Ocarina sales plummeted.
> (*Can You Hear, Bird*, 3)

Ashbery's emphasis on fun has always been refreshing, and it is still a point worth making that poems don't have to be anxious. In 'The Problem of Anxiety' he refers to the things he has 'carefully left out: / descriptions of pain, and sex, and how shiftily / people behave toward each other' (*Can You Hear, Bird*, 121). This can start to seem merely evasive, and the replacement of these experiences by endless camp irony is deadeningly inhuman and even supercilious.

The fact that Ashbery has made camp boring is disturbing because it's not just a question of writing dull poems – it means he's turned what was previously a subversive gesture into a predictable one. So instead of making his readers rethink their outlook he is now reassuring them, lulling them with what increasingly looks like flippancy. What started as a kind of polyphony has become monotonous, like listening to someone who always sounds sarcastic. The gender implications of this are disquieting, especially because the culture has changed since Ashbery first started doing this – camp has been thoroughly absorbed into popular culture, which it often mimicked to begin with but in which, now, its effects tend to be conservative.

This means that Susan Sontag's essay, curiously, is more accurate about camp now than it was in 1964: she said it was apolitical and it has *become* apolitical. This is partly because the achievements of gay liberation, and the general unsettling, in the culture, of assumptions about gender, mean that gays no longer have to be as secretive about their sexuality as they did in the 1960s. So where before the camp stress on the aesthetic was crypto-political, now it has been drained of that political content. So Ashbery's camp refusal of *angst*, and camp habit of making everything aesthetic, now make him seem monotonous. His vision flattens hierarchies so systematically that it is drained of any consciousness of power relations, and eerily anaesthetised. His poems are similar in this respect to Andy Warhol's paintings and their camp celebration of commodification, which leads to the replication and multiplication of iconic images. Like Warhol's paintings, Ashbery's poems turn into clones of each other, and what seemed radically defamiliarised becomes all too familiar.

Ashbery is the most famous contemporary gay poet. His deployment of a tactic that now looks like a refusal ever to speak directly or deal straightforwardly with felt experience has the effect of trivialising gays, of insinuating the idea that gays are evasive and frivolous. Camp was a brilliant device for self-advertising, for letting straight culture know that gays were around and were a sophisticated cultural and ideological force, but straight culture no longer needs telling that. There are serious contemporary issues for poetry to deal with which will require all its wit and irony in combination with other qualities – and this makes Ashbery's tired jokiness all the more exasperating.

8

Creeps and Bastards:
C.K. Williams as Voyeur

I have suggested that Robert Lowell and John Berryman are both, in their different ways, exceptionally conscious of the gender issue for men of their generation. C.K. Williams (born 1936) is a man of the generation after theirs and was still young as the women's movement gathered momentum. It's not surprising, then, that Williams, *more* than either Lowell or Berryman, is preoccupied with what is gendered in his own responses, that he gives the issue more explicit priority than either of them. The unease about masculinity which Lowell starts to express in mid to late career, especially in 'Near the Ocean'[1] is a component of Williams's outlook from the start and becomes important as early as his second volume *I Am the Bitter Name*[2] whose horrified vision of violence and suffering is obsessively expressed through sexual imagery juxtaposed with references to the oppressiveness of state institutions in a manner that suggests a loosely Reichian outlook:

> the nations have used up their desire
> the cunts of the mothers the cunts
> of the bad daughters stinking
> of police stations of the sisters
> and generations of men saying
> look cunt what about me
>
> (67)

This critique of bureaucratic authoritarianism locates the political malaise it is diagnosing specifically in masculine compulsions to dominate and control which pervert and exhaust desire and oppress women.

The early C.K. Williams is New Left in his outlook – his poems are deeply disturbed by a sickness they are driven to diagnose in the body politic, whose symptoms are a mutually reinforcing compound of (mostly sexual) repression and mostly hidden but occasionally explicit and violent oppression. 'In the Heart of the Beast' (116–21) is only the most obvious expression of these ideas in its protest against Vietnam and the killings at Kent State. It is partly because these poems seem so thoroughly identifiable so much of the time as the product of a 1960s sensibility that makes them unsatisfactory. In retrospect, however, they can be seen to show signs already of the mature Williams and it's crucial that these signs are most especially related to the preoccupation with gender which Williams adds to his routinely Reichian/Marcusian mingling of Marx and Freud.

Much of what makes these poems so agonised is their habit of accusing the State but at the same time locating its abuses in the masculinity of the State's character and behaviour, and so simultaneously indicting the man who is doing the indicting. The poems are convinced that there is a malaise which is prevalent but also systematically hidden or ignored – they find signs of this everywhere, even if these signs can't always be fully interpreted, as when he refers to men urinating staring determinedly at the wall, 'so we won't covet each other's cocks' (69). I'll be discussing in detail Williams's preoccupation with the gaze, but what is symptomatic for him in this image, and what is the implicit source of his protest, is the human habit of looking *away*. What will come to define Williams's sense of himself as a poet is his insistence on looking at what others routinely turn away from. This image is introduced apparently enigmatically in a context focused on violence but thereby suggests that such violence is a product of routine repression, that there is a conspiracy that enforces a looking away from collective maleness and its works which allows those works to flourish unchecked. The victims here are women and children and the reference to bullets going into them immediately precedes this apparently much more mundane reference, so that mundane maleness is anxiously defamiliarised.

The starting-point of this poem, 'Poor Hope' is clearly the My Lai Massacre (March 16, 1968) and it's interesting that there's a poem by Robert Lowell on the same subject – 'Women, Children, Babies, Cows, Cats'[3] which also focuses on the maleness of its American perpetrators. The horrified critique of 'martial masculinity' which preoccupies Lowell in his middle age preoccupies Williams in his youth – both indict the war in Vietnam as patriarchal. In 'The Nickname of Hell' (101) the president is said to have a face 'flushed

/horribly like a penis' and his actual penis is said to be lined with buttons and to be primed by 'commanders' deep inside it. Here again though the poet is regarded – because of his own gender – as complicit with this patriarchal violence, so that the president tells him 'you are my penis'.

At times Williams seems to regard male biology itself as the culprit and to regard war as the product of something akin to the male sex drive. The addressee of 'Bad Mouth' (103) is said to 'know how to beat women so they love you afterwards' and 'even his sperm hurts / like napalm'. 'The Nut' (98) refers to a male drive which is like 'hammering' in its frustrated and impatient violence. Its viciousness is like 'fucking a bad whore' but the hammering is endless and also 'like murdering'; so that the 'woman screams men what / is this?' – this drive is incomprehensible to women who are its (apparent) object. The political result of this male drive is that 'feminine' qualities of altruism, nurturing and the like are systematically erased – here the early Williams seems to offer a crude version of the political vision of the mature Adrienne Rich which was to be expressed in the decade following *I Am the Bitter Name*. So 'The Admiral Fan' (81) refers to breasts which represent 'dawn amity peace exaltation' but which are withered by patriarchy. The symbolic woman who owns them is used up in Washington which in this way visits a metaphorical sterility on the American landscape.

However, what is most significant about this for Williams's mature poetic is his sense of complicity with the malaise he is diagnosing. He knows that his identity is thoroughly implicated in the masculinity which he indicts; and he knows, also, that his indictment is subtly compromised by his own feelings of guilty excitement which are aroused by this masculinity which he simultaneously identifies with and eschews. 'The Beginning of April' (84) expresses his thrill at his own dominating maleness, declaring that he feels 'terribly strong today' which reminds him of how he once won an arm-wrestling contest so conclusively that he sprained his opponent's wrist, and of how he once made a beautiful woman love him when she hadn't wanted to. This sense of thrill is characteristically followed by anxiety, however, because his sense of his own strength is contrasted with the fragility of a starving Biafran child. Because he feels so powerful he feels he would only have to touch the child to kill him. His response to this represents a crucial clue to Williams's later career: he feels compelled – from the powerful masculine position he has defined – to respond by attempting to understand and sympathise with the suffering of the child, and to call into question his own feelings of dominating power.

Questioning is the most characteristic mode of Williams's mature work and replaces the tendency towards statement (and overstatement) in his mostly unsuccessful first two volumes. It's his switch to this mode and his simultaneous finding of the perfect form to express it, in his long free verse lines, that facilitate the astonishing leap forward in quality that he makes with his third volume *With Ignorance* (1972, reprinted in Poems 1963–1983). The assertiveness and expressionism of his earliest work are too frenetic and unfocused. These early poems are undermined by their formal flux and unpunctuated slither so that they seem to be slipping through their own fingers; their form evokes an elusiveness that their content is constantly and unsuccessfully trying to master.

Elusiveness is the most recurrent quality of the subjects of Williams's mature poems but one that is now admitted and often assumed and focused upon interrogatively. The form that he invents for himself and which is his most distinctive poetic achievement allows him to introduce a discursive idiom which he deploys to question the nuanced ramifications of his subject. This makes Williams's use of the long line the opposite of Whitman's. Where Whitman deploys it to reach out and encompass all experience in the embrace of transcendentalist acceptance, Williams uses it to hold experience at arm's length and analyse it with troubled scepticism.

The posture he adopts is one of looking and then questioning what he sees, but this very posture is also reflected upon as the poem simultaneously looks at and questions the poet and his poetic posture. This is especially crucial because the poems worry about their own voyeurism. As with his response to the Biafran child, Williams depicts himself looking and sympathising – but not, now, from a position of strength. 'The Beginning of April' depicts the poet as masterfully self-sufficient and troubled by the starving child only reluctantly and then as a rebuke to his masterfulness. In his mature work, by contrast, Williams depicts himself as vulnerable and implies that his need to look is itself a symptom of his vulnerability. So in 'Bob' (148–50) he refers to himself as without work and loveless and friendless, 'helpless, self-pitying, angry, inert' (149); in 'Bread' (151–2) he castigates himself for all he has done, to himself and to others, which has caused him to end up in a slum; in 'The

Gift' (187–9) he calls himself a 'sorrowing brute' – 'bitter ... brutal, abrasive, corrosive'.

Williams does adopt a version of confessionalism though his focus is never as thoroughly on himself as it is in the confessional poems of Lowell and Berryman. What these lines reveal is how he lacerates himself for the disturbingly weak combination of violent feelings and passiveness. The violence is the negative side of a stereotypical masculinity. Any glamour this might have, however, is erased by its being hobbled by inertia, so that the violence is directed inwards and becomes 'corrosive'. So he's shown self-destructively eating away at himself. He's rendered contemptible by the extent to which he falls short of the masculine ideal of powerful autonomy which is characterised by its ability to deploy its energies to act successfully to achieve its desires – by contrast he is haunted and damaged by his 'sexual hunger, how a breast could destroy me, or a haunch: not having the beautiful haunch' (188).

What is remarkable here is how Williams focuses, more or less explicitly, on his sense of diminished masculinity – as confessions go this is more than usually daring. This is at its clearest when Williams brings this depiction of himself into a gender interaction. So in 'Shame'[4] he remembers himself 'in 1971, when I was living by myself, painfully lonely, bereft, depressed' talking to a woman

and I realize it wasn't my then irrepressible, unselective,
    incessant sexual want she meant,
which, when we'd been introduced, I'd naturally aimed at
    her and which she'd easily deflected,
but that she thought I really was, in myself, the way I looked
    and spoke and acted,
what she was saying, creepy, weird, whatever, and I am taken
    with a terrible humiliation.

Creepiness is gender specific. It's especially likely to be applied to a man by a woman who is accusing him of disturbingly displaying qualities conventionally thought to be feminine, especially a kind of vulnerable attentiveness which, in a man, seems weak and even 'weird'. The kind of man Williams depicts himself as being in 'The Beginning of April' (84) – who wins at arm-wrestling and wins over a woman against her will – is the opposite of a creep. The term 'bastard' – again gender specific – would be more likely to be applied to him, half-admiringly. Creeps are too passive: bastards are too active; creeps are too 'feminine': bastards are too 'masculine'. When this same man is troubled by the starving child he may start to appear admirably well balanced: if, however, he becomes too troubled, if he wants to look *too* closely at the child, he starts to seem creepy.

When Williams presents himself looking and questioning it's clear that the explicit project he has set himself is the compassionate one he outlines in 'The Beginning of April' – that, however strong he might feel, he will understand and sympathise with the sufferings of others. What happens, however, is that the self he defines in the poems – which is usually an earlier self – is shaken and fragile and therefore is looking, by implication, in response to his own neediness. Much of the power of Williams's mature work arises from its enactment of the problematic interaction between what is seen and the man who sees; and the man's neediness charges his gaze with the edginess of voyeurism.

Voyeurism is gendered in a similar way to creepiness – it's masculine, but tainted uncomfortably with passiveness. Yet both, too, mingle this passiveness with a desire to control – the creep, for example, may attempt to master a woman deviously, insinuatingly. Voyeurism, similarly, attempts to frame what it sees with the mastering gaze. Both, moreover, are linked to the taste for pornography which also combines elements of passiveness and control, a combination far more difficult in actual sex. It allows its male consumer a sexual pleasure that does not require him to take an initiative, and yet it also fixes the object of that pleasure in a thoroughly visual frame that does not allow her to respond with any threatening unpredictability.

It's unsurprising, therefore, especially considering that Williams also speaks about the relentlessness of his own sexual hunger, that he has written two poems about pornography. Both poems refer to how the pornographic vision frames its objects of desire – 'Old Man'[5] refers to the 'glare of ink'; 'Floor' (199–201) refers to how the copulating couple have been posed in their turn-of-the-century photograph. Curiously, though, both poems are unusually interested, for Williams, in history. 'Old Man' shifts away from the soft-core magazine it starts with to a contrasting photograph of naked Jews 'lined up in snow waiting to be shot and thrown in a ditch'; 'Floor' imagines the lives being lived at the time the photograph was being taken, police violence against strikers and racial minorities, and girls working in sweatshops. He refers to the couple's 'surprisingly sophisticated self-distancing' which refuses to allow the camera to possess them with any thoroughness, and he later unfreezes the photograph to imagine them after their pose is broken – the man then taken by a 'manly focus' and the woman softened by tenderness.

What this indicates is that Williams is acutely aware that the gaze may simply reify its object, and that he's above all concerned to eschew that reification. He therefore moves away from the pornographic image in order to evoke the lives lived away, as it were, from desire in order to define the place of desire, its status, in the larger context of identity and experience. More challengingly he ends 'Old Man' with a surprising celebration of the pornographic image he began with, in order to redeem the desiring gaze itself:

> Vamp, siren, seductress, how much more she reveals in
> her glare of ink than she knows;
> how she incarnates our desperate human need for regard,
> our passion to live in beauty,
> to be beauty, to be cherished, by glances if by no more,
> of something like love, or love.
>
> (78)

Most feminists would be highly sceptical that this model incarnates anything as exalted as this, but Williams's insistence that she does is a sign of how much he wants to invest in the act of looking, how much he wants to believe that it does not simply reify and represent a voyeuristic need to pry and possess. These lines therefore transform the gaze into 'regard', which combines associations of looking with those of respect and even love, and subtly switch from the desire to look to the desire to be looked *at*, so that the two are made to seem symmetrical with each other. This does strike me as suspect in this pornographic context but I'm less concerned to condemn this than to draw attention to the pressing need it represents on Williams's part to invent a notion of the gaze which is creatively sympathetic.

This is so important to him because it's so thoroughly bound up with his own notion of what poetry should do, and with his own most repeated poetic strategy which starts from looking, often at what a stranger is doing, and then following the ramifications of his response to what he sees. The volume *Flesh and Blood* is composed entirely of eight-line poems that mostly show this process at its starkest, almost like notebook starting-points for his longer poems. 'The Dirty Talker: D Line, Boston' (6) starts by describing a man ('shabby, tweedy, academic') old enough to be the father of the woman he's talking to, but standing too close to her for that. So he thinks they are lovers and that he's ending their affair but that the girl won't let him go. This then seems to explain the spasms in her shoulders which he thought at first were laughter. But then:

> We were in a station now, he pulled back half a head from
>   her the better to behold her,
> then was out the hissing doors, she sobbing wholly now so
>   that finally I had to understand –
> her tears, his grinning broadly in – at *me* now though, as
>   though I were a portion of the story.

This is characteristic, then, of Williams's work in finding its material in something closely observed in a city environment and then painstakingly interpreting it. As elsewhere there is some discomfort in the sense of the poet observing a moment in someone else's life, and this is increased because we as readers are made to participate in the act of observing. There's tension in the implied covertness of this, like watching the sympathetic hero of a film searching someone's flat as its owner is approaching. What is gendered in this, however, is precisely the edge of voyeurism I've been describing and it is here especially acute because the 'dirty talker' is engaged in what may worryingly be regarded as an analogously creepy activity involving an unwanted intrusion. When this man looks back at the poet in the last line this sense of dismaying complicity is confirmed when this makes Williams feel as though he were 'a portion of the story'.

This self-reflexiveness is characteristic of Williams in his insistence that he can have no privileged position from which to judge what his poems report – the judgements that he makes are necessarily compromised by his own emotional investment in what he is seeing. Much of this is specifically related to his sense of his own gender bias. His guilty sense of complicity with the dirty talker is clearly related to the rueful declarations he repeatedly makes about his horniness which still thrives, he notes in 'Old Man', even as he approaches 60:

> Maybe coming of age in the American sensual darkness,
>   never seeing an unsmudged nipple,

an uncensored vagina, has left me forever infected with an
    unquenchable lust of the eye:
always that erotic murmur – I'm hardly myself if I'm not in a
    state of incipient desire.

(The Vigil, 76)

His most extensive exploration of this inextricability of the self and
desire is in 'With Ignorance' (165–72) where he evokes the existen-
tial meaning of desire's unquenchability. In 'Floor' he celebrates the
pornographic moment because it represents a brief 'peace' (201)
amidst the social upheaval surrounding it: in 'With Ignorance' he
regards such tranquillity as fleeting and regards that fleetingness as
symptomatic of the human inability to find a resting-place of being,
to find a moment that is not the unstable threshold of another
moment.

    The word 'peace' is indicative in this context of a larger sense in
Williams's work that desire is a form of conflict. This has briefly
been stayed in 'Floor' but mostly Williams regards it as endless, so
that 'With Ignorance' links the 'hunger again, need again' to 'every
slip or leap into rage, every war, flame, sob' (165). It's a cause, that
is, of internal conflict because it leads to a sense in Williams of
always being at war with himself – but it's also linked, as in
Williams's earlier work, to the sense that this masculine hunger
runs alongside the drive to agitate for domination. This leads to the
belief that 'War … happens and stops happening but is always
somehow right there, twisting and hardening us' (138) because
sexual hunger and the hunger for power are cognate with each
other and 'love is battle and we watch ourselves in love / become
maddened with pride and incompletion'.

    So in 'Combat' Williams describes how, when he was 21, he and
the woman he was trying to seduce 'struggled on that narrow bed,
twisted on each other, mauling one another like demented athletes'
(196). In this case, though, this routine aggression, however 'strenu-
ous' (196), which arises in ordinarily immature sexual interactions,
is a component of a much more specific conflict between the young
man and the young woman. He is Jewish and she is German and
the older Williams in retrospect considers that she and her mother
allowed him his limited liberties in order to cleanse them of their
contamination by Nazism. This means that although at the time
Williams fancied himself in the role of sexual aggressor, 'of beast,
primed, about to pounce' (196) that it was he who was the victim of
a more complex aggression. His actual role as he now recreates it is

closer to that of scapegoat – ironically a traditional one for Jews – in being the paradoxical victim of an apparent privilege that is really a form of humiliation. Activeness and passiveness as he perceived them at the time are reversed in retrospect: it is not the young woman who is reduced to a sex object, but the young man who is reified as a mere representative of his race. What he has participated in is a battle scene in the sex war which is used as a purging re-enactment of the depredations of the Second World War, in which he will be allowed all the symbolism of a merely illusory dominance. That this makes him subtly the victim is confirmed by the poem's point of departure, which is that the young woman is conjured into his mind by a victorious boxer who has 'the same rigorous carriage, same facial structure' as her. This subtly associates her with an aggressive masculinity and confirms the retrospective role reversal which 'Combat' enacts.

Being turned into a puppet like this is especially offensive to masculinity as it is traditionally understood. It's precisely this which Williams depicts himself struggling against in 'My Mother's Lips' (178–9) – the sense of being the subject of his mother's ventriloquy, as she 'seemed to be saying under her breath the very words I was saying as I was saying them', the fear that she actually *'caused'* what he said. Asking her to stop is clearly enough expressive of his wish for manly autonomy. It's equally important, though, that the next step in development Williams describes is being alone in a hotel declaiming his earliest poems from a window. This attempt to acquire his own 'voice' is paralleled with his earlier wish to speak for himself, so that he's shown at the end of the poem learning to be his own man as a poet. What is most characteristic of Williams, though, is that in this very moment of becoming himself he stresses how this is involved with being drawn out of himself 'and beyond' – the acquisition of his poetic identity involves transcending the boundaries of identity. His mature poems can be read as consistently enacting this and showing that autonomy is both impossible and irrelevant. Their consistent concern with looking and questioning places them on the far threshold of self, or on the meeting-point of selves.

This means that some of the most memorable moments in Williams's poems are when the objects of his gaze suddenly return that gaze. These are moments of mutual recognition which still retain crucial elements of the unknown – they enact how selves interact with significantly limited mutual understanding and how that understanding can suddenly grow and also increase self-understanding. In 'The Dirty Talker' this takes the form of a shock of potential self-recognition. In 'Bread' Williams describes how he and a grocer were apparently the only people still living in a neighbourhood subject to urban renewal, how one day Williams shouted at some boys misbehaving on the grocer's roof, and then their eyes met and the grocer smiled and Williams smiled back, 'as though we were lovers, as though, like lovers, we'd made speech again / and were listening as it gutted and fixed the space between us' (152). In 'From My Window' Williams watches a man pushing the wheelchair of a Vietnam veteran until they both tumble over and the man has to haul his friend back into the wheelchair – and then 'leans against the cyclone fence, suddenly staring up at me, as though he'd known / all along, that I was watching'. The men in both these poems are observed in moments that are curiously touched with intimacy to such an extent that they take on a sexual edge. The grocer is rubbing himself with the cream 'he used to use on his breasts'; the veteran's friend accidentally jerks off the paraplegic's jeans so that his shrivelled penis is revealed.

This deliberately raises the question of the poet's voyeurism – part of the impact of these poems arises from the discomfort they arouse. Much of their importance, however, comes from how they draw on this discomfort to question inter-relationships; they transcend voyeurism in the end because they enact the investment of each individual self in other selves. The gendered aspect of voyeurism is crucial here because it refers to how the traditional image of masculinity as both emotionally distant and controlling can lead men to adopt an attitude to others which is thoroughly cold and reifying. Williams's mature poems, by contrast, deconstruct voyeurism and so reveal this gendered malaise at work, and then transcend voyeurism to suggest an entirely different model of interaction. Where voyeurism requires the object of the gaze to be fixed at a stable distance, Williams's poems destabilise the gaze so that its objects are brought suddenly and humanly close. This means that what starts as 'lust of the eye' is transformed into 'regard'.

In this way, the neediness that lies behind the gaze in Williams's poems is referred to as motivating their 'lust of the eye' – the poet's fragility leads him to look at others with a vulnerability that may seem creepy. However, it's largely by admitting this that they transcend mere voyeurism and enact genuine moments of human

contact and understanding that involve the interaction of vulnera-
bilities, which motivate both the desire to look and the need to be
looked at. This is why the meeting of gazes is so representatively
important; when, in 'Bob', Williams meets the gaze of the epony-
mous retired hit man, he says

> It's impossible to tell how much that glance weighed: it was like
>   having to lift something,
> something so ponderous and unwieldy that you wanted to call
>   for someone to help you

> (148)

This is the product of the bar-room interactions described in this
poem, interactions devoid even of the mock-heroism attributed to
barroom colloquies by John Berryman who tends to glamorise,
however ruefully, that form of masculine self-destructiveness. Here
again Williams is more dismissive, more sceptical about such gender
displays than the men of his father's generation. What these lines
more broadly suggest, though, is the contrast between the distance
and, as it were, lightness of the solo voyeuristic gaze and the repre-
sentative closeness and emotional heaviness when gazes meet.

This is where Williams most clearly represents the shifts in
gender attitudes that have taken place in the last thirty years. He's
acutely aware of the qualities associated with traditional masculin-
ity. He's interested in heroism – 'Cowboys' (*Flesh and Blood*, 28)
describes the 'extra-lovable second lead' who will 'teach us to die, /
in his buddy's arms, stoical, never losing sight of our side's virtues:
community and self-denial'. 'Herakles' (*Flesh and Blood*, 5) describes
the hero as 'self-forged, self-conceived, hammered out in outrage,
trial, abandon, risk'. He's deeply fascinated by manual labour and
its attendant culture – his realist depictions of men at work consti-
tute some of his best writing, as in the crew working on the roof of
his building in 'Tar' who 'hack away the leaden layers of asbestos
paper', whose 'ladders flex and quiver' (217).

By contrast with such manly and risky activity, Williams himself
may seem feminised by watching and commenting – or at least to
resemble the retired men in 'The Regulars' (209–11) who sit in the
'Colonial Luncheonette on Sixth Street' and pontificate on the activ-
ities in their neighbourhood. It's by self-consciously adopting this
role however that Williams questions gender assumptions and
bravely creates a gender position for himself in his poems which is

masculine but also deconstructs masculinity. By displaying the neediness of his gaze and even taking the risk of appearing creepy, Williams evokes the possibility of a masculinity that is driven to explore its own emotional life in relation to the emotional lives of others. Partly by defining himself as often passive in relation to those he observes, Williams invents a new form of masculine poetic activity in which the poet, for example as father and lover, uses his long line to register each complex ramification, each nuanced response that arises through mutual 'regard', through loving interactions:

> Instead I'd step into my train: how rich, I would think, is the
>   lexicon of our self-absolving;
> how enduring our bland, fatal assurance that reflection is
>   righteousness being accomplished.
>
> The dance of our glances, the clash; pulling each other
>   through our perceptual punctures;
> then holocaust, holocaust: host on host of ill, injured presences
>   squandered, consumed.
>
> Her vigil, somewhere, I know, continues: her occupancy, her
>   absolute, faithful attendance;
> the dance of our glances: challenge, abdication, effacement,
>   the perfume of our consternation.
>
>   (The Vigil, 74–5)

Notes

Introduction

1. Barbara Ehrenreich, 'The Decline of Patriarchy' in Maurice Berger, Brian Wallis and Simon Watson (eds), *Constructing Masculinity* (New York: Routledge, 1995) 284.
2. R.W. Connell, *Masculinities* (Cambridge: Polity, 1995) 186. This book henceforth Connell.
3. Robert B. Shoemaker, *Gender in English Society 1650–1850: the Emergence of Separate Spheres?* (Harlow: Longman, 1998) 6.
4. Thomas Foster, 'Dickinson in Women's History', in Joseph A. Boone and Michael Cadden (eds), *Engendering Men: the Question of Male Feminist Criticism* (New York: Routledge, 1990) 239–53.
5. Mary P. Ryan, *Womanhood in America* (Irvine: University of California Press, 1983) 165.
6. David T. Evans, *Sexual Citizenship: the Material Construction of Sexualities* (New York: Routledge, 1993) 48.
7. R. Brannon quoted in Nigel Edley and Margaret Wetherell, *Men in Perspective: Practice, Power and Identity* (Hemel Hempstead: Harvester Wheatsheaf, 1995) 77.
8. Stephen Heath, 'Male Feminism' in Alice Jardine and Paul Smith (eds), *Men in Feminism* (New York: Routledge, 1987) 26.
9. Alice Jardine, 'Men' in Alice Jardine and Paul Smith (eds), *Men in Feminism* (New York: Routledge, 1987) 61.
10. Judith Butler, *Gender Trouble* (New York: Routledge, 1990).
11. Calvin Thomas, *Male Matters* (Urbana and Chicago: University of Illinois Press, 1996) 3.
12. Ted Hughes, *Shakespeare and the Goddess of Complete Being* (London: Faber, 1992).
13. Peter Middleton, *The Inward Gaze: Masculinity and Subjectivity in Modern Culture* (New York: Routledge, 1992) 145.
14. Robert Bly, *Iron John: A Book About Men* (New York: Addison-Wesley, 1990).
15. Robert Lowell, *Robert Lowell's Poems: A Selection* (ed.), Jonathan Raban (London: Faber, 1974) 101–4.
16. Ted Hughes, *Birthday Letters* (London: Faber, 1998) 96.
17. John Berryman, *His Toy, His Dream, His Rest* (New York: Farrar, Straus and Giroux, 1968) 307.

1 Men and Mermaids: Robert Lowell's Martial Masculinity and Beyond

1. Robert Lowell, *Life Studies* (London: Faber, 1959) 19–59. This volume henceforth LS.
2. Robert Lowell, *The Dolphin* (London: Faber, 1973).
3. Victor J. Seidler, *Rediscovering Masculinity: Reason, Language and Sexuality* (London: Routledge, 1989) 125. This volume henceforth Seidler.
4. Judith Butler, *Gender Trouble* (London: Routledge, 1990) 59.
5. Quoted in *Robert Lowell: A Biography* by Ian Hamilton (London: Faber, 1983) 201. This volume henceforth Hamilton.
6. Robert Lowell, *Near the Ocean* (London: Faber, 1967) 13. This volume henceforth Ocean.
7. Sandra M. Gilbert and Susan Gubar, 'Tradition and the Female Talent' in *The Poetics of Gender* (ed.), Nancy K. Miller (New York: Columbia University Press, 1986) 202. This essay henceforth Gilbert and Gubar.
8. Mark Seltzer, 'The Love Master' in *Engendering Men* (eds), Joseph A. Boone and Michael Cadden (New York: Routledge, 1990) 140.
9. Alan Williamson, *Pity the Monsters: the Political Vision of Robert Lowell* (New Haven and London: Yale University Press, 1974) 102. Henceforth Williamson.
10. Robert Lowell, *History* (London: Faber, 1973) 38. This volume henceforth History.
11. Robert Lowell, *For the Union Dead* (London: Faber, 1956). Henceforth UD.
12. Terri Witek, *Robert Lowell and Life Studies: Revising the Self* (Columbia and London: University of Missouri Press, 1993).
13. Robert Lowell, *Day by Day* (London: Faber, 1978) 61.
14. Robert Lowell, *Collected Prose* (London:Faber, 1987) 122–5.
15. Mary Ellmann, *Thinking About Women* (London: Virago, 1979) 34.
16. Tom Ryan, 'Roots of Masculinity' in *The Sexuality of Men* (eds), Andy Metcalf and Martin Humphries (London: Pluto Press, 1985) 26–7.
17. Lynne Segal, *Slow Motion: Changing Masculinities, Changing Men* (London: Virago, 1990) 116. This book henceforth Segal.
18. Katherine Wallingford, *Robert Lowell's Language of the Self* (Chapel Hill: University of North Carolina Press, 1988) 54.
19. Vereen M. Bell, *Robert Lowell: Nihilist as Hero* (Cambridge, Massachusetts: Harvard University Press, 1983) 111.
20. Robert Lowell, *Poems 1938–1949* (London: Faber, 1950) 18–24.
21. Luce Irigaray, *Speculum of the Other Woman* (Ithaca, New York: Cornell University Press, 1985) 185–6.
22. Adrienne Rich, 'Caryatid: A Column', *American Poetry Review*, vol 2, 1973, 42.

2   John Berryman and the Buried Women

1. John Berryman, *Seventy-Seven Dream Songs* (London: Faber, 1964) 33.
2. John Bayley, 'On John Berryman' in *Contemporary Poetry in America* (ed.), Robert Boyers (New York: Schocken Books, 1974) 64 and 76.
3. John Haffenden, *The Life of John Berryman* (London: Routledge, 1982) 209–10. Henceforth Life.
4. John Haffenden, *John Berryman: A Critical Commentary* (London: Macmillan, 1980). Henceforth Critical Commentary.
5. John Berryman, *Homage to Mistress Bradstreet and Other Poems* (London: Faber, 1959).
6. Paul Mariani, *Dream Song: the Life of John Berryman* (Amherst: University of Massachusetts Press, 1996). Henceforth Mariani.
7. Christopher Benfey, 'the Woman in the Mirror: Randall Jarrell and John Berryman', in *Men Writing the Feminine: Literature, Theory and the Question of Genders* (ed.), Thais E. Morgan (Albany: State University of New York Press, 1994) 125.
8. John Berryman, *His Toy, His Dream, His Rest* (New York: Farrar, Straus and Giroux, 1968) 259. This is the second volume of *Dream Songs*, comprising numbers 78–385. These are referred to as *Dream Songs* in the text and each is identified by their *Dream Song* number.
9. Helen Vendler, 'John Berryman' in *The Given and the Made* (London: Faber, 1995) 36. Henceforth Vendler.
10. See Stephen Frosh, *Sexual Difference: Masculinity and Psychoanalysis* (London: Routledge, 1994) 13.
11. Lewis Hyde, 'Alcohol and Poetry: John Berryman and the Booze Talking', in *Recovering Berryman*, (eds), Richard J. Kelly and Alan K. Lathrop (Ann Arbor: University of Michigan Press, 1993) 217.
12. Tony Eardley, 'Violence and Sexuality', in *The Sexuality of Men* (ed.), Andy Metcalf and Martin Humphries (London: Pluto Press, 1985) 104.
13. John Berryman, *Recovery* (London: Faber, 1973) 7.
14. Julia Kristeva, *Powers of Horror: An Essay on Abjection* trans. Leon S. Roudiez (New York: Columbia University Press, 1982).
15. Calvin Thomas, *Male Matters: Masculinity, Anxiety, and the Male Body on the Line* (Urbana: University of Illinois Press, 1996) 13–16.
16. Jerold M. Martin, 'Things are Going to Pieces: Disintegration Anxiety in *The Dream Songs*' in *Recovering Berryman*. Martin is here quoting from George E. Atwood and Robert D. Stolorow, *Structures of Subjectivity* (Hillsdale, NJ: Lawrence Erlbaum Associates, 1984) 94.
17. George F. Wedge, 'The Case of the Talking Brews: Mr. Berryman and Dr. Hyde', in *Recovering Berryman*, 236.
18. Joel Conarroe, *John Berryman: An Introduction to the Poetry* (New York: Columbia University Press, 1977) 101–2.
19. J.M. Linebarger, *John Berryman* (New York: Twayne, 1974) 110–11.
20. M.M. Bakhtin, *The Dialogic Imagination* (ed.), Michael Holquist, trans. Caryl Emerson and Michael Holquist (Austin: University of Texas Press, 1981) 76.

21. 'The Art of Poetry: An Interview with John Berryman' by Peter Stitt in *Berryman's Understanding* (ed.), Harry Thomas (Boston: Northeastern University Press, 1988) 44.
22. Robert Pinsky, *The Situation of Poetry* (Princeton, New Jersey: Princeton University Press, 1976) 34.
23. John Berryman, *Love and Fame* (London: Faber, 1971) 67.
24. Adrienne Rich, 'Living with Henry' in *Berryman's Understanding*, 127.
25. Eileen Simpson, *Poets in their Youth: A Memoir* (New York: Random House, 1982) 226.

3 Ted Hughes and the Goddess of Complete Being

1. Ted Hughes, *Shakespeare and the Goddess of Complete Being* (London: Faber, 1992) 327. This book henceforth Shakespeare.
2. Jacqueline Rose, *The Haunting of Sylvia Plath* (London: Virago, 1991). Henceforth Rose.
3. Ted Hughes, 'Poetry and Violence' in *Winter Pollen: Occasional Prose (ed.)* William Scammell (London: Faber, 1994) 251–67. This book henceforth Winter Pollen.
4. Ted Hughes, *Lupercal* (London: Faber, 1960) 26 and 52. This book henceforth Lupercal.
5. Ted Hughes, *Poetry in the Making* (London: Faber, 1967).
6. Ted Hughes, *New Selected Poems 1957–1994* (London: Faber, 1995).
7. Ted Hughes, *Wodwo* (London: Faber, 1967) 155–7. This book henceforth Wodwo.
8. Ted Hughes, *Wolfwatching* (London: Faber, 1989) 10–11. This book hence forth Wolfwatching.
9. Peter Middleton, *The Inward Gaze: Masculinity and Subjectivity in Modern Culture* (London: Routledge, 1992) 190.
10. Tom Paulin, 'Laureate of the Free Market? Ted Hughes' in *Minotaur: Poetry and the Nation State* (London: Faber, 1992) 270.
11. Ted Hughes, *Moortown* (London: Faber, 1979) 104.
12. Ekbert Faas, *Ted Hughes: the Unaccommodated Universe* (Santa Barbara: Black Sparrow Press, 1980), henceforth Faas. Keith Sagar (ed.) *The Achievement of Ted Hughes* (Manchester: Manchester University Press, 1983).
13. Cynthia Enloe, *The Morning After: Sexual Politics at the End of the Cold War* (Berkeley and Los Angeles: University of California Press, 1993) 63.
14. Keith Sagar, 'Fourfold Vision in Ted Hughes' in Keith Sagar (ed.), *The Achievement of Ted Hughes*, 299–300.
15. Ted Hughes, *The Iron Man* (London: Faber, 1968).
16. Lynne Segal argues that soldiering is predominantly masochistic. See *Is the Future Female?* (London: Virago, 1987) 197.
17. Michael Schmidt, *An Introduction to Fifty Modern British Poets* (London: Pan, 1979) 388. This book henceforth Schmidt.
18. Lynne Segal, *Slow Motion: Changing Masculinities, Changing Men* (London: Virago, 1990) 102.

19. Sylvia Plath, *Collected Poems* (London: Faber, 1981) 156.
20. Jessica Benjamin and Anson Rabinbach, 'Foreword' to *Male Fantasies* vol II by Klaus Theweleit (Oxford: Polity Press, 1985) xix.
21. Margaret Dickie Uroff, *Sylvia Plath and Ted Hughes* (Urbana: University of Illinois Press, 1979) 183. This volume henceforth Uroff.
22. Ted Hughes, *Crow* (London: Faber, 1972).
23. Annie Schofield, 'The Oedipus Theme in Hughes', in Keith Sagar (ed.), *The Achievement of Ted Hughes*, 186–209.
24. Jarold Ramsey, '*Crow* or the Trickster Transformed' in Keith Sagar (ed.), *The Achievement of Ted Hughes*.
25. Thomas West, *Ted Hughes* (London and New York: Methuen, 1985) 69.
26. A.C.H. Smith, *Orghast at Persepolis* (London: Eyre Methuen, 1972) 113.
27. Julia Kristeva, *Revolution in Poetic Language* trans. Margaret Waller (New York: Columbia University Press, 1984) 26.
28. Ted Hughes, *Cave Birds* (London: Faber, 1978) and *Gaudete* (London: Faber, 1977).
29. Craig Robinson, 'The Good Shepherd: *Moortown Elegies*', in Keith Sagar (ed.), *The Achievement of Ted Hughes*, 266.

4   Able Semen and the Penile Canon: Derek Walcott's 'Adamic Utterance'

1. Derek Walcott, 'Leaving School' and 'Meanings' in Robert D. Hamner, (ed.), Critical *Perspectives on Derek Walcott* (Washington DC: Three Continents Press, 1993), 28 and 45 respectively. This collection of essays by and about Derek Walcott henceforth Critical Perspectives.
2. Derek Walcott, *Omeros* (New York: Farrar, Straus, Giroux, 1990).
3. Derek Walcott, *Collected Poems 1948–1984* (London: Faber, 1992), 504. This volume henceforth CP.
4. Rei Terada, *Derek Walcott's Poetry: American Mimicry* (Boston: Northeastern University Press, 1992), 6. This book henceforth Terada.
5. Derek Walcott, 'The Muse of History' in The Post-Colonial Reader (ed.), Bill Ashcroft, Gareth Griffiths, Helen Tiffin (London: Routledge, 1995) 370–4.
6. Edward Hirsch, 'An Interview with Derek Walcott', in William Baer (ed.), *Conversations with Derek Walcott* (Jackson: University Press of Missouri, 1996) 63. This book henceforth Conversations.
7. Derek Walcott, *The Bounty* (London: Faber, 1997) 56.
8. Derek Walcott, *The Arkansas Testament* (London: Faber, 1988) 48–51.
9. Kadiatu Kanneh, 'Feminism and the Colonial Body' in Bill Ashcroft, Gareth Griffiths and Helen Tiffin (eds), *The Post-Colonial Studies Reader* (London: Routledge, 1995) 346.
10. Ted Hughes, *New Selected Poems 1957–1994* (London: Faber, 1995) 346.
11. Elleke Boehmer, *Colonial and Postcolonial Literature* (Oxford: Oxford University Press, 1995) 224.
12. Derek Walcott, 'Dream on Monkey Mountain' in *Dream on Monkey Mountain and Other Plays* (New York: Farrar, Strauss, Giroux, 1970).

13. Tejumola Olaniyan, 'Derek Walcott: Islands of History at a Rendezvous with a Muse', in *Scars of Conquest/Masks of Resistance* (Oxford: Oxford University Press, 1995) 109.
14. Elaine Savory, 'Art and Macho Attitudes: The Case of Walcott', in *Postcolonial Literatures: Achebe, Ngugi, Desai, Walcott* (Basingstoke: Macmillan, 1995) 245–57.

5   Sons of Mother Ireland: Seamus Heaney and Paul Muldoon

1. Seamus Heaney, *Preoccupations: Selected Prose 1968–1978* (London: Faber, 1980) 61–78. This volume henceforth Preoccupations.
2. Seamus Heaney, *New Selected Poems 1966–1987* (London: Faber, 1990) 1–2. Unless otherwise stated all references to Heaney's poems are to this volume.
3. Seamus Heaney, *Seeing Things* (London: Faber, 1991) 23.
4. Blake Morrison, 'Speech and Reticence: Seamus Heaney's *North*' in Peter Jones and Michael Schmidt (eds), *British Poetry Since 1970: A Critical Survey* (Manchester: Carcanet Press, 1980) 103–11.
5. Michael Parker, *Seamus Heaney: the Making of the Poet* (Basingstoke: Macmillan, 1993) 62. This book henceforth Parker.
6. Terry Gifford and Neil Roberts, 'Hughes and Two Contemporaries: Peter Redgrove and Seamus Heaney' in Keith Sagar (ed.), *The Achievement of Ted Hughes* (Manchester: Manchester University Press, 1983) 93.
7. Ted Hughes, *Shakespeare and the Goddess of Complete Being* (London: Faber, 1992) 157.
8. Margaret Dickie Uroff, *Sylvia Plath and Ted Hughes* (Urbana: University of Illinois Press, 1979) 199.
9. Jacqueline Rose, *The Haunting of Sylvia Plath* (London: Virago, 1991) 151.
10. See Kadiatu Kanneh, 'Feminism and the Colonial Body' in Bill Ashcroft, Gareth Griffiths and Helen Tiffin (eds), *The Post-Colonial Studies Reader* (London: Routledge, 1995) 346.
11. Clair Wills, *Improprieties: Politics and Sexuality in Northern Irish Poetry* (Oxford: Oxford University Press, 1993) 57. This volume henceforth Wills.
12. Elleke Boehmer, *Colonial and Postcolonial Literature* (Oxford: Oxford University Press, 1995) 224.
13. Paul Muldoon, *Selected Poems 1968–1983* (London: Faber, 1986) 34. Unless otherwise stated all references to Muldoon are to this volume.
14. Fredric Jameson, *Postmodernism or the Cultural Logic of Late Capitalism* (London: Verso, 1991) 17.
15. Paul Muldoon, *Madoc* (London: Faber, 1990) 10–11.
16. Paul Muldoon, *The Annals of Chile* (London: Faber, 1994).
17. Ted Hughes, *Winter Pollen: Occasional Prose* (ed.), William Scammell (London: Faber, 1994) 241 and 240.
18. Paul Muldoon, *Meeting the British* (London: Faber, 1987) 16.
19. Paul Muldoon, *Why Brownlee Left* (London: Faber, 1980) 7–8.

6 'Insofar as they are embodiments of the patriarchal idea': Women Representing Men

1. Adrienne Rich, *The Fact of a Doorframe: Poems Selected and New 1950–1984* (New York: Norton, 1984) 35–9. Unless otherwise stated all references to Rich's poems are to this book.
2. Adrienne Rich, *On Lies, Secrets, and Silence: Selected Prose 1966–1978* (London: Virago, 1980) 248. Henceforth On Lies.
3. Ezra Pound, 'Vorticism', *Fortnightly Review*, September 1, 1914, 461–71.
4. Adrienne Rich, *Blood, Bread and Poetry: Selected Prose 1979–1985* (London: Virago, 1987) 50.
5. Wendy Martin, 'Adrienne Rich', in *An American Triptych* (Chapel Hill and London: University of North Carolina Press, 1984) 231.
6. Adrienne Rich, *A Wild Patience Has Taken Me This Far: Poems, 1978–81* (New York: W.W. Norton, 1981) 5.
7. Liz Yorke, *Adrienne Rich: Passion, Politics and the Body* (London: Sage, 1997) 65. All references to Yorke are to this book.
8. Adrienne Rich, *Your Native Land, Your Life* (New York: Norton, 1986) 3–27.
9. Adrienne Rich, 'When We Dead Awaken: Writing as Re-Vision (1971)' in *Adrienne Rich's Poetry* selected and edited by Barbara Charlesworth Gelpi and Albert Gelpi (New York: W.W. Norton, 1975) 91. Henceforth Gelpi.
10. Sylvia Plath, *Collected Poems* (ed.), Ted Hughes (London: Faber, 1981) 129–30. All references to Plath are to this volume.
11. Jo Shapcott, *Electroplating the Baby* (Newcastle Upon Tyne: Bloodaxe, 1988) 54–62.
12. Jo Shapcott, *Phrase Book* (Oxford: Oxford University Press, 1992) 26–7.
13. Carol Ann Duffy, *Selected Poems* (Harmondsworth: Penguin, 1994) 47–8. All references to Duffy are to this volume.
14. Sharon Olds, *Satan Says* (Pittsburgh: University of Pittsburgh Press, 1980) 24.
15. Sharon Olds, *The Gold Cell* (New York: Knopf, 1987) 48.
16. Sharon Olds, *The Dead and the Living* (New York: Knopf, 1984) 48. Henceforth The Dead.
17. Sharon Olds, *The Father* (London: Secker and Warburg, 1993).

7 The Politics of Camp: Frank O'Hara and John Ashbery

1. David Bergman, *Gaiety Transfigured: Gay Self-Representation in American Literature* (Madison: University of Wisconsin Press, 1991) 48. This book henceforth Bergman.
2. Nancy Chodorow, *The Reproduction of Mothering: Psychoanalysis and the Sociology of Gender* (Berkeley: University of California Press, 1976) 167–9.
3. See my discussion of Morgan in *Contemporary Poetry and Postmodernism: Dialogue and Estrangement* (Basingstoke: Macmillan, 1997) 133–50.

4. Geoff Ward, *Statutes of Liberty: the New York School of Poets* (Basingstoke: Macmillan, 1993) 51.
5. David T. Evans, *Sexual Citizenship: the Material Construction of Sexualities* (London: Routledge, 1993) 97.
6. Susan Sontag, 'Notes on Camp' in *A Susan Sontag Reader* (Harmondsworth: Penguin, 1983) 105–19.
7. See Fredric Jameson, *Postmodernism or the Cultural Logic of Late Capitalism* (London: Verso, 1991) 6.
8. Kenneth Rexroth, 'Introduction' to *Selected Poems by Pierre Reverdy* (London: Jonathan Cape, 1973) 9. Henceforth Rexroth.
9. Marjorie Perloff, *Frank O'Hara: Poet Among Painters* (New York: Braziller, 1977) 214–15.
10. Frank O'Hara, *The Collected Poems* (ed.), Donald Allen (New York: Knopf, 1979) 195. All references to O'Hara are to this volume.
11. See Roger Gilbert, *Walks in the World* (Princeton: Princeton University Press, 1991) 182.
12. John Ashbery, *Selected Poems* (London: Paladin, 1987) 31–2.
13. John Ashbery, *Can You Hear, Bird* (Manchester: Carcanet, 1996) 141.
14. Gregory W. Bredbeck, 'Body odor: Gay male semiotics and *l'ecriture feminine*' in David Porter (ed.), *Between Men and Feminism* (London: Routledge, 1992) 100.

8 Creeps and Bastards: C.K. Williams as Voyeur

1. Robert Lowell, *Near the Ocean* (London: Faber, 1967) 25–7.
2. C.K. Williams, *I Am the Bitter Name* reprinted in *Poems 1963–1983* (Newcastle Upon Tyne: Bloodaxe, 1988). Unless otherwise stated all page numbers refer to this volume.
3. Robert Lowell, *History* (London: Faber, 1973) 199.
4. C.K. Williams, *Flesh and Blood* (New York: Farrar Straus Giroux, 1987) 41.
5. C.K. Williams, *The Vigil* (Newcastle Upon Tyne: Bloodaxe, 1997) 76–8.

Index

Index